Human Rights

Human Rights:
Concept and Context

Brian Orend

broadview press

National Library of Canada Cataloguing in Publication Data

Orend, Brian, 1971-
    Human rights : concept and context / Brian Orend.

Includes bibliographical references and index.
ISBN 1-55111-436-4

    1. Civil rights. 2. Civil rights—History. I. Title.

JC571.O773 2002   323   C2002-901698-3

Broadview Press Ltd. is an independent, international publishing house, incorporated in 1985

North America
Post Office Box 1243, Peterborough, Ontario, Canada K9J 7H5
3576 California Road, Orchard Park, NY 14127
Tel: (705) 743-8990; Fax: (705) 743-8353;
e-mail: customerservice@broadviewpress.com

United Kingdom and Europe
Plymbridge North (Thomas Lyster Ltd.)
Units 3 & 4a, Ormskirk Industrial Park, Burscough Rd, Ormskirk,
Lancashire L39 2YW Tel: (1695) 575112; Fax: (1695) 570120;
E-Mail: books@tlyster.co.uk

Australia
St. Clair Press, P.O. Box 287, Rozelle, NSW 2039
Tel: (02) 818-1942; Fax: (02) 418-1923

www.broadviewpress.com

Broadview Press gratefully acknowledges the financial support of the Book Publishing Indus-try Development Program, Ministry of Canadian Heritage, Government of Canada.

Typesetting and assembly: True to Type Inc., Mississauga, Canada.
PRINTED IN CANADA

This book has been printed on 100% post consumer waste paper, certified Eco-logo and processed chlorine free.

Contents

Acknowledgements

I must first thank all those at Broadview Press for everything done to bring this book into being, from the original proposal to the final edition.

Continued thanks to all my colleagues at the University of Waterloo, especially those in philosophy. Particular gratitude, for all his support, is due to my chair, Richard Holmes. The idea for this book developed out of a seminar on human rights I offered during the summer of 1999. Thanks to all participants, especially Jan Narveson.

I wish to extend a special thank you to all the teachers who have had me as a student in the past. Educators have played an important and positive role in my life, no doubt influencing my own decision to become a professor. So thanks to all those who taught me, either as a young Brian Pearson or in my older form as Brian Orend. There are too many good ones to mention, but I would like to single out John English, Thomas Pogge, and that great group who taught at St. David CSS in the mid- to late-1980s.

While I was writing this book, my wife Jane was even more busy being pregnant. I like to joke that we were both working on our babies at the same time. Thanks to her for her patience during the writing period, and moreover for giving me a son, to whom this book is dedicated.

For Sam

Preface

This book contains a number of features that commend it to the reader. First, and as the subtitle indicates, this work contains two parts. The first part deals with the conceptual foundations of the idea of human rights. It seeks to explain the basic ideas, arguments, and controversies behind human rights, in a way that is both clear and comprehensive. Each chapter in this section has a convenient summary, and there are some diagrams to illustrate core ideas. The book's second part deals with the real-world history of human rights, from their origins to their latest manifestations and implications. There, we move from ancient and medieval sources of the rights idea to the realities of the twentieth century—and the challenges of the twenty-first. This combination of theory and history—of concept and context—is rare in a book on human rights, most of which are *either* theoretical *or* historical.

Although there are many cross-references between the book's two parts, they can, if desired, be read and treated separately. Whether to read the theory part or the history part first is up to the reader. One note on the history section: reasonable people can disagree on what counts as a vital event in, or contribution to, human rights history. The intent of the section is not to satisfy everyone's preference; rather, it is to provide a substantive sketch of how human rights have developed over time. Even so, the account offered compares well—in terms of depth, detail, and readability—with similar versions currently on offer.

This book is not an edited anthology, though it can be used to complement one of the many available, whose number seems to be growing daily. While such collections are useful, there is still something to be said for the older textbook tradition, in which one coherent and consistent understanding is developed and then defended. Of course, readers need to know the diversity of opinion about human rights, but sometimes reading how another person has processed such information can ease one's way, and add to one's own insight and choice. This is especially true if that person adopts an approach which is balanced, informed and moderate—something I strive to achieve in these pages.

In two appendices, this book contains four primary human rights documents, plus a human rights research tool. The documents, in Appendix A, are both national and international, since the entire text views human rights as both national and international in importance. Recent books, unfortunately, convey the impression that human rights are only international—as if only for distant, impoverished strangers and not of vital concern for everyone. The documents in Appendix A are, in chronological order: the American Bill of Rights (1789), the French Declaration of the Rights of Man and Citizen (1789), the United Nations's Universal Declaration of Human Rights (1948), and the Canadian Charter of Rights and Freedoms (1982). Why these four? The answer arises from a sense of their relevance to the expected reader. While there are other important human rights documents, both national and international, reasons of space dictated that the choice should be limited to those of immediate importance for the intended readership of this work. In any event, each of these four documents has proven itself to be compelling not only in its own right but also in terms of the impact it has had on human rights history around the world. Particularly influential, of course, has been the Universal Declaration of Human Rights.

The research tool, in Appendix B, provides the reader with a long list of prominent human rights documents, organized by theme and time of ratification. Moreover, the Appendix contains web-site addresses that direct the reader to some of the very best online human rights research sites. No other human rights textbook of which I am aware has this useful information.

The goal of this book is to provide some satisfying "one-stop-shopping" in connection with human rights. While drawing on the latest material, it explains the conceptual issues in clear language; it explores the historical trends; it exposes readers to some primary documents; and it suggests sources for further research. I hope and expect the reader to come away from this book with a strong and timely grasp of the core issues surrounding human rights in our time.

Part One: Concept

Chapter 1

Basic Vocabulary
and Core Concepts

The human rights community, like any other community, has a certain way of speaking. Such speech can at first seem peculiar, or even forbidding, to those not familiar with it. As with learning any language, though, it is both possible and pleasant to learn the human rights language, provided one has a welcoming introduction to it, and one is willing to put in the effort required. The language of human rights is an important one to know at this point in our shared history. It is especially influential in moral, legal and political debate and like other languages is possessed of its own brand of logic and inner beauty. It is, moreover, a language designed to be spoken universally—by each and every one of us—and so we all have reason to inquire into its structure and significance. It is therefore essential, at the earliest moment, to grasp the basic vocabulary and the core concepts employed in discussions of human rights.

accepted universally? / Has implicit morality built in

Human

One cannot say "human rights," of course, without saying both "human" and "rights." The assumption will be made, for now, that there is no need to define exhaustively what a human being is: we are, I suggest, rather well acquainted with such creatures. The importance of drawing attention to the "human" component of "human rights" is to introduce a core concept: that of a right-holder. A right-holder, very simply, is the person who has the right in question. Part of the distinctiveness of the human rights idea is the belief that *all* human beings have, or hold, human rights. While this seems to follow rather obviously when one looks at the language, it is actually a bold and substantive moral claim, and one which, when first introduced, went against the grain of history.

For the longest time, a person was considered a right-holder only if possessed of certain select characteristics, like being an able-bodied, land-owning adult male. The contemporary human rights idea, by contrast, suggests that *every* human being—man or woman, rich or poor, adult or child, healthy or sick, educated or not—holds human rights. We are all members of the human community, and so hold any and all of those rights referred to as "human rights." It is astonishing how often even human rights activists overlook this fundamental feature, often referred to as the "universality" of the human rights idea.

Overlooking universality is, of course, the very bread-and-butter of those who violate human rights, such as repressive governments. Officials in such governments often claim many things for themselves—rewards and resources, access and influence—which they deny to their fellow citizens. They thus fail to grasp, or respect fully, the twin commitments to *universality* and to *a form of equality* inherent in the human rights idea. Particularly vicious human rights violators, like the Nazis, often claim that those whose human rights they violate are not even human and so are not entitled to claim human rights. The first step on the road to mass human rights violations is, invariably, to denigrate the very humanity of the person(s) targeted. The sad psychology seems always the same: denying the humanity of the hated person(s) dislodges both conscience and sensitivity, which normally prevent innocent people from being brutalized. Crude propaganda is sometimes used to cement such bizarre beliefs about the inhumanity of those targeted for persecution. One thinks, for instance, of the Nazi "news-reels" depicting Jewish people either as rodent-like vermin at the very bottom of the social scale, or else as fat-cat capitalists at the very top.[1] While these opposing images are not consistent, nonetheless the beliefs expressed in them are at odds with the core commitment to *a baseline level of equality for all*, present in the idea of human rights.

This notion—that as human beings we all share a basic level of equal moral worth in some significant respect—is a thoroughly modern concept. It is morally moving yet surprisingly difficult to defend; it is inspiring yet constantly subject to critical challenge. This is not to suggest that the core commitment to elemental equality has no basis other than raw conviction or personal temperament: human rights advocates offer reasons to justify this commitment. It is, indeed, crucially important to justify it; otherwise the rights violator will ask why he should treat as respected equals those he rejects, spurns, and ultimately abuses and brutalizes. So we must face up to some difficult questions: What makes us think that we are all equally entitled to human rights? What makes us think that, just because we were born biologically human, we are entitled to rights, regardless of what further qualities we possess? A fuller discussion of this complex topic, which combines issues of holding rights with rights justification, must wait for a subsequent chapter.

Rights

We turn now to the "rights" element in "human rights." What is a right to begin with? The Oxford English Dictionary (OED) offers a helpful introduction, suggesting a three-fold definition of a right:

1. "that which is morally or socially correct or just; fair treatment."

2. "a justification or fair claim."

3. "a thing one may legally or morally claim; the state of being entitled to a privilege or immunity or authority to act."

We do well here in noting, for the time being, how the concepts of morality and justice in general, and of fairness in particular, are implied in each of these definitions. Central, too, is the reference to being entitled to something, to being able to claim something as one's own or as one's due.

It is important to be mindful of a meaningful yet subtle distinction between "right" and "*a* right." In general, "*a* right" has a more narrow and concrete reference than "right" does. After all, a correct answer to an exam question is *right* but is not, presumably, something students have *a right* to ask their professor for during exam time. To have a right is to have something more specific and meaningful than abstract rightness on one's side: it is to have a well-grounded and concrete claim on the actions of other people and on the shape of social institutions, in particular governments.

 There is considerable consensus amongst rights advocates that a right can be defined, at least initially, as a justified claim or entitlement. *A right is a justified claim on someone, or on some institution, for something which one is owed.* The right-holder, in claiming a right, is asserting that he is entitled to be treated in certain ways by other people and by social institutions. The need for justifying rights is obvious: we cannot be required to jump up and obey on somebody else's mere assertion. Right-holders must offer us sufficient reasons why we should treat them the way they want. What counts as a sufficient reason is one of the most important issues in rights theory. It is a topic to which we will return and it demands that we offer plausible answers to the following questions: what can we reasonably require of people in social and political life? What, if anything, is so valuable that we can oblige, perhaps even force, other people and social institutions to provide for us?

Rights are Reasons, not Properties

The fact that a person claiming a right must offer the rest of us sufficient reasons why we should respect his claim provides us with an insight into the ultimate nature of a human right. A human right, like any other right, is *not* a property of persons; rather, it is *a reason to treat persons in certain ways*. This is a crucial distinction, for on it rests the difference between a dated and discredited theory of natural rights and a more compelling and contemporary theory of human rights.

If one believes that human rights are properties of persons—an essential part of human make-up, as it were—then one is immediately confronted with sharp questions, like "Where are they?" If human rights are literally properties of personhood, then one should be able to display them for all to see. But, of course, nobody can *show us* his human rights. Human rights are, after all, not material things like cars, houses or oil paintings. Nor are human rights more immaterial things like personality traits or psychological dispositions, which in general are also observable, albeit in a different way, over time. With enough observation, for instance, one can discern that Jimmy is an angry young man; but all the observation in the world will not allow one to see Jimmy's human rights. This must mean that human rights are either non-visible properties of persons, or else not properties of persons at all.

Older natural rights theorists, such as English philosopher John Locke,[2] tried to suggest that human, or "natural," rights are non-visible properties of personhood. These older theorists, in other words, relied on a metaphysical conception of human nature to ground their claims about natural rights to things like life and liberty. We have rights, they said, in the same way that we have a soul.

The prickly problem with likening rights to souls is that one is injecting needless, and excessive, controversy into the discourse surrounding rights. If one goes the route of metaphysics, then one has to tell a very elaborate story about non-visible properties that will come to rest on premises which are necessarily speculative and hotly disputed. Such metaphysical premises often include the existence of a certain kind of God and of an enduring yet unseen structure of humanity, like an immortal soul endowed with free will. A simpler and sounder strategy, it seems, would be to decline the metaphysical option and to accept instead one rooted in moral reasoning, to be detailed below. While such a strategy will not itself be free of controversy, it is clearly less fraught with peril than the metaphysics of the various natural rights accounts.

Another problem which older natural rights theorists wrestled with was the issue of forfeiture. Many of us want to say, for example, that convicted criminals forfeit—or lose, or give up—their human right to liberty for the duration of their imprisonment. You do the crime, you do the time. But how can imprisonment be justified if human rights are properties of persons, part of the very fabric of their being as people? Some natural rights theorists responded by saying that imprisonment is thus unjustified, while others such as Locke said that a felon committing a crime somehow renounces his very humanity and becomes "a noxious Creature, like a Wolf or Lyon."[3] Both responses seem unsatisfactory. There is nothing wrong with sending a convicted criminal to prison as punishment and it is palpably untrue that a criminal can no longer be considered a human being. The most plausible conclusion to draw here is that we should reject the assumption that human rights are properties of persons, woven into the very fabric of our being.

The nail in the coffin of the idea that rights are properties is this: to view rights as natural properties is, mistakenly, to mix up a fact (or description) with a value (or prescription). Make no mistake about it: human rights are *not* facts about us; rather, they are values committing us to treating each other in ways we think we all deserve. Human rights do not tell us who or what we are; rather, they tell us how we should treat our fellow human beings. Human rights do not describe our nature; rather, they prescribe our behaviour. *Rights, most generally, are reasons to treat persons in certain respectful ways.* This does not mean that such reasons never refer to facts about the kinds of creatures we are, or about how we are motivated to act. It does mean that such reasons are not themselves part of our constitution as human beings. We do well here to note Jan Narveson's instructive phrase: "a person's rights are as real as his reasons are strong."[4] When someone says, "Respect my rights!", we can always respond, "Why should we?" A person's reasons for others to respect his rights thus become all important: so important, I submit, that after peeling away all the layers we find, at the very heart of human rights, a set of especially powerful reasons informing us how we should treat each other and how we should shape our shared social institutions. *In the final analysis, rights are reasons.*[5] This only underlines the importance of considering what counts as a strong reason—how we are to know whether a "justified claim" is, in fact, justified. The forthcoming chapter on the justification of human rights will examine several of the most influential views on this vital issue.

Trumps

Contemporary rights advocates agree that a right is not merely any claim, justified by a sufficient reason, to a certain kind of treatment; rather, it is an especially powerful and weighty claim. The very word "right" clearly connotes something serious and compelling, something that should not be denied lightly. Many rights defenders agree with Ronald Dworkin's famous declaration that "rights are trumps." Just as, in certain card games, a trump card beats all others, a rights claim "beats" such competing social values as the growth of the economy, the happiness of the majority, the promotion of artistic excellence, and so on. A rights claim is thought to be heavier—a better reason for action, something more deserving of our attention and protection—than these other social goals. Rights stand at the very foundation of political morality in our era. A standard assertion about human rights, in this regard, is that respect for them is a necessary condition for a government to be considered minimally just and decent on the world stage. Respect for human rights is the price of admission for political respectability; it is the touchstone of legitimacy for those with ambitions to rule.

Dworkin's declaration is sometimes taken to be an expression of absolutism about rights. Absolutism would be the belief not merely that rights are trumps but, moreover, that they are *always* trumps: that under no conditions can rival social goals beat out a rights claim in the competition for our attention, protection and social investment. It is important to note that this is not Dworkin's actual position. In fact, absolutism is an extreme view of rights which is not often defended nowadays. Dworkin's actual position is that rights are trumps *only if other things are equal*. If other things are not equal—if certain exceptional circumstances hold—then rival social goals may actually have a greater claim on our attention. Consider a case of serious and widespread national emergency, such as war, famine, or epidemic. We might think, for instance in a country being swept by the deadly Ebola virus, that those afflicted should be quarantined and that the antidote, if there is any, should be made available to all who need it. We might think, further, that these things should be done, in such an extreme crisis, even if those afflicted are forced into quarantine against their will and even if the medical supplies have to be appropriated by force from a company which claims them as its property. In truly exceptional cases, such rival social claims as national survival, or the avoidance of widespread disaster, may be compelling enough to outweigh rights claims, maybe even some human rights claims. But Dworkin correctly emphasizes the rarity of such occasions and suggests that, in daily life in a normal society, we still feel the force of the claim that rights are trumps. It is reasonable, then, to note that it adds to our definition of a right to say that it is a *high-priority* justified claim to a certain kind, a respectful kind, of treatment.[6]

Hohfeld's Analysis

More can, and should, be said about the nature of a claim and its connection to the essence of a right. For this, we should turn to W.N. Hohfeld. Hohfeld, a former law professor, is one of the most cited authorities on rights: it would be a real challenge to find a contemporary book on rights that does not contain at least one approving reference to him. Hohfeld famously claimed, back in 1919, that a right may be one of four kinds: a claim, a liberty, a power, or an immunity.[7]

The OED informs us that a claim is defined as "a demand or request for something considered as one's due." A Hohfeldian claim-right is a demand for something *from* some person or institution. It is a claim *on* somebody *for* something. A claim-right imposes an obligation on other people and/or on social institutions. In the language of rights theorists, a claim-right imposes a correlative duty. The duty literally co-relates with the right. There is no claim right-holder without a correlative duty-bearer. For example, if I claim that this book is copyrighted by me, I am demanding that, among other things, other people not copy it without my permission and perhaps even some royalty be paid to me from its sale. My copyright is a claim on other people's behaviour, as well as upon such social institutions as the legal system. We shall return shortly to consider Hohfeld's important assertion that, of the four kinds of rights, only claim-rights are "rights in the strict sense."[8]

A liberty, according to the OED, can be defined as "the right or power to do as one pleases." A Hohfeldian liberty-right is quite different from a claim-right: whereas a claim-right imposes correlative duties, a liberty-right is, so to speak, duty-free. Liberty-rights survive and flourish only in an environment where there are no duties. Hohfeld's technical definition of a liberty-right runs something like this: Bob has a liberty-right with regard to an action only if no one else has a claim on him with regard to that action. Only if Bob bears no duties to refrain from the action can he be said to be at liberty to perform it, should he choose. If there is no claim to tie him down, Bob is a free man. Suppose, for example, that Bob is single and owns his house. Suppose further that, in his basement, he wants to install a private, full-length bowling alley. Now, the rest of us may find this lacking in taste (and may not be surprised that he is single!) but none of us have any claim on Bob that he not go ahead with it. It is, after all, his house; he bears no duties to anyone to refrain from refurbishing his basement in this way. He thus enjoys a liberty-right to do so.

The definition of power, in the OED, is "the ability or authority to do or act." Sally enjoys a Hohfeldian power-right to perform an action if some other person, such as David, can and will—or at least should—be affected by her action. For Sally to enjoy the power-right, David must be in some sense liable to her, in the sense that he is subject *either* to her power (i.e., her actual ability to act) *or* to her authority (i.e., her entitlement to act), or perhaps both. For example, holders of public office, whether it be the local mayor or the President of the United States, enjoy numerous power-rights. They frequently have both the power and the authority to affect our lives in a substantial way: by setting rates of taxation, for instance, or by their decisions about public investment in health care and education, or by sending our soldiers off to fight a war. Parents also have many power-rights over their children, rights that erode over time as the children grow into adulthood.

The OED defines immunity, in the relevant sense, as "freedom from an obligation." Hohfeld himself would be hard-pressed to improve upon this conception. For him, an agent like Jim has an immunity-right from the action of Alison if Alison has no power-right over Jim with regard to the action in question. If Alison has neither power nor authority over Jim, then Jim is immune from Alison's action. An example of an actual immunity-right would be the fact that, in most Western democracies, elected members of public legislatures are immune from being sued for anything they say during a debate in the legislature. Elected members of legislatures do not have to worry about being sued for slander, libel, or fraudulent misrepresentation for anything they say during the course of such debates. The goal of granting our elected officials such immunity is to encourage the maximum freedom of expression during legislative debates, in the hopes that such will ultimately forward the public good.

There are at least two different ways of interpreting Hohfeld's important argument that, of these four kinds of rights, only claim-rights are rights "in the strict sense." The first way is literal: only claim-rights are worthy of the narrow and high-priority status synonymous with rights, whereas the other kinds of "rights" are merely pretenders to the throne, so to speak. It is only those entitlements that make concrete claims on other people, or institutions, that deserve to be called "rights." The problem with this literal way of interpreting Hohfeld is that, while it makes for a meaningful distinction between claim-rights and liberty-rights, it fails to do so between claim-rights and power-rights, or between claim-rights and immunity-rights. For power-rights also make claims on others—claims of liability—and immunity-rights claim that others either cannot or may not have power over the right-holder with regard to the action at hand. Indeed, even liberty-rights seem to make, or contain, a claim of a kind: Bob, in our example, seems most centrally to be claiming that no one interfere with his liberty to install a bowling alley in his basement.

This leads us to the second, preferred way of interpreting Hohfeld: to say that a right "in its strict sense" has the nature of a claim is to say that, whatever other elements may be present—such as power, liberty, or immunity—the element of a claim *must* be present. A claim that other people, or social institutions, either should do something or should refrain from doing something is a necessary condition for a rights-claim. *A claim is at the core of a right.* Consider Peter Jones' compelling idea that, in any familiar kind of right, there is typically found a cluster of Hohfeldian rights:

> [I]f I have a property right in a car, that right is likely to consist of a complicated cluster of Hohfeldian rights. Typically these would include the claim-right that others should refrain from damaging my car or using it without my permission, my liberty-right as owner of the car to use the car, the power to sell the car or to permit others to use it, and my immunity from any power of others to dispose of the car without my consent. In other words, a single assertion of right might, on inspection, turn out to be a cluster of different types of right.[9]

To this notion, I suggest we add the further proposition that it is the claim-right within the complex cluster which is necessary; it is what genuinely causes the assertion to strike with the force of a right. It is the concrete claim on our personal behaviour, and on the structure of our shared social institutions, which gets our attention and demands our respect.

Claim, Right, Entitlement

A cautionary note about claiming is in order. The impression should not be gained that, for the rest of us to respect Brenda's rights, she actually has to claim her rights in the strict sense of verbalizing these claims, constantly letting us know what her rights are. The sense of claim here is not the very narrow one of *uttering* a claim. The sense, rather, is that of *being entitled to utter* such a claim, and to expect that it be fulfilled. We see this clearly when we consider as an example Brenda's being unable to speak because she is asleep. Her inability to speak, at that point, does not mean that Brenda lacks rights. She still has claims on others even when she is not shouting them at the top of her lungs, or filing a lawsuit in court. Indeed, it seems that verbal claims are necessary *only* when things have gone wrong and when the duty-bearer needs to be explicitly reminded of his duty, or punished for having violated it. It is perhaps most appropriate, then, to view a right as the combination, or fusion, of *both* a claim *and* an entitlement. (It is interesting to note that the OED underlines this very tight conceptual connection by defining an entitlement as "a just claim, a right.") A right is an entitlement that endures even when the right-holder is not actually making a verbal claim and yet, most crucially, a right remains a justified claim, or demand, on the behaviour of others and the shape of social institutions. In other words, a right is a justified claim that remains justified even in the absence of verbal assertions: the reasons for the duty-bearer(s) to treat the right-holder in the appropriate way still exist, even if unstated. These observations only underline the key insight that, in the final analysis, rights are reasons. Rights are enduring grounds for treating the right-holder in a respectful way.

Moral vs. Legal Rights

So a right is a high-priority entitlement, justified by sufficient reasons, to something one claims as one's due. But it is important to note that rights, thus defined, can be of two kinds: moral or legal. It is crucial to make this distinction, since far too often the two are run together. Legal rights are those rights, as just defined, which 1) are actually written into legal codes, such as the US Bill of Rights, or the Canadian Charter of Rights and Freedoms; and 2) when violated have concrete legal remedies, notably lawsuits seeking restitution. An example would be the legal right, codified in the American Bill of Rights, not to be put on trial twice for a serious crime such as murder, provided one has already been found innocent of the same charge in a previous trial. This is the legal right of American citizens not to be put in "double jeopardy."

Moral rights need not be written into actual legal codes: maybe they are, maybe not. Moral rights exist either as rights within social moralities *or* as rights within what we might call a critical, or justified, morality. A social morality is a widely believed and practised code of conduct in a given society. For instance, in most cultures it seems to be a widely recognized moral right not to be lied to: we believe we are entitled to be told the truth and we condemn, criticize and shun those who lie to us. Though there are some cases when we excuse lying, in general nobody praises a liar, and no one enjoys being lied to. Being told the truth is something we feel is a reasonable claim on the behaviour of other people and on social institutions, especially our governments. A critical or justified morality, by contrast, is a complex and well-defined theoretical system of morals: it need not be widely believed and practised. It is more systematic and logically coherent than social moral codes and, at times, criticizes such social codes on grounds of inconsistency, incompleteness, or hypocrisy. A prominent example here would be utilitarianism, an elaborate ethical code designed to maximize the greatest happiness for the greatest number of people. Perhaps another example would be human rights theory itself, as developed by professional theorists who devote their careers to understanding human rights and to extending their development.

It is important to note that there may be some overlap between legal rights and moral rights: moral rights, in either sense—but especially the first, social code sense—often find expression in particular legal codes which provide concrete remedies for their violation. For instance, the moral right not to be lied to is at least partially codified in most Western democracies in the form of the law of perjury: lying to a court, while under oath during a proceeding, is a crime for which there is legal punishment. Another relevant observation here is this: the fact that the US Constitution has remained comparatively stable over more than 200 years may well be because the rights that it includes and protects are rights that Americans largely endorse as part of their actual social morality. Widespread agreement between moral rights and legal rights will lead to relatively stable legal systems, as well as to reinforced social moral codes.

He believes M. Rights exist

The degree of overlap between legal and moral rights does not diminish the differences between them. Two differences, in particular, must be noted. The first is that moral rights need not have legal codification for their existence and claim on our attention, nor effective legal remedies for their violation. There is no such thing as a legal right for which there is no law; but moral rights, in either sense, can exist and be real for people regardless of whether they are recognized in law or not. Indeed, changes in laws over time are frequently brought about because there has been a change in the social morality of the people, a change that is often first seen in the theoretical works of the professionals developing critical moralities. An example of a moral right not generally codified into law might be, say, the right in most Western cultures not to be betrayed sexually by one's partner, unless in the context of an "open marriage." You cannot throw your cheating partner into jail—it is not a legal right—but I suggest that most of us believe sexual fidelity from one's partner is a moral right, a reasonable claim on the behaviour of the partner, unless both have come to an explicit alternative arrangement. The social stigma surrounding adultery counts as some evidence in favour of this claim.

The second key difference between legal and moral rights is that legal rights need not be rights that are morally justifiable, either to the social morality of the particular culture or, perhaps more frequently, to plausible critical moralities. Many of us, for example, would say that the legal rights granted to slave-owners over their slaves in the American South before the Civil War were legal, but not moral. The same holds true for the legal rights granted to whites, in preference over blacks, during apartheid-era South Africa. It is interesting and important to note that, sometimes, the rights held in social moralities may themselves be subjected to moral criticism from critical moralities. As a critical moralist would say, just because it is widely believed or done does not make it right. Sometimes even society-wide beliefs and actions need critical correction from a gifted expert or inspired leader. Such figures, when successful, are often referred to in the history books as "moral reformers." The question arises: are human rights moral or legal? This is a surprisingly difficult question to answer fully. The short answer is both. Many human rights have, in a number of countries, been written into legal codes, and they can enjoy effective legal protection. For example, one of the most codified rights in the various constitutions of the Western liberal democracies is to "life, liberty and security of the person." Claims to personal security and personal liberty are some of the most plausible human rights claims there are. But all too often, human rights are either not written into the laws at all, or are written into laws but not actually protected on the ground. History is relevant here: human rights came into being first and foremost as rights developed by philosophers and theologians in critical or justified moralities. They were then incorporated into social moralities, for instance through the pro-rights revolutions in America and France in the late 1700s. Since the end of World War II in 1945—and spurred especially by reaction to the horrors of the Holocaust—social commitment to the idea of human rights has both widened and deepened to the point where it is now one of the most influential moral and political concepts of our time. So human rights are sometimes, in some places, legal but they began and continue in many places to exist only as moral rights. The contemporary human rights

Terrible Question [handwritten marginalia]

movement has, as probably its main goal, the effective translation of the moral values inherent in human rights theory into meaningful and concrete legal rights. Making human rights "real," in this sense of translating fine thoughts and warm feelings into guaranteed legal protections, is what animates many human rights activists today.

A word about international law is appropriate at this point. In addition to being written into the national constitutions of various countries, human rights have been written into the body of international law. International law refers to various rules agreed to by different countries in order to regulate their interactions. Governments come together to sign international treaties endorsing these rules and regulations. They then each return to their own countries and pass these treaties into law within their own borders. This procedure is referred to as "ratifying" the treaty, and in most countries this is done through the various constitutional means for turning a bill into a law. It may surprise some readers to know that there exists something called the International Bill of Rights, composed of the Universal Declaration of Human Rights (1948), the International Covenant on Civil and Political Rights (1966), and the International Covenant on Economic, Social and Cultural Rights (1966). Most countries—almost all, in fact—have by now ratified this International Bill. In theory, this means that such countries have committed themselves to making human rights real within their borders. The trouble, though, with calling human rights "legal" in this sense of being codified into international law is that the enforcement mechanisms of international law are very weak, at least in comparison with those of national law. If one lives in a well-run country, one can have considerable confidence in the law being effectively enforced by the police and the courts. But if one's distant relative lives in a country that is not well-run, then not only is the relative worse off, there is also little that one can do to ensure that the relative will be treated well by his own government. There just is not the same network of effective social institutions connecting countries together as there is connecting people together within the borders of a well-run country. As a result, it is sometimes said that "international law" does not even deserve to be called "law" in its proper sense, since it is so much more difficult to bring outlaw governments to justice internationally than it is to bring criminals to justice domestically. There are, in practice, precious few international guarantees for the human rights of persons living in countries that refuse to make human rights real within their borders, even if those countries have signed all the international human rights treaties currently on offer. It thus seems justified to suggest that human rights exist first and foremost as rights in critical and social moralities, rights that many people hope to translate into effective legal rights throughout the world's many nations through a process of long-term political struggle, educational engagement and institutional reform.

General vs. Special Rights

General rights are those rights that make claims on all other people and all relevant social institutions. For example, human rights are general moral rights, held against all. No one has the right to violate, or perhaps even to ignore, the legitimate human rights claims of others. Special rights, by contrast, are rights that make claims only against particular persons or institutions, and usually only at particular times and under certain circumstances. A kind of special legal right would be, for example, the set of rights that a landlord in a particular country or state has against his tenants regarding the terms of the lease, and vice-versa. Such precisely defined entitlements are not claimable against all humanity; their scope is specially confined to the particular relationship in question.

Rights vs. Their Objects

It is crucial not to confuse a right, whether it is general or special, with its object. A right's object is sometimes also called the right's substance. The difference, once grasped, should never be lost sight of: a right is a justified claim *to* something, whereas the object of the right is that very something being claimed. Consider a property right, say, in a house. The right is the justified claim, or entitlement, to the house, whereas the house itself is the object of that claim. To use a metaphor, a right is like an airplane ticket: it is one's claim, or entitlement, to get on the plane when the flight is ready to go. But it is the flight itself that is one's main want, or object. This distinction is crucially important for all talk of making rights, especially human rights, real. To make a right real, it is not enough to get the right written into a legal code, nor even to get the majority of people in a culture to endorse it in their social morality. *To make a right real is to bring it about that the right-holder actually possesses the object of his right-claim.* Think of the airplane ticket metaphor: one does not really care about the ticket itself—the small scrap of paper—except insofar as it allows one to get on board the flight, which is what one really wants and why one bought the ticket in the first place. Likewise, one does not care so much about the mere entitlement to one's house or car, to one's raw right to vote in elections, or to enjoy personal security. What one really cares about is actually having a house, a car, a vote, reliable security, and so forth. Rights are always rights *to* something, and it is *the something* that we most want. This does not mean that rights themselves are valueless: try getting on board an airline flight without a ticket. Rights have, historically, proved rather useful in helping us get our hands on the things we want to claim as our due. First came the claim, and the object followed. The point here is that the value of rights rests mainly in the way they facilitate and help secure our possession and enjoyment of the objects we claim from society as those things which we are owed.

What exactly are the objects of *human* rights? This is a controversial question, one for which no two rights theorists will offer the same answer. We will examine this question intensively in a subsequent chapter. It has already been suggested that, most generally, rights are justified, high-priority claims to a certain kind of treatment. Human rights, in particular, are justified, high-priority claims to that minimal level of decent and respectful treatment which we believe is owed to a human being. But what exactly is meant by "decent and respectful treatment"? How do we measure it? How do we know when we have received it? How do we know, conversely, when our claim to such treatment has been ignored or violated? It seems fair to say that we tend to measure and rate the calibre of treatment we receive from society by the degree to which we are secure in our possession of the following items: freedoms and opportunities, protections from serious threats, elemental regard and recognition from others, and also concrete objects, such as cars and houses. We know we are being treated decently when we actually possess, or otherwise enjoy, secure access to these important objects. It should, of course, be noted that these objects are not just "objects" in the familiar sense of the term. We can, and do, have just and high-priority general claims to things other than concrete objects: just because an object is abstractly defined, it does not make it less vital to the minimal level of respectful treatment we are demanding when we demand that our human rights be satisfied. Indeed, we might judge that such abstractly-defined objects as security, liberty and recognition are just as important—perhaps even more fundamentally important—than the more concrete objects of our rights claims. It is, furthermore, quite plausible to suggest that our claims to concrete objects are justified precisely by the fact that they are connected to the satisfaction of our claims to the more abstractly-defined objects. For example, many people have argued that owning private property is a justified right insofar as it is implied by the prior, more abstract, right to human freedom. One gets to claim the concrete object as a way of making real one's prior claim to the abstract object, which contains the overriding general value and reason for action.

Perhaps the most encompassing description for the objects of our rights claims is that they are important benefits: concrete goods, freedoms, protections, respectful treatment are all beneficial and all things we place great value on. Indeed, they must be: otherwise, why would we bother to claim them as objects of our rights? We deeply want things that benefit us importantly, be they material goods, security from violence, or the freedom to make our own choices in life. Which mixture of these important benefits provides us with the minimum level of decent treatment that every human being can rightfully demand? That is a topic whose answer must await fuller development in a future chapter.

Civil and Political Rights vs. Social and Economic Rights

We saw that, in the International Bill of Rights, there are two International Covenants: one on civil and political rights, the other on economic, social and cultural rights. This split has become controversial in recent times. The notion behind the split is that there are two kinds of human rights, distinguished by the unique set of objects to which each lays claim. Civil and political rights claim various freedoms and legal protections: freedom of personal conscience and expression; freedom of movement and association; freedom to vote and run for public office; reliable legal protection against violence; and the various due process rights, like the right to be considered innocent before proven guilty of a crime and the right to a public trial before an impartial jury. Civil and political rights are sometimes called "first generation" human rights, because they were the first claimed by human rights activists. Such rights are the classical, traditional, canonical human rights recognized in the history of political struggle in the West. Economic, social and cultural rights, by contrast, claim concrete material goods and various social benefits, such as a subsistence level of income, basic levels of education and health care, clean water and air, and equal opportunity at work. These rights are sometimes labelled "second-generation" human rights, for obvious reasons: after the first generation had been secured and the Industrial Revolution brought about sweeping social change, different objects started to be claimed by social activists as a matter of human right. There has even been talk, very recently, of a "third generation" of human rights—the latest set of claims, focussing on recognition and equality—but consideration of these is best reserved for later, since the aim in this section is to introduce the storied clash, or so-called clash, between first- and second-generation rights.

Contemporary human rights defenders, led in this matter by Henry Shue and James Nickel,[10] deny that this supposed split between first- and second-generation human rights constitutes a split in kind. Most want to say that there is but one correct list of human rights, and it contains objects from both of these supposedly separate "kinds" or lists. Hence their use of the "generations" metaphor: the one set of claims is not utterly different from the other; it merely came later and seeks to complete the same task. More pointedly, the subsequent rights originated from, and remain sustained by, the same family of concepts and core values that are implied by those in the first generation. This inclusive contemporary view, however, remains hotly contested in some circles: there are still a number of theorists who insist that *only* civil and political rights are *really* human rights, whereas socio-economic "rights" are merely desirable goals dressed up in the more powerful rhetoric of rights. Such skeptics, like Maurice Cranston, argue that if the objects of socio-economic rights were provided to everyone, that would impose outrageous costs on society.[11] Civil and political rights, by contrast, supposedly entail duties which are both affordable and readily assumed. It is not too much to ask for the standard civil and political freedoms, as well as for a well-functioning legal system. But it would cost society far too much, and prove far too burdensome, to provide everyone with drinkable water, basic education and health care, and a subsistence level of income—and that is assuming we could even arrive at an agreement on what defines such a level. The response from defenders of socio-economic rights points out that defenders of civil and political rights also staunchly defend the right to own private property, a right with socio-economic consequences if ever there was one. Furthermore, they suggest that civil and political rights also impose costly burdens: no one can suggest that running the legal system, for example, comes cheap. Yes, realizing human rights costs money, and absorbs real time and resources, but this is a price worth paying, owing to the great importance of providing everyone with the objects they need to be treated decently as human beings.

Negative vs. Positive Rights

This distinction has probably the highest profile, and is also the one that always generates the most discussion and debate. A negative right can be defined as one which imposes a correlative duty which calls only for *inaction* on the part of the duty-bearer, be it a person or institution. The duty-bearer can fulfil his duty merely by refraining from acting. For example, it is sometimes said that all a duty-bearer has to do, to fulfil his duty correlative to the right of free speech, is not to interfere with the speech of others. One fulfills one's duty by doing nothing. (This does not imply, of course, that one must sit there and listen to the speech; it means merely that one fulfills one's duty by refraining from attempts to suppress the speech in question.) A positive right, by contrast, can be defined as one which imposes a correlative duty which *does* call for action on the part of the duty-bearer. The duty-bearer must do something to fulfil his duty in this regard. For instance, if the right is to a subsistence level of income, then social institutions have to provide that income to those who do not have it. They can do this through such means as social welfare transfers.

Many thinkers in the past, such as Cranston, were tempted to claim that negative rights line up with civil and political rights, whereas positive rights line up with social and economic rights: the former kind only demand forbearance and non-interference on the part of duty-bearers whereas the latter kind demand action, provision, assistance and aid on the part of duty-bearers. These thinkers concluded that, since it is both reasonable and affordable to require non-interference, and both unreasonable and costly to demand provision and aid, civil and political rights are the only genuine human rights in existence. Strictly speaking, this equation does not seem sustainable. For example, the construction and maintenance of an effective legal system clearly require that a series of actions be taken, and yet a well-functioning legal system is something very near and dear to the defenders of civil and political rights. So here is a case of a civil and political right imposing correlative duties that are positive in nature. Thus, the older equation breaks down.

Not all rights theorists agree with the definition of negative and positive offered above. We will consider their objections in a subsequent chapter. The point that the present distinction between negative and positive underlines, regardless of whether or not it is ultimately sustainable, is this: what duties can we reasonably require of people and institutions? What does respect for human rights really cost—and is it a price we are willing to pay? These issues are fundamental to the human rights debate: who, or what, should bear the duties correlative to human rights? Which exact duties are these? Where should we locate the line between a duty that is reasonable and fair, and one that is excessive and destructively burdensome? Indeed, what objects of human rights claims are so vital that it makes sense to say that we can require that they be made available to everyone, perhaps on penalty of being subjected to force?

Rights Violation

Much of our concern with respecting human rights is to avoid violating them. In general, a human right is violated when a duty-bearer fails to perform his correlative duty without just cause. Since human rights are designed to provide elemental protections and benefits, it follows that just causes for ignoring them, or for putting correlative duties to the side, are few and far between—and must be of exceptional and overriding importance. One is reminded here of our earlier discussion of rights as trumps. Human rights are not absolute: there are very rare personal and social emergencies when the duties correlative to human rights may, with sufficient reason, be put aside. Certain cases of self-defence, or war, come to mind. In the ordinary course of life, however, human rights outweigh all rival claims and inclinations. So for a person to take away an object of one's human rights—be it security or liberty—is for that person to violate one's human rights. Such a person may be resisted, and subsequently subjected to proper punishment. For a social institution to fail to provide the protections or benefits in question would be for it to violate human rights. It is important to consider whether such failure is intentional and deliberate or not. Intentional failure is the clearest form of violation and calls for the reform of a morally decrepit and wicked social structure. Non-intentional failure, while still a violation, calls for institutional reform of a different kind. In this non-intentional case, the institution usually lacks the wherewithal to do its part in making human rights real. It may therefore require assistance, or restructuring, or an injection of resources. But it does not deserve to be under the same dark cloud of disapproval as institutions of the first sort. Institutions which intentionally violate human rights are wicked, and have neither legitimacy nor grounds for complaint against those who resist them. Institutions that unintentionally violate human rights are merely disadvantaged, albeit seriously so. These regimes may yet earn their legitimacy by locating and prioritizing the resources they need to become rights-respecting. Such disadvantaged regimes may call, in the first instance, for assistance rather than resistance.

Conclusion: Overall Initial Definition of a Human Right

A human right, then, is a general moral right that every human being has. Sometimes it finds legal expression and protection, sometimes not. This legal variability does not undermine the existence and firmness of the moral right, and actually provides focus for contemporary human rights activism, where the goal is often to translate the pre-existing moral claim into an effective legal entitlement.

A human right is a high-priority claim, or authoritative entitlement, justified by sufficient reasons, to a set of objects that are owed to each human person as a matter of minimally decent treatment. Such objects include vitally needed material goods, personal freedoms, and secure protections. In general, the objects of human rights are those fundamental benefits that every human being can reasonably claim from other people, and from social institutions, as a matter of justice. Failing to provide such benefits, or acting to take away such benefits, counts as rights violation. The violation of human rights is a vicious and ugly phenomenon indeed; and it is something we have overriding reasons to resist and, ultimately, to remedy.

Notes

1 The connection between hate propaganda and the promotion of brutalities against a targeted group can also be seen, very sadly, in the more recent case of the Rwandan civil war of 1994. Most estimates place the death toll for that near-genocidal strife somewhere between 500,000 and one million human beings. For more, see G. Prunier, *The Rwanda Crisis: History of a Genocide* (New York: Columbia University Press, 1995). For more on the Holocaust perpetrated by the Nazis against the Jews, and other groups, during the Second World War, see M. Gilbert, *The Holocaust* (New York: Henry Holt, 1987). Most estimates of the death toll from the Holocaust coalesce around the figure of at least six million.

2 John Locke, "Second Treatise" in his *Two Treatises of Civil Government*, ed. P. Laslett (Cambridge: Cambridge University Press, 1988), first published in 1688-89, chap. 2, sections 8-16.

3 Locke, "Second Treatise," section 16.

4 J. Narveson, *Moral Issues* (Oxford: Oxford University Press, 1983), 22.

5 I first made this claim in my *War and International Justice: A Kantian Perspective* (Waterloo: Wilfrid Laurier University Press, 2000), 90-109.

6 R. Dworkin, *Taking Rights Seriously* (Cambridge, MA: Harvard University Press, 1977).

7 W.N. Hohfeld, *Fundamental Legal Conceptions Applied to Judicial Reasoning* (New Haven, CT: Yale University Press, 1919).

8 Hohfeld, *Fundamental Legal Conceptions*, 15-16.

9 P. Jones, *Rights* (New York: St. Martin's, 1994), 12-24.

10 H. Shue, *Basic Rights: Subsistence, Affluence and U.S. Foreign Policy*, 2nd ed. (Princeton: Princeton University Press, 1996); J. Nickel, *Making Sense of Human Rights* (Berkeley: University of California Press, 1987).

11 M. Cranston, *What are Human Rights?* (New York: Basic Books, 1973).

Chapter 2

Who Holds Human Rights?

In the last chapter, we were introduced to the core concept of a human rights-holder. It was suggested at that time that, since we are well acquainted with human beings, we would not have to dwell for long on the identity of human rights-holders. Who holds human rights? All human beings, of course: hence the name of the very concept in question. Human rights, after all, are general moral rights, claimable by everyone and held against everyone, especially against those who run social institutions. The twin commitments to universal entitlement and to a baseline level of equality for all are hallmarks of the contemporary human rights movement, and are part of its special contribution to world history. Human rights are designed to be shared by all of us, no matter what our nationality, age, race, gender, language, occupation, religion, income, social standing, sexual orientation, hair colour, or taste in ice cream. Prominent human rights documents enthusiastically proclaim that all human beings have rights. For instance, in the United Nations's Universal Declaration of Human Rights—part of the International Bill of Rights mentioned last chapter—it is stated that "all members of the human family" hold human rights. "All peoples," "all human beings," "every individual," "everyone," has human rights.

Reflections on Difficulties

This defence of equality and universality sounds sublime but, upon reflection, how plausible is it? Granted, where human rights are also legal rights, then the answer to the question of who holds them is straightforward: whomever is referred to, in that law, as a rights-holder. Fans of international law, citing documents like the Universal Declaration, are thus inclined to suggest that such proclamations settle the issue of rights-holding definitively: all human beings hold human rights. While that is a relevant contention, and while we might want to agree with it, we must be sure that such endorsement is not given loosely, or without full consideration and a satisfying rationale. What happens, for example, when we step back from the law and reconsider the issue from the point of view of moral reasoning—of human rights as general moral rights? Do we really believe that all human beings have human rights in this sense? Do Nazis have human rights? Serial rapists? Mass murderers? Terrorists? Soldiers of an enemy country, attacking us during war? Corrupt officials of an oppressive government? Are these contemptible kinds of people entitled to *exactly the same* baseline level of dignified treatment as the rest of us, who are decent, reasonable and law-abiding? Does it even make sense to suggest that people who violate the human rights of others nevertheless retain human rights themselves?

Criminals and rights-violators are not the only ones posing problems here: consider all those human beings who are not, in the relevant sense, normal, healthy or well-functioning. Do the comatose or the insane, for instance, have human rights—exactly the same set of rights as the rest of us? Do infants, or the enfeebled elderly? What about those who have a lethal and highly contagious disease?

Note that these possible counter-examples all deal with existing, actual human beings. There is an additional, and very heated, controversy over whether human beings who are not yet actual can be said to have human rights, whether they be fetuses in the womb or entire future generations not yet conceived. None of the international law documents answer this question: do non-existing, or merely potential, human beings count? Do they have high-priority and justified moral claims on us actual human beings, here and now? Does a fetus have a human right not to be aborted, for instance? Do future generations have a human right to a clean environment? Of course, such potential human beings cannot literally utter such claims but, as we saw in the last chapter, the key is whether we have sufficiently strong reasons to act in such a way, here and now, to ensure they will enjoy a certain baseline quality of life once they are born. The key is not whether they are actually in the act of asserting their human rights but whether we have reasons strong enough to acknowledge that we are under some kind of important correlative duty towards them. Human rights, after all, are more about enduring entitlements than about explicitly uttered claims.

One important question, in this connection, is this: if we allow for these kinds of distinctions and discriminations—if we say some people have human rights while others do not—then are we not thinking in essentially the same way as those brutal human rights violators we want to condemn? Such violators are, after all, quite keen on the idea that some human beings do not really deserve human rights, or perhaps are not even worthy of being called "human" in the relevant sense at all. This raises a whole hornet's nest of problematic questions: are we so confident that we know what being "human" in the relevant sense really is?

Are the comatose, or fetuses, fully human? What about the severely disabled, or the pathologically insane? Is it truly compelling to suggest that this way of making distinctions is "essentially" on the same level as the human rights-violator? Perhaps this way of making judgments is simply leading us to the most defensible and sober conclusion: that only those normal, well-functioning, adult human beings who do not violate the human rights of others truly enjoy full status as holders of human rights. If that is the most defensible conclusion, with regard to status as a human rights-holder, however, it would appear to bring with it an unfortunate consequence.

This consequence would be that the contemporary human rights movement cannot defend two of its most cherished beliefs: in universal entitlement, and in a baseline level of moral equality genuinely shared by all. If the movement has to give up these two bedrock beliefs, then it might fear losing much of its special contribution to history, namely, how it has widened our moral horizons and brought previously excluded groups of people "inside the circle" of genuine moral concern and shared status. If human rights are not really shared by all human beings, then do we lose the global reach and cosmopolitan concern—the "one world" quality—that has long seemed part of the idea's real promise?

The purpose of this second chapter is to pursue plausible and well-developed answers to many of these difficult questions surrounding the status of being a human rights-holder. Before we get to it, though, one disclaimer must be made. The question of human rights tends, for whatever reason, to bring with it questions regarding whether non-human animals, plants and perhaps even inanimate objects (such as rare works of great art) also have rights. My belief is that one's perspective on human rights has little, if any, necessary connection to whether one believes that other species, or things, also have rights. There are human rights theorists who are also passionate animal rights activists, as well as human rights activists who could not care less about whether cows should be created only to be carved up into juicy steak. In any event, the sole focus of this book is on *human* rights: the reader must look elsewhere for a discussion of animal rights and the moral status of plants and inanimate objects.[1]

Necessary and Sufficient Conditions

To come to a firm grasp of who holds human rights, we need to employ an important distinction. This is the one between a necessary and a sufficient condition. A necessary condition for human rights-holding status would be something that one *cannot do without* if one is to have such status at all. It is necessary in the sense that the condition is required: without the condition or characteristic in question, one is excluded from further consideration as to whether one has human rights or not. An example of a necessary condition in general would be this: for a student like Alice to get an "A+" on her upcoming exam in "World History," she is required to write the exam. If she does not write it, it is impossible for her to get an "A+" on it. Writing the exam is thus a necessary condition for scoring an "A+" on it. Of course, the fact that she writes the exam is by no means *enough to earn* the desired "A+"; she might, after all, write the exam but fail it miserably. This illustrates nicely the difference between a necessary condition and a sufficient one. Whereas a necessary condition for x is whatever one cannot do without in order to have x, a sufficient condition for x is whatever is enough to have x. Writing the exam, while needed for an "A+," is not enough to earn it. A sufficient condition for getting an "A+" would be something like offering an exam answer that answers all questions clearly and comprehensively, and doing so in an exceptionally good and insightful way.

Why not another example to hammer the point home? Having $250,000 is a necessary condition for being a millionaire but it is obviously not of itself sufficient. One needs the full, cool million to earn the status of millionaire. Conversely, having $10 million is certainly sufficient for being a millionaire but not all of that cash is necessary to merit such status. Sometimes sufficient conditions give us "surplus," above and beyond what we strictly require. Of particular interest to us is the set of conditions that are *jointly* necessary and sufficient. An example of such a joint set would be having, let us say, exactly two bundles of $500,000 for status as a millionaire. Both bundles are genuinely needed, and only when combined together are they sufficient, to produce the sought-after status of being a millionaire.

The relevance of this distinction between necessary and sufficient conditions to the question of who holds human rights is this: what conditions, or characteristics, must a creature have in order to be a human rights-holder? What other characteristics are enough to earn such status? What conditions are necessary, and what others sufficient, for us to pronounce a person a fully-fledged human rights-holder? Do all human beings sport both the necessary, and the sufficient, conditions required, or can only a special sub-set of humanity fit the bill? For the remainder of the chapter, point-by-point consideration will be given to various properties, conditions, and characteristics that have often been proposed as being important to one's status as a human rights-holder. We will consider whether such proposed properties are necessary or sufficient, or perhaps neither. Our aim is to achieve an understanding of the unique set of characteristics that is jointly necessary and sufficient for human rights-holding status, i.e., the set that perfectly fits our sense of who holds human rights.

Biological Humanity

Perhaps the clearest way to ground the universality and equality of human rights is to insist that human rights are ultimately rooted in human biology. We all have human rights because we are all, quite literally, human beings. One is a human rights-holder if, and only if, one is born of human parents. We all must, additionally, have the same set of human rights because we are all equally human: no one is "more" biologically human than the next person. This very straightforward view of biological humanity possesses both strengths and weaknesses.

The main strength of this view is that it does establish a clear and uncontested necessary condition for being a human rights-holder: you must be a human being, and moreover a living one. You must have human blood pulsing through your body. Thus, when we talk of human rights, it simply will not do to refer to the "human rights" of dead bodies, or of future generations, or of different living species. Dead bodies, or non-existent people, are inappropriate objects for our high-priority moral concern, the way human rights-holders clearly must be. How, after all, can the claims of the dead have high priority against those of the living? A dead body—even if it is a human corpse—is not a moral subject, has no moral status. A corpse values nothing, has no vital (i.e., life-sustaining) interests, feels neither pleasure nor pain, and so on. Indeed, a dead body is nothing save an inert clump of physical tissue. Non-existent people—future generations yet to be conceived—likewise fail to have high-priority claims against those currently alive. For one thing, those currently alive have definite and identifiable needs and interests, whereas talk of future generations is very vague: we have little idea of the kind of people they are going to be, or of the kinds of circumstances they are going to face. Future generations, as the non-living, likewise have no vital interests, value and feel nothing, *et cetera*. So even though we might plan prudently for the future, and hope that our descendants enjoy the good things in life, it seems a wild exaggeration to refer to non-existent people as having high-priority moral claims on us the living, here and now. As for the fetus, I put the matter aside for another project. The fetus exists and is alive, so is importantly unlike a corpse or future generations yet to be conceived. The fetus also has human parents. But for more on the thorny issue of fetal rights, and whether they are equivalent to human rights, I refer the reader to the relevant literature on abortion.[2]

Defenders of animal rights, and the rights of other non-human species, sometimes contend that the language of human rights is discriminatory. Peter Singer and Richard Ryder, for example, suggest that limiting human rights to human beings is a form of what they call "species-ism," an arbitrary and primitive preference in favour of our own kind, simply because it *is* our own kind. Animal rights activists like Singer would note here that animals exist and are alive, can feel pleasure and pain, have vital interests, and so on.[3] My response is that saying *only* human beings are entitled to *human* rights is not somehow to prefer, or privilege, the human species in an arbitrary and groundless way, analogous to a form of racial or sexual discrimination. Just because one believes that only human beings are entitled to human rights does not mean that one cannot also endorse animal rights. What it does mean—at least, probably—is that animals, if they do have entitlements, do not enjoy the same kind of entitlements that human beings enjoy. Such an assertion is far from being arbitrary or groundless, since it is rooted in real and morally important differences between species. We might want to say, for example, that we human beings have the right to participate in, and shape, those social institutions that have deep impact on the quality of our lives. To this end, we believe that people should have the right to run for public office if they wish, have the right to vote in free and fair elections, have the right to be treated in a respectful way by social systems of education and health care, and so on. But it is silly to say that animals should be able to run for public office, or to vote in public elections, or to show up for school one day eager to learn calculus or chemistry. Maybe animals do have rights of a kind: that is not our main concern in this book. But even if they do it is clear that such animal rights are not exactly the same thing as human rights, which *is* our main concern. I leave it to others to worry about animal rights; I return our attention to those of our fellow human beings.

The main weakness with the biological humanity perspective is that, while it is necessary, it is not sufficient to ground human rights claims. For instance, if one believes that biological humanity is sufficient for human rights-holding status, then one is confronted with a forfeiture problem. Most of us want to say that a person can, by committing certain crimes, forfeit some, perhaps all, of his human rights claims. If one has rights *simply because* one has human biology, then one can never give up such rights while on this side of the grave. To view human biology as sufficient for human rights-holding status is to view human rights as properties of persons, instead of the more appropriate view—suggested in the last chapter—of *rights as reasons to treat persons in certain respectful ways*. We simply do not come born with human rights the same way we come born with two eyes and a nose. Human rights are not physical facts. Thus, this perspective mistakes values for facts. More precisely, this view resorts to a fact-like appeal as a disguised way of persuading us to adopt a certain set of values. But the raw fact of our biological humanity seems to carry with it no intrinsic moral significance: from a purely physical point of view, we are just a living clump of cells, complex structures of meat, blood, and bone. Biology is but brute fact; it alone provides no reason for treating other people in a respectful way. Human biology *can* serve as a meaningful category of exclusion, in order to fix what group of creatures we are talking about, namely, living human beings and them alone. But it does not of itself give morally sufficient reasons for respectful treatment.

The point needs to be driven home because it is very common to mix together talk of what is "natural" with what is "good." It is equally frequent to mix together talk of what is "good" or "right" with what is "humane." Indeed, in many of the most famous human rights documents, the phrase "humane and dignified treatment" occurs with remarkable repetition. One always needs to remind oneself, though, that the "humane" treatment we all owe each other is rooted not in biology but, rather, in morality. "Humane" treatment is a value-laden term, not a factual one; and to be "inhumane" is not to be an alien from another planet; rather, it is to violate a core code of conduct to which we believe every living human is duty-bound. References to our shared humanity *are* rhetorically powerful, often serving to move people to act in morally appropriate ways. This reference is part of what gives the biological humanity perspective its first-glance appeal. It must be stressed, however, that reference to a shared humanity in this raw biological sense is really a short-hand way of speaking about a set of values that we wish were shared by everyone, that we believe *should* be endorsed by everyone. Citing the fact that we all share some of the same biology may help to persuade some people to act in ways they should. They do say, after all, that blood is thicker than water. If such appeal to biological similarity helps such people access the appropriate, human rights-respecting mind-set, then it does play a positive role. But this role seems persuasive rather than justifying; it appears to be psychological rather than moral.

Presumably, what we ultimately want are reasons for respecting human rights that are not only persuasive but also have the force of justification behind them.

Most people, upon reflection, would say that biology does not of itself impose moral duties on us; rather, we impose such duties on ourselves through our beliefs and values, through our agreements and actions, through what we find good and desirable about life. Morality is not a naturally occurring biological product: it is not bred into our bones. Morality is constructed socially by our shared responses to the blessings and burdens of our biology, by our knowledge about each other and the world, and by our values regarding what constitutes a worthwhile existence. Human rights must thus remain grounded in strong moral reasons, not in a core collection of organic chemicals pulsing through our bodies. Human biology, while necessary, is not sufficient for human rights-holding status. What characteristics, when coupled with biological humanity, might suffice?

Metaphysical Humanity

To refer to metaphysical humanity, we saw in the last chapter, is to suggest that there is an important property shared by us all which is literally "above" or "beyond" the physical. It is to posit the existence of a substance shared by all of us which demands dignified regard. An enduring example of such a shared metaphysical property would be something like a soul. We are rendered morally special in the universe, and deserving of respectful treatment, not because of our brain-heavy biology but, rather, because we each have an immortal soul and it is this soul that is the seat of our true interest, identity and worth as individuals. A related metaphysical appeal would be to claim that we all have human rights, and the exact same set of such rights, because we are all children of God, and no one is more a child of God than the next person. Everyone, since they have the imprint of the divine on their person, must be treated with some baseline level of dignity and respect. To fail to do so is not merely to violate those people, but also to debase oneself in front of God and, moreover, to violate one of God's most important commands.[4]

There is no denying the fact that such religious appeals are both rhetorically and emotionally powerful. One also cannot deny the important role religion has played, in all cultures, in deeply influencing what people believe about things like morality and politics. Religious, and other metaphysical, appeals *have* played positive roles at points during humanity's moral evolution. But, as was mentioned in connection with the biological humanity perspective, we should be seeking a perspective that is not merely rhetorically persuasive, or psychologically comforting, but also justified from the point of view of a critical morality, of a reasonable and principled argumentative appeal. Even though we saw in the last chapter that metaphysical appeals can never, strictly speaking, be proven false—since they are inherently speculative matters—this very "un-prove-ability" also limits the degree to which we can appeal to metaphysics to ground important claims about what people are duty-bound to do, and how social institutions ought to be shaped. For example, to tell people they must behave a certain way because God commands them to do so runs afoul of a real problem when some such people respond, in all sincerity, with "Who are you to tell me what God commands?" What if such people do not believe in God, or in an immortal soul, to begin with? Or what if they do indeed believe in God but do not endorse the particular vision of God which this view would have them support? After all, a number of religious traditions require adherents to discriminate sharply between believers and unbelievers—or between the chosen and the excluded—and thus they may reject the universality and equality sought through such an appeal. Far from uniting us all behind the ideal of respect for human rights, religious appeals might serve only to exaggerate differences of opinion regarding who has equal moral status and why. Religion, as we all know, has generated deep social divisions throughout history and thus, in spite of its positive and inspiring qualities, might not make for the most accessible, inclusive or successful grounding for human rights.

Metaphysical appeals are thus double-edged swords: while they cannot be disproved, they cannot be proven either. The lack of evidence behind them means they cannot be shown to be false, but their speculative nature also means it is very difficult to show those who reject the initial speculative premises that they are true, or even just more likely. To those who dismiss metaphysical appeals as hopelessly out of date, or as stale conceptual leftovers from an earlier and utterly different era, there seems to be nothing this perspective can offer to make them endorse the human rights idea. Before we write such people off, we should consider alternative methods for conceiving the essence of human rights claims, and who exactly is entitled to make them. In the face of assertions about faith, souls and God, many reasonable people are left asking for more. In my judgment, appeals to metaphysical properties are neither necessary nor sufficient to ground human rights-holding status.

Rational Agency

Another time-honoured perspective on the question of who holds human rights is that it is only by virtue of being a rational agent that one is a human rights-holder. The roots of this view, which is still influential in philosophical circles, can be found as far back as Aristotle, who famously pronounced that man is a "rational animal."[5] It is our rationality that makes us special in the universe. Rationality is the most distinctive and valuable thing about us, the very essence of our most fundamental identity and aspiration as human beings. It is not our genes, or our souls, which ground human rights; rather, it is our ability to act in a rational manner. After all, are we to grant rights to the irrational?

We should examine the connection between rationality and action inherent in this rational agency perspective. It is not our cognitive ability to reason that is important here. The fact that we can think logically, perform mathematical calculations, and process information in a valid manner is no doubt very useful, but that is not what this view is getting at. If it were, computers might have as strong a claim to status as rights-holders as human beings, which seems absurd. The idea, rather, is that it is our unique ability as human beings *to apply rational thought to how we act*, especially with regard to considering how our actions affect each other, that is the core element on which this perspective focuses.

How do we apply reason to action? The answer: by selecting ends of action in the first place, and then by taking the intermediate measures reason tells us we need to, if we are to arrive at the end successfully. In other words, reason aids us *both* in helping to select which ends of action, amongst various alternatives, to adopt as our goals, *and then* in helping to select which means of action, amongst various alternatives, we need to take to move toward them. This everyday, applied use of reason has been called, in contrast with purely theoretical uses, our faculty of "practical reason." Defenders of the rational agency perspective maintain that it is because we have practical reason that we have human rights.

Alan Gewirth, an influential philosopher of human rights,[6] suggests that, as a matter of practical reason, all human beings endorse the following proposition: "I do act A for end E." Whether A is "study" and E is "to earn a university degree," or whether A is "stare out the window at the scenery" and E is "to relax," Gewirth contends that all human action contains this aspect of purposiveness. Everything we do, we do for a reason. All human action—from the heroic to the mundane—has a purpose. This is not, of course, to suggest that every reason for action is equally good, or that every purpose has equal value. The idea, rather, is that every human action is done for *some* reason, whether good or bad, strong or weak. Every human being, as a rational agent, inescapably makes use of the faculty of practical reason in every action taken. Our faculty of practical reason is, after all, our foremost guide in making choices in life. Sometimes we use it well, other times we use it poorly—but we always use it. The idea, indeed, is that we cannot help but to use it, since it is so strongly an integral part of who we are as human beings.

Gewirth continues by suggesting that if, for instance, I say, "I do A for E," then I must endorse E. I must personally find E good in some sense. Otherwise, why would I pursue it? Now, for me to endorse E is for me to endorse those things I must have, and do, to get E. If I endorse the end, then I must logically endorse the means required to achieve it. Gewirth contends that, for whatever end E that I might be pursuing through action—be it a university degree, a business deal, or even simple leisure—I must have those things I need to be capable of purposive action in the first place. What do I need to be capable of purposive action at all—to be a being capable of deploying my faculty of practical reason in daily life? Gewirth suggests two things: freedom and well-being. I am incapable of purposive action unless I am free to make decisions about which ends I want to pursue. If I am coerced, or under extreme duress, then I cannot be said to "pursue" an end at all: my action is, rather, the product of necessity, more like a mechanical reflex response than a voluntary and purposive human action. By "well-being," Gewirth means the basic material necessities of life: if I am starving, or have been beaten and am at death's door, then I cannot be said to be a purposive agent. I am just barely clinging to life. Gewirth concludes that every human being must claim—and is entitled to claim as a matter of high priority—those elements, like freedom and well-being, that are necessary conditions for purposive human action.

Our practical rationality tells us that, no matter what ends we want to pursue in life, we must have access to freedom and well-being, or our action will be doomed to failure right from the start. Freedom and well-being, it is sometimes slyly said, are *what we want, no matter what we want*. Freedom and well-being are necessary conditions for any kind of purposive action at all; they form the baseline we need to have access to, in order to get whatever else we might desire in life. Freedom and well-being are thus things we can all reasonably claim to have access to, and so should be thought of as the core objects of our human rights claims. Since we all vitally need freedom and well-being as the kinds of creatures we are—i.e., purposive creatures possessing practical reason—we are all entitled to have access to them.

Even if this argument of Gewirth's gives *me* very good reason to claim freedom and well-being as the objects of *my own* human rights, why should I recognize the similar claims of *all other* human beings? Gewirth responds to this important question with his "Principle of Generic Consistency": if I can claim freedom and well-being because I need such things to be a purposive agent, then I must recognize that all other purposive agents may likewise claim freedom and well-being for themselves. They need freedom and well-being for their action as much as I need them for mine. So for me to claim freedom and well-being for myself while denying it to others would be for me to be arbitrary and irrational: I would be claiming that I am different in exactly the same respect in which I am identical with all other human beings. We are all, in the final analysis, purposive beings, possessing practical reason, who want in life to pursue ends of our own choosing. All humans need freedom and well-being, and as rational agents we all know it. Thus, not only do we have human rights because we are rational agents, but reason itself informs us that we ought to respect the human rights claims of all human beings.

Gewirth's work is impressive in many ways, and he takes this rational agency perspective farther and deeper than anyone else. His proposals on behalf of liberty and well-being are eloquent, but does he succeed in showing that truly *everyone* is entitled to freedom and well-being? What about those unfortunate human beings who do not seem, under any plausible description, to be capable of the kind of purposive activity he talks about? Can we really say, for example, that infants are "purposive" in any meaningful sense? Infants, alongside the severely disabled and most clearly the comatose, do not seem capable of any kind of purposive self-direction whatsoever. To what extent, on this view, should we grant them the things they require for such direction? If rational purposiveness is the reason for respecting human rights, then those people who are not, or cannot, be rationally purposive will fall outside the scope of human rights membership, and thus universality will be sacrificed. Criminals also pose a problem for Gewirth. Most of us believe there is nothing wrong with throwing into jail people convicted of a serious crime. Yet if such criminals are rational agents and purposive beings—and surely most of them are—then Gewirth says they are entitled to freedom. How, then, can we justify taking away the freedom criminals have if, by the very nature of their rational agency, they are entitled to freedom?

While philosophically distinguished and nicely packaged, the rational agency perspective does not seem capable of delivering either universality or equality with regard to human rights-holding status. For not all human beings are practically rational—e.g., the insane, infants, the comatose, the enfeebled elderly—nor are they all practically rational to the same degree. So if it is our capacity for practically rational action which ultimately grounds human rights, these classes of people will be excluded, or at the least we will have a hierarchy of human rights that seems opposed to the very concept. Some holders of the rational agency view accept these conclusions, and simply state that the commitment to universality and equality in the human rights idea is only metaphorically and not literally true: it is more a matter of rhetoric than logic. Relative to nearly every preceding moral and political code, the human rights idea is clearly more inclusive and more egalitarian. Yet, strictly speaking, it is indefensible to suggest that all human beings are entitled to exactly the same set of human rights. On this view, it stretches all plausibility to pretend that infants and adults, or the able-bodied and the comatose, share the same set of core entitlements. In each of the pairs, one group is capable of purposive rational action, the other is not.

Reason is indeed a marvellous faculty that we have the great fortune to be endowed with. It is hard to imagine the kinds of life we would be condemned to live without the resources of reason to draw on. But it is quite another thing to say that rational agency is necessary to be a human rights-holder, since that view means we have to give up on universality and equality. Considerably large groups of people—notably children under the age of reason—will be excluded if we adopt this view. What about sufficiency, then? It may be true that, in connection with other characteristics, rational agency is relevant for rights-holding status. It is not sufficient on its own, though, for reasons of criminal forfeiture outlined above. We are looking, above all, for a joint set of necessary and sufficient characteristics that will pick out every human being as a human rights-holder yet also allow for forfeiture. It is difficult to see rational agency, on its own, giving us either.

Emotional Responsiveness

If reason on its own is neither necessary nor sufficient for granting us status as human rights-holders, what about our emotional capacities? Reason and passion, often dramatically contrasted, are obviously both prominent parts of our make-up as human beings. So perhaps if reason is not what we are looking for, then maybe our passions will prove more promising. Moreover, looking at emotion provides some much-needed balance to the disproportionate attention given to reason in the human rights literature. This is especially true for the philosophical subset of the literature, which often focuses entirely on complex issues of justification.

Perhaps what makes us fit objects of moral concern is not the fact that we are thinking creatures, capable of applying the canons of rationality to our habits of action, but rather the fact that we are feeling creatures: creatures with sensitivities to the world and to other people; creatures that can feel pleasure and suffer pain. Let us first consider these most basic emotions, the primal sensations of pleasure and pain, before proceeding to consider more refined and complex emotional capacities and what they might reveal, if anything, about our moral status.

Someone might suggest that, since we all feel pleasure and pain—whether we are normal or insane, young or old, healthy or handicapped, law-abiding or criminal—we should all be entitled to the fundamental kinds of protections and benefits that human rights are designed to provide. Since human rights constitute the very minimum for decent treatment in the modern world, it follows that not having the objects of human rights—whether through deprivation or violation—can only cause enormous pain and suffering, perhaps even culminating in death. We need only reflect on the lives of those people bearing the burdens of life in a country governed by a brutal regime to feel the force of this claim. Since a central purpose of a sound system of morality and politics must be to ward off severe and preventable pains, and to afford the basics for a pleasant life, it follows that we all should enjoy the objects of human rights.

This view has undoubted strengths to it, not the least of which is its core premise that, other things being equal, pleasure is good and pain bad. Who can deny the truth of that claim, or the fact that such sensations play a powerful role in motivating us to act? Since pleasure and pain are so central to our experience of life in general, then surely they must find a central place in our particular understanding of morality and politics, i.e., in our understanding of how we ought to treat each other. This view, additionally, appears at first to secure the universality of human rights quite readily: we all do indeed feel pleasure and pain, and we all no doubt prefer the former to the latter. This way babies, the insane, the enfeebled elderly and even criminals would be entitled to human rights.

The exceptional case of the comatose may, however, reveal cracks in this view's façade of universality, since it is unclear whether people in comas feel pleasure and pain. In general, they are unresponsive to external sensory stimulation. Another critical consideration is that, on this pleasure/pain view, there could be no such thing as forfeiture. Criminals and gross human rights violators, after all, still feel pleasure and pain. If it is such sensations alone which ground human rights, then it is clear that we all, always, retain our human rights claims as long as we remain alive. Is this a strength or a weakness? Its strength, of course, is that it allows for (near-) universal entitlement, and moreover entitlement which endures throughout the course of our lives. A potential weakness, though, is that it here runs afoul of our beliefs about appropriate punishment for people who violate the human rights of others.

It is a complex issue whether this pleasure/pain perspective will give us equality of human rights for all. Presumably its defenders would insist that it does, since we all feel pleasure and pain: we all, obviously, have this primordial sensate capability hard-wired into our very fabric as human beings. Nevertheless we do not all feel pleasure and pain in the same ways, nor to the same degree. Would that imply on this view that some people deserve more human rights than others? Does human rights-holding depend on some degree of sensory sensitivity, some particular intensity of emotional responsiveness? Additionally, it is clear that we do not all find the same objects, actions and experiences pleasurable or painful. Why anyone would want to be a race-car driver, for example, is beyond me, and why anyone would want to read—much less write—a textbook on human rights is beyond a lot of other people. Does this diversity of responsiveness imply, on this view, that there should be a difference in which objects different people get to claim as a matter of human right? Everyone, after all, has their own taste. The serious problem with such a "live-and-let-live" consequence, in connection with human rights, is this: what if one person gets a lot of pleasure out of being a horrible human rights-violator? We know it is a grim fact about our world that there are such human predators: there are monstrous freaks who get pleasure out of inflicting brutal pain on others. Does that mean, on this understanding, that such a predator can claim the entitlement to perform such violations, on the grounds that the violations nevertheless generate pleasure, which is agreed by all to be a very enjoyable part of life, a central motivator in human action? If one objects, on the sensible grounds that a person ought not to be entitled to perform an action that inflicts great pain on another, then one has to admit that such an objection introduces new and different considerations—beyond mere sensation—into the issue of who counts as a human rights-holder. It seems to show that raw sensate capacity, or elemental emotional responsiveness, cannot suffice for status as a human rights-holder. Consider also the converse case: what if a person like Drew experiences great pain at the fact that someone else he despises, and feels nothing but contempt for, gets to enjoy certain pleasures, for instance upon being elected to public office? Should Drew's resentful suffering, under this view, be sufficient to undermine the claim of the latter person, call her Jessica, to political participation and the fruits thereof? Presumably not. Both these examples point toward the following conclusion: the very variability and sheer idiosyncrasy of emotional response—of the sensation of pleasure and pain—make one skeptical that it can provide a firm foundation for exactly the same set of human rights for every human being. Even though (nearly) all of us have the raw capability to feel pleasure and pain, this raw capability may be too thin and flimsy to serve as a necessary, much less a sufficient, condition for human rights-holding status. For beyond the broadly shared capability, too much subjectivity intrudes, bringing with it serious ambiguities about both universality and equality.

The main ambiguity about universality is this: if we make the capacity to feel pleasure and pain a necessary condition for human rights-holding status, then the comatose will fail to have human rights. Likewise for the otherwise insensate. Who are they? Think of those who go in for a minor surgical procedure, whether at the hospital or at the dentist's. When such people are "put under" with anaesthetic, they become insensate. So if emotional or sensory responsiveness is a necessary condition for holding human rights, such people would at that juncture have no human rights. But surely such a conclusion is mistaken: one does not give up one's human rights at that point, and health care practitioners who take nefarious advantage of one's insensate condition are, as they should be, subject to severe criminal and civil law penalties. The main ambiguity about equality, in connection with this view, has to do with the variability of emotional response and sensory capacity. If emotions ground rights, then variability of emotion would seem to imply variability of rights. If the pursuit of pleasure alone grounds rights, then what if someone's pleasure involves the violation of another's rights? Elemental emotional responsiveness forms neither a necessary nor a sufficient condition for holding human rights.

Maybe this is too hasty. For presumably one reason why we take claims of human rights seriously is that we are generally quite pleased at the thought, and the experience, of living in a society where human rights are respected and real, which is to say where everyone has secure possession of the objects of his or her human rights. And one reason, surely, why we condemn human rights violations is because we often have very strong emotions of disgust and outrage when we witness, or are informed of, such brutalizing behaviour. Maybe we should, therefore, pay more attention to our emotional responses: maybe they are important clues as to what we find, ultimately, most defensible and compelling in moral and political life. Perhaps, for example, our analysis thus far will change if we move to consider emotions more deep and complex than mere sensate responsiveness to our pleasure/pain receptors. As David Hume once wrote,[7] surely morality has much to do with the emotion of sympathy, or empathy—i.e., with our feeling some kind of emotional connection to the welfare of other people, and being moved to act by it. To have sympathy or empathy is to feel pain of a kind when another so suffers, and to be pleased when the other so feels. In other words, what about the emotions which connect us together, instead of the pleasure and pain we each feel separately as individuals, sometimes at the expense, or to the indifference, of others?

Hume believed that the ultimate impulse to be moral comes not from an imperative of reason, nor from biological inclinations, nor from a soul yearning for God but, rather, from our emotional identifications with other people and how well they are doing. Most of us are pleased when those we are connected to do well, and are pained when they suffer hardship. There is no reason to suppose that we only feel such things with reference to those we are intimate with, though obviously our feelings about family and friends will be much more intense. Many of us can, I believe, feel genuine empathy with a total stranger, or with someone suffering human rights violations on the other side of the world. Such emotional bonding, such sensitive responsiveness to others, seems one of the cements of civilization.

We might want, in light of such reflections, to say that if one does elicit empathy from another person, then that suffices to make one an object of high-priority moral concern, a holder of human rights, a member of the moral community. If Sam's welfare is cared for by Jane, such that Jane feels empathy with Sam and is moved to act as a result, then that seems a compelling clue that Sam's life is important, that it counts from a moral point of view. But to make one's status as a human rights-holder *depend* on whether another person has such feelings still seems too flimsy a foundation for what we are concerned with here. Emotions and passions, while powerful and strong, can also be inconstant, in some people notoriously so. Sometimes people simply lack the emotional sensitivity we often feel they should have. The emotional responses of normal, well-balanced people may indeed serve as compelling reasons to treat people in respectful ways. But it is the fact that they are the emotional responses *of normal and well-developed people* that is all-important here: the emotional responses of deviants who get perverse pleasure out of harming people, or those of merely insensitive clods, are obviously of very little, if any, weight in moral debate. The desires of deviant rights-violators form no overriding reason for action for anybody. It also seems an error to locate the source of one's status as a human rights-holder in the hands of another, so to speak. Status as a human rights-holder should be granted more in terms of one's own characteristics and merits, than in terms of how others happen to respond to oneself. The reasons that ground human rights should ultimately be about who we are as individual people rather than about others' responses to us. We should not want to entrust our fate, in something so vital as whether or not we get human rights, to the comparative tastes and sensibilities of other people. One's capacity to elicit from others the feeling of empathy with oneself might appear sufficient for human rights-holding status but is by no means required to deserve it. Second thoughts about sufficiency should be raised as well. For belief that being an object of empathy suffices for human rights-holding status might be at odds with forfeiture. Presumably *someone* feels sympathy for hardened criminals, whether it be members of their family or fellow cellmates. It may interfere with our beliefs about forfeiture to suggest that such criminals enjoy human rights so long as somebody out there feels sympathy for them. Are we, after all, to let them out of prison, in spite of their violation of another's human rights, on the grounds that, since somebody out there still loves them, they retain all their human rights, including that to liberty? The answer, I suggest, is no. So emotional responsiveness, though a large part of life, is neither necessary nor sufficient for status as a human rights-holder.

Contractarian Reciprocity

Some thinkers, such as Jan Narveson,[8] believe it false to say that all human beings have the same human rights, since not all human beings can limit their claims on others to what is reasonable. The idea here is something like this: to be able to make reasonable demands on others is to be a source of moral obligation. To be a source of moral obligation is, moreover, to be capable of reciprocating the obligation, were the situation reversed. Some people are incapable of this kind of other-regarding reciprocity and thus cannot be considered human rights-holders. Morality, as well as politics, is seen under this perspective as a two-way street, a conventional agreement about mutual treatment between beings who are capable of both giving and receiving treatment. This reasoning views morality and politics as the products of a social contract, and so gets referred to as a "contractarian" perspective. Only fully-functioning participants in the social contract count as fully-fledged human rights-holders. But not all living human beings are such participants.

The list of non-participants includes infants, the insane, the severely disabled, and the enfeebled elderly. Such people cannot really, of their own accord, enter into mutually beneficial contractual agreements; thus, on this view it makes little sense to say they enjoy human rights. Such persons are not capable of endorsing a deal of the kind whereby one affirms, "If you respect my human rights, then I will respect yours." They are not able to consent to such an arrangement, nor can they act in reciprocal fashion as both right-holder and duty-bearer. It appears, in other words, that such people can only take, and never give, and thus they cannot count as beings of equal moral status with the rest of us. This is to say that contractarians, in general, are committed to the view that *only* normal, adult, non-criminal human beings enjoy full status as human rights-holders. Why non-criminal, in addition to being full-grown, well-functioning and capable of entering into a mutually beneficial arrangement for reciprocal treatment? The contractarian answer is that criminals violate their side of the contract, and freely take themselves out of the deal, so to speak. In so doing, criminals subject themselves to appropriate punishment by the rest of us who keep our word and perform our fair share of the social burden.

Contractarianism appeals to those skeptical of biological, or metaphysical, groundings for moral beliefs. Its notion that morality and justice are social conventions—values we agree on—possesses a certain sober strength to it. But the fact that it cannot endorse genuine universality with regard to human rights may reveal a flaw. The controversial claim in the contractarian world-view is that a being is incapable of being a source of moral obligation *unless* it is capable of returning the favour. Against this claim, we might ask rhetorically, does a human baby fail to be a source of moral obligation merely because, through no fault of its own, it is too young to be able to return the favour at this exact moment? Has a young child no human rights? In other words, contractarianism may commit a similar kind of mistake as one referred to last chapter when we discussed the difference between uttering a claim and being entitled to utter a claim. Just as one can *have* a justified claim without actually *uttering* it, perhaps one can also be owed the performance of correlative duties from others even if, at present, one is incapable of performing duties on their behalf.

It should be noted that a contractarian might actually agree with this argument, revising his beliefs only slightly. He could agree that a baby is owed a certain kind of respectful treatment from the rest of us *while at the same time* insisting that the baby has no human right to claim that kind of treatment from us. His revised belief would rely on this principle: while a human right *does* imply correlative duties, it does *not* follow that a duty always implies a correlative right, much less a correlative *human* right, which is the most powerful rights-claim of them all. A contractarian might therefore speak sincerely of duties to babies, or to the insane, or even to animals and the environment, without suggesting that all these things have *a right* to such treatment. These things do not have rights because they are not the kinds of creatures that can have rights: they are not capable of participating in a reciprocal social contract. This does not mean, though, that the rest of us can treat these things however we wish. Why, if these things fail to have rights, should we nevertheless consider ourselves duty-bound to them? The duty, the contractarian might suggest, is rooted in a distinction mentioned last chapter: while these things have no concrete *rights*, it remains *right*, in a broader sense, not to harm them. It is right, or morally correct, to refrain from harming these things because it is obvious that a society in which babies are not tortured, nor the environment trashed, is much preferable to, and more pleasant than, a society in which such actions are permitted.

Narveson's perspective on this issue is that a baby, or an insane person, is owed the duty of non-harming because, and only because, it is closely related to another fully developed, normal, non-criminal adult human being who would be pained greatly if it were harmed.[9] The duty is transitive, so to speak: Caroline has a duty to baby Bobby because Caroline has a prior duty to Bobby's mother Ann, and Bobby is very closely connected indeed to Ann. One has a duty not to cause great pain to another human rights-holder, and harming Ann's baby would cause *her* great pain; thus one has a duty not to do so, even though the baby has no human rights.

This move shows great liveliness of mind but, in my view, injects a needless artificiality into the debate. It simply strikes a false note to say that children are owed only indirect duties *via* those adults closely connected to them, whereas the rest of us are directly owed duties. An even larger problem is this: in Narveson's example, baby Bobby has no human rights at all against his own mother, Ann. While we certainly expect mothers to love their children deeply, sometimes this does not happen, in tragic fashion. Does a baby have no right not to be harmed and abused at the hands of those who should, but sometimes fail to, nurture it? I expect most of us agree that the baby should not be seen as morally exposed, so to speak, to the whims of those who have the greatest amount of power over it.

The main issue here with contractarianism, in my judgment, is the difference between a necessary and a sufficient condition. Perhaps it is true to say, assuming biological humanity, that actually displaying the traits of contractarian reciprocity—adhering faithfully to the social contract— is sufficient for human rights-holding status. But it is quite another thing to say that, unless you are such a person, you fail to have human rights at all, since surprisingly vast numbers of human beings will be summarily excluded from human rights-holding status. While contractarianism is a compelling way to model rights relationships, especially legal ones, between normal, responsible adults, it does not follow that it is the best way to model all of our rights relationships, especially this most vital one of human rights. Since contractarianism is excessively exclusive, it cannot in my judgment find its way into the preferred set of jointly necessary and sufficient conditions for human rights-holding status: it gives too much, so to speak, with regard to normal, responsible adults, and far too little with regard to everyone else.

A superior view seems to be that human beings who are *incapable* of contractarian reciprocity might remain human rights-holders. This preserves the universality and equality residing at the heart of the human rights ideal. So children, the insane, the developmentally challenged, the enfeebled elderly, and so on, are properly seen as human rights-holders. They remain biologically human, after all, and they have vital interests in a minimally good life. They can suffer harm in connection with such fundamental interests, and so on. As such, these people are suitable subjects of high-priority moral concern—sources of moral obligation— alongside the rest of us who are otherwise more capable than they.

One should admit, though, that our understanding of what such people—infants, etc.—are owed as a matter of human right differs from our understanding of what normal, responsible adults are owed. This claim follows from two compelling considerations. The first is the fact that we can define the objects of human rights only in general terms anyway, thus allowing *some* space for different interpretations of them. The second consideration is the fact that the differences between these different groups of people *require* such different interpretations. More on this slight variability when we turn our minds, in a subsequent chapter, to considering what the objects of human rights exactly are. The general idea, for now, is this: if we talk about a human right to liberty, for example, then our interpretation of what liberty fully implies for a normal adult will involve different, and perhaps more, things than what it means for a young child. We might plausibly say that an adult should have, as part of her human right to liberty, the right to run for public office but deny that same object to a child on the very plausible grounds that it cannot really make use, much less good use, of that right. So a child's human right to liberty might naturally imply a more narrow range of objects than an adult's human right to liberty, but this does not mean that the child therefore lacks a human right to liberty, much less human rights altogether. A more limited scope for fit objects of its freedom does not mean a child has no grounds to complain should someone lock it in a closet, or kidnap it away from its parents. We should note as well that these reflections on object variability do not imply that children, or the otherwise differently-abled, will always have fewer objects implied by their human rights. For example, it seems clear that we all have the human right to physical security. Since an infant is clearly weaker and more vulnerable, in general, than a fully-developed adult, we might expect that a child may claim more things for its physical security than normal adults can. The child needs more to achieve the same level of ele-mental physical security as the rest of us. Having the same human rights *is compatible with* having slightly different sets of objects, as soon as one understands that different sets might be needed to secure for different kinds of people the same kind of respectful and humane treatment.

The contractarian correctly calls our attention to criminals in our midst. What about those normal, (apparently) well-functioning adults who *are capable of* engaging in contractarian reciprocity but instead deliberately choose to be free-riders or, worse, predators and violators within our shared social contract? Do such people have human rights? What is necessary or sufficient in this regard? This raises interesting questions about the relationship between being morally good and being a human rights-holder.

Moral Goodness

An even more exclusive perspective on who holds human rights is this: only morally good human beings are entitled to human rights. Ancient thinkers like Aristotle would have been quite comfortable with this view: he believed, for example, that only certain well-educated, well-off and properly cultivated men should govern a political community. He even went so far as to suggest that some people are so morally deficient that they are best thought of as "natural slaves."[10] At first glance, it is this view itself that seems seriously deficient. It might even be the most intol-erant and self-righteous of all the perspectives discussed thus far. At its worst it seems opposed to the very spirit of the human rights idea. For who is entitled to decide which human beings are morally "good enough" to be entitled to the objects of human rights claims? What theory of morality is so well-defended, or so obviously "true," that we can use it to distinguish between good and bad people, granting human rights to the former and denying them to the latter? The whole thing seems to smack of the most provincial and narrow-minded of moral mind-sets.

But is this perspective so clearly wrong, so irredeemably hidebound? It does seem, for one thing, to be consistent with our intuitions about criminals: since they have proven themselves morally deficient, they are not entitled to exactly the same set of core entitlements as the rest of us. What about grievous human rights violators? Is anyone really prepared to say that someone like Hitler or Stalin is entitled to the same basic rights as the rest of us who have never engaged in genocidal massacre? There is also the question of incentives in favour of better behaviour: if we deprive bad people of the objects of human rights, this should provide them with a very effective inducement to get their act together and play nice with others, ultimately improving society. Why should we treat bad people the same way we treat good people? To use a revised version of a familiar phrase: why should we let good things happen to bad people? Let us treat them in the decrepit way they deserve, and thus spur them on to self-improvement, to worthiness of reception into the club of human rights-holders. It would seem that only a *morally* good person, after all, could be entitled to *moral* rights, which we have seen are what human rights are in the first instance. Anyone who denies this view would seem to be committed to the ethically perverse, and perhaps logically paradoxical, proposition that immoral people have moral rights.

That might be a bit too forceful a way of putting the point, which revolves around forfeiture. The idea behind forfeiture is simply this: a person can, by performing horrible deeds, give up or lose his entitlement to the objects of his human rights claims. The kind of horrible deed in question would be violating another's human rights, as defined in the last chapter: depriving a human right-holder of an object of her human rights without just cause for doing so. It would be wrong, I suggest, to allow human rights-violators to escape unscathed in spite of their crimes. It would be wrong because to do so would show disrespect to the ideals that human rights represent, and more importantly to the person actually victimized by the violation. Such failure to punish would also send out perverse signals to other, would-be rights violators. Above all, failure to punish violation is unfair to those who do not violate. Human rights, if they are to be real, must be enforced, respected and fulfilled in fair fashion. Those who thwart this process without just cause deserve punishment.

A sense of proportionality tells us that the punishment should fit the crime. There should be an elemental balance between the degree of rights violation and the degree of rights forfeiture. It would seem disproportionate and wrong, for example, to torture to death a criminal convicted of stealing an automobile. This recognition of the natural need for proportionality between crime and punishment implies that, in general, there remain firm moral limits to how we are permitted to treat criminals. I do believe there are very rare cases—relating to self-defence individually and war collectively—where the proportion called for between the degree of violation and the need for defence can entail complete forfeiture of a person's rights, including the right to physical security.[11] But such emergencies are truly exceptional and do not usually provide good guidance during the ordinary course of life. Most criminals are caught after the fact of their deed, and so the imperatives of a swift and successful emergency response are not so nearly acute, and often not to the point at all. My own judgment as to punishment in general is this: one loses what one abuses. What all criminals abuse, in the course of their violation, is their freedom to be at large in society; thus this is what they must lose through forfeiture, entitling us to throw them in jail for a time and regulate their conduct. Criminals most centrally forfeit their human right to liberty. Ordinarily, then, they do retain some of their human rights. This seems in line with our beliefs. Very few people argue that we should treat criminals however we want, inflicting on them things like starvation, gratuitous beatings, savage acts of torture, and so forth. Statements banning the deliberate infliction of "cruel and unusual punishment" are, indeed, frequently encountered in prominent human rights documents. The bottom line here is this: some people can and do, of their own accord, violate human rights. In doing so, they deserve punishment and forfeit their claims to liberty. When they so forfeit, they justify the imposition of jail time of a length and severity proportionate to both their degree of violation and their varying needs for behaviour modification.

It is important to see that such punishment, such forfeiture, does *not* violate the principles of universality and equality which are so central to the human rights tradition. Everyone is treated as an equal to begin with: we all have the same set of human rights, and we are all equally responsible as duty-bearers correlative to human rights-holders. Should someone, of their own accord, violate the terms of such responsibility, then they will have forfeited some (and only exceptionally all) of their human rights. They may therefore be subjected to such punishment as the rest of us deem reasonable and proportionate to the offence. Such people will, through their own behaviour and fault, have given up their claims to some of the objects of their human rights. In doing so, these people entitle the rest of us to treat them in ways that would ordinarily be deemed rough and inappropriate, but as part of punishing a serious crime are seen as being needed, for the reasons mentioned above about respecting the victim, ensuring fairness and establishing incentives in favour of respecting human rights principles.

This is to say that some version of the moral goodness perspective is indeed a necessary condition for status as a human rights-holder. This necessary condition is best stated negatively, however: the idea is more about the avoidance of serious moral badness than it is about the achievement of some controversial level of moral goodness. It seems wrong to agree with Aristotle that moral goodness demands that we accord human rights only to those who display moral excellence or great virtues of character. We should, rather, accord human rights equally to all human beings, at least initially. If someone performs a horrible deed—if his actions fall below the minimum demanded from all as duty-bearers and as decent human beings—then that person, of his own accord, gives up some of his human rights, notably to liberty. Should someone break their responsibilities, as a duty-bearer, by violating another's human rights while at large in society, then they forfeit their own human right to liberty and are thus appropriately subjected, upon conviction, to be taken out of social circulation and thrown in jail, subject of course to constraints of proportionality in punishment.

It is worth noting how this view of forfeiture is compatible with the view of rights as reasons, suggested in the last chapter. If rights are properties of persons, whether biological or metaphysical, then they can never be "given up" or "lost." Thus, if one supports the idea of forfeiture, one cannot believe in the rights-as-properties view; one must acknowledge the strength of the rights-as-reasons view. According to this view, forfeiture boils down to this: by committing his crime of rights-violation, the criminal has now *changed the reasons that govern our treatment of him.* Before he committed an act of rights-violation, we had no reason to seize him by force, put him on trial against his will, and then on conviction to lock him in a miserable cage for years on end, subjecting him to further measures of behaviour modification. As soon as he performed that violation, however, he of his own accord and responsibility changed the equation and altered the weight of reasons. His initial entitlement to freedom at that moment became less important than showing respect to the human rights principle he broke, respecting the victim he violated, reforming his conduct through corrective measures, ensuring fair treatment for all, and deterring further violations in the future. The conclusion, then, is this: if some fail to treat others with the baseline kind of universality and equality defended in the human rights idea, then those people provide others with overriding reasons to treat them in a way that is very particular and quite unequal, namely, in a way expressive of proper and proportionate punishment.

Having Vital Interests
in a Minimally Good Life

We have reached the point in our discussion where the following can be said: the necessary conditions for being a human rights-holder of equal status include biological humanity and non-violation of anyone else's human rights. This is indeed a surprisingly thin account of what makes for a human rights-holder, and we should wonder whether there is more to add. What we are most concerned with is discerning the set of characteristics that is *jointly* necessary and sufficient: the set that selects exactly those persons we acknowledge as having human rights. Do we have it already, in the set of biological humanity and non-violation of another's human rights? Is that all there is to holding human rights: being human and not acting like an animal, so to speak? Is that enough to ground an authoritative entitlement, sufficient to render one a fit subject for high-priority moral concern on the part of others and of social institutions? It might seem so: the set offers both universality and equality as we have understood them here in this chapter. Moreover, it does so in a way that is not nearly as controversial as some of the rival views, notably metaphysical humanity. My own sense, though, is that something more must be added to secure the requisite moral importance of being a human rights-holder. Given, as I contended earlier, that there is no intrinsic moral significance to biological matter—raw flesh and bone—there seems to be more needed to imbue one with the moral status of a human rights-holder than the simple fact that one avoids violating the human rights of others. There needs to be something morally positive about oneself, so to speak, in addition to the moral negative of not violating another's human rights. I suggest this moral positive is having fundamental interests in, or vital needs for, living a minimally good life.[12]

To *have an interest* in something, first off, is not the same thing as *taking an interest* in something. To take an interest in something—like football, fashion or photography—is for the thing in question to capture one's curiosity and attention, one's time and energy. To have an interest in something, by contrast, is for one to have a stake in it; it is for one's well-being to be affected by it. This is to say that taking an interest in something is generally much more personal, emotional and subjective than the question of what one has an interest in. The categories might overlap, but they also differ. For instance, the scope of what we can take an interest in is larger than the category of what we have an interest in, and much larger than what we have a *vital* interest in. We can take interest in a whole range of things in which we have very little, if any, of our well-being genuinely at stake. Such plurality, of possible things to take an interest in, is one of the joys of living in an advanced and civilized society where there is much on offer. The two categories do overlap in the sense that we should expect that people take an interest in those things in which their interests are at stake. But this is, curiously, not always the case. For instance, a surprisingly large number of people fail to take much interest in how exactly their personal finances are run, even though the fate of such finances clearly impacts upon their own well-being. Such lack of interest, in something people have an interest in, creates large demand for financial services providers, investment managers, tax attorneys, and so on. Many other people—or perhaps they are the same group—could not care less about the whole world of politics and politicians. They do not take any interest whatsoever in the political arena. Yet there is no denying that decisions politicians make—about the use of public resources, for example—both can and do have a material impact upon the well-being of these very same people, and the rest of us more broadly. So sometimes one can fail to *take* an interest in something that one *has* an interest in, just as often as one can take an interest in something in which one's interests are not at stake.

Some interests, of course, are absolutely vital to one's well-being. A vital interest, as here conceived, would be the same thing as a vital need. To need something, of course, is to require it, to be dependent on it in some important sense. Importantly, to need something is to be harmed if one is deprived of it, or is lacking it to begin with. To vitally need something is for it to be required to sustain one's functioning as the very kind of creature one is. For one to fail to have an object of one's vital needs is for one to suffer grievous harm—for one to face a grave threat to one's ability to lead a minimally good life, or perhaps even any life at all. David Wiggins has made important contributions to this line of thought. He suggests that, for someone to vitally need an object, call it x, three things need to hold: 1) the deprivation, or lack, of x would harm that person's very functioning in life as a human being; 2) there are no acceptable substitutes for x available to that person; and 3) x is integral to that person's living a life of minimal value.[13]

I contend that there are five abstractly defined items that meet each of Wiggins's three criteria for the vital needs of the human person living in our time: 1) personal security, 2) material subsistence, 3) elemental equality, 4) personal freedom, and 5) recognition as a member of the human community. I submit that these five vital needs are also the ultimate objects of our human rights claims. I refer to them, subsequently, as the "foundational five" objects of human rights.

Full discussion of exactly which objects are fully implied by each of these five abstractly defined items will be reserved for the upcoming chapter on the objects of human rights. But some immediate, provisional comment can be made here. Personal security means reliable protection from, or freedom from, a context of violence that poses a threat either to one's very life, or at least to the core aspects of one's physical and mental well-being. Material subsistence means having secure access to those resources one requires to meet one's biological needs—notably a minimal level of nutritious food, clean water, fresh air, some clothing and shelter, and basic preventative health care. Elemental equality means our need to be regarded as equal in initial status with other moral agents, and not to suffer from vicious and groundless social discrimination. Freedom means the need to follow one's own path in life, not subject to coercive interference with one's critical life choices. Liberty also implies the need to have some space to enjoy some privacy, and above all to develop a degree of personal identity, integrity and autonomy. Finally, recognition means our deep need as social beings for acknowledgement from others of our own humanity, of our own worth, and of our own belonging to, and full membership within, the human community.

Not having any one of these five core elements does real damage—verifiable harm—to one's functioning as a human being. This is perhaps clearest with physical security and material subsistence, but it does not take much imagination to realize that lacking the other elements also harms human functioning: why else, for example, would we make the deprivation of liberty the core ingredient in criminal punishment? Similarly, it is clear that there are no acceptable substitutes for any one of these five core elements of vital human need: what, for instance, would one trade one's physical security for, or one's need for social recognition as a human being? Such are goods beyond price and measure, so instrumental are they to one's present and future. Finally, all five elements together appear necessary for living a minimally good life in the modern world. We know this by reflection on the alternatives: without enough food and water, without basic medical care, without freedom from serious violence, we clearly cannot live minimally well, or even for long at all, in this world. To suffer from vicious social discrimination, or to be forced to live a life not of one's choice, is to suffer grievous harm as a human being. It is to endure a life that none of us would find worth living considering the kinds of creatures we are and with respect to the kind of decent and respectful treatment we deserve. However we each, individually, understand the full picture of the good life, we need these five core elements to pursue it. These five elements are what we truly and vitally *need*, no matter what else we might *want* out of life. Of course, we should want what we vitally need, and most of us as rational agents do so. But wanting what one vitally needs is not necessary to ground one's entitlement to the objects of those needs. As we will discern more clearly in the next chapter, the grounding of the entitlement comes not from one's subjective wanting but, rather, from one's objective needing—and, moreover, from the core principle that *one should not be inflicted with grievous harm in connection with one's vital needs.*

Conclusion

In this chapter we sought a joint set of necessary and sufficient conditions for status as a human rights-holder, conditions that are consistent with the universality and equality residing at the heart of the human rights idea. After canvassing many options, we came to some conclusions. To hold human rights, one must be biologically human, one must avoid violating another's human rights, and one must have fundamental interests in, or vital needs for, living a life of minimal value. One's having these three characteristics gives everybody else overriding reasons to acknowledge one's status as a fully-fledged holder of human rights.

Notes

1 P. Singer, *Animal Liberation* (London: Avon/Hearst, 1991); T. Regan, *The Case for Animal Rights* (Berkeley: University of California Press, 1983).

2 See J. Thomson, "A Defence of Abortion," *Philosophy and Public Affairs* 1 (1976): 47-66 and D. Marquis, "Why Abortion is Immoral," *Journal of Philosophy* 86 (1989): 183-202.

3 Singer, *Liberation*, which refers at 17-21 to Ryder as the coiner of the term "species-ism."

4 Someone might here interpret the Ten Commandments, and/or the Golden Rule, as specifying a set of crucial moral duties, demanded by God, from which we can infer correlative human rights. See also M. Perry, *The Idea of Human Rights* (Oxford: Oxford University Press, 2000).

5 Aristotle, *The Nicomachean Ethics*, trans. W.D. Ross (Oxford: Oxford University Press, 1998), Book One, chap. 7.

6 A. Gewirth, *Human Rights: Essays on Justification and Application* (Chicago: University of Chicago Press, 1982); A. Gewirth, *The Community of Rights* (Chicago: University of Chicago Press, 1996).

7 D. Hume, *An Enquiry Concerning the Principles of Morals*, ed. T. Beauchamp (Oxford: Oxford University Press, 1998).

8 J. Narveson, *Moral Matters*, 2nd ed. (Peterborough: Broadview, 1999), 1-38, 133-42.

9 Narveson, *Moral Matters*.

10 Aristotle, *The Politics*, trans. C. Lord (Chicago: University of Chicago Press, 1985), Book 3.

11 For more, see my *War and International Justice: A Kantian Perspective* (Waterloo: Wilfrid Laurier University Press, 2000), 156-60.

12 J. Nickel, *Making Sense of Human Rights* (Berkeley: University of California Press, 1987); J. Feinberg, *Rights, Justice and The Bounds of Liberty* (Princeton: Princeton University Press, 1980).

13 D. Wiggins, *Needs, Values and Truth* (Oxford: Basil Blackwell, 1986).

Chapter 3

What Justifies Human Rights?

We now have a substantial understanding of what human rights are, and who holds them. All of us have human rights—i.e., high-priority moral claims *on* others and social institutions *for* them to do their fair part ensuring we possess the objects of our vital needs and fundamental interests. In return, each of us commits to doing our own fair part in ensuring that the human rights of others get satisfied. This responsibility as a duty-bearer—which comes hand-in-hand with status as a human rights-holder—most centrally implies that we not violate the human rights of another. Such violation is, on this side of the grave, the one and only thing that leads to the loss of our human rights. Even then, such forfeiture must still be proportional to the degree of human rights-violation and so complete forfeiture is truly an extraordinary event. One's moral status as a rights-holding human being, while not literally absolute, is nevertheless a quite resilient thing, an enduring entitlement to minimally decent treatment.

Knowing what human rights are, and knowing who holds them, leads one to the next question: *why* do human rights-holders hold human rights? What sufficient reasons can we come up with to show that those whom we like to think hold human rights—namely, all of us—do in fact hold them? In other words, we need to offer a justification for human rights.

Elements of a Good Justification

To justify something is literally to show that thing's justice, rightness, or correctness. In general, to justify some claim is to show adequate grounds for people to believe in that claim and to guide their conduct accordingly. So to justify human rights is to show adequate grounds, or sufficient reasons, why people should believe that human rights exist and are important—why people should adjust their conduct in light of the claims that human rights make on all of us.

Justifying a moral or political claim—such as that human rights exist and are vitally important to respect—is not the same sort of thing as justifying a proposition of science, or one of mathematics and logic. In science, one justifies a claim, or hypothesis, by testing it under rigorous, repeatable conditions until sufficient similarities in the experimental results force any reasonable observer to concede that the hypothesis is actually borne out, i.e., that it accurately describes the way the world really is, according to the best evidence available at the time. In math and logic, one proves a claim by any number of so-called proof procedures, showing that the claim follows from the application of a sound system of derivation to given concepts or numbers. Repetition of the procedure often serves to solidify the claim in one's own mind but is not needed to show the force of the claim—the truth of the conclusion—to a reasonable observer. One does not need, for example, to run thousands of experiments to prove that two and two together make four; if one does it properly, one proof procedure is all one needs to grasp it for good.

Aristotle once wrote, wisely, that ethics and politics do not afford the same kind of rigorous proof standards that math and science demand.[1] This does not mean that ethics and politics are less important; indeed, the converse may well be more true for our daily lives. What it does mean is that it would be wrong to hold ethics and politics to the same exacting standards of justification as are used in math and science. To do so would be to compare apples and oranges: they simply are not the same kind of thing. Thus, we cannot expect, in ethics and politics, to prove a claim with absolute certainty, the way we can in math and logic. It is less a matter of truth versus falsehood, and more a matter of being better supported, and more acceptable, versus being more poorly supported, and more objectionable. In this sense, ethics and politics are more like science, searching for the most compelling and useful understanding, the most adequately supported claim given current information. Of course, the information in question can be quite different: appeals to evidence in moral and political debate generally include more references to values and preferences than do such appeals in science. Furthermore, there is less assurance in ethics and politics about connections between cause and effect than there is in science: one cannot, after all, run repeat experiments using human beings, again and again, to verify the strength of a supposed connection or correlation. But this fact of lesser assurance does not mean that ethics and politics are nothing more than a cognitive crap-shoot. It does not mean that morality is a case of hopeless "he-said/she-said" subjectivity, without any further means of determining what is more, and what less, compelling. Custom, history and common sense reflection on our values and preferences inform us, to a meaningful degree, about cause and effect in human relationships, along with what calibre of treatment from others we want and what kinds of social system enhance life and what other kinds detract from it and need to be reformed.

A good justification, like any other good argument, has to rest on some basic set of premises and principles which are themselves *not* argued for. This is the case because we cannot keep arguing forever: philosophers have referred to such a never-ending chain of reasoning as an "infinite regress," and thus as something that we finite creatures, with lives to live and choices to make, should avoid. *Every argument has to rest somewhere*: it is thus part of the art of argument to decide where one is going to rest content, on which core premises and principles one is going to stand satisfied.[2] Usually, in moral and political debate, these premises will involve some conception of human nature and some understanding of a foremost requirement of morality and justice. For example, one justification for human rights we will be looking at in this chapter rests on a *conception* of human nature that assumes a set of vital needs we all share, and a *core principle* that it is deeply, and manifestly, wrong to inflict harm on people in connection with their vital needs. Such harm is grievous and unjust, falling below the threshold of minimally decent treatment we have the right as human beings to expect and demand. The only justification for intentionally inflicting such grievous harm is to protect others from suffering such grievous harm themselves.[3]

A good justification not only starts out from plausible initial premises and principles on which it ultimately rests, it also arrives at plausible conclusions using a consistent and compelling chain of reasoning. In this case we already know the conclusion we are after, and are assuming its power and strength: that we all have human rights, and that such ought to be respected and made real in concrete social contexts. It is more a matter, in this chapter, of sampling influential views about the initial premises and how, exactly, it is appropriate to move from such premises to the sought-after conclusion of respecting human rights.

A final preliminary remark about pluralism in justification. It is often a hallmark of philosophical treatments of human rights to search for one, and only one, chain of justification. Philosophers tended to focus on discovering The One True Principle and then deducing human rights from that principle. In doing so, they take exceptional pains to show that their pet justification is the only one that "works," while all other competing justifications must fall to the side and stare at it in awe and honour. We can admire the competitive striving behind such an endeavour, and we can certainly agree that some justifications seem to succeed where others fail to satisfy. But from these agreements it does not follow that there is one, and only one, true justification—one, and only one, chain of reasoning that stands head and shoulders above all the other ideas on this issue. It is more plausible, I suggest, to view the justification of human rights as lawyers tend to view the justification of a legal claim. Almost never will a good lawyer get up in court and do as the philosopher does: develop one, and only one, line of reasoning and argument on behalf of his client. A good lawyer will take pains to show that his favoured conclusion is supported, to some degree, by a number of different lines of reasoning, a number of different sources of appeal, value and authority. The aim of the lawyer, after all, is to persuade the judge and jury that a certain decision is more justified than its alternative, and the lawyer knows that such persuasion has to appeal to different people with different life experiences, responsive to various emotional and cognitive factors. It seems compelling to observe that different people can support human rights for a variety of reasons, and that there is probably more than one good reason that provides powerful support for the existence of human rights and the force of their claim on our behaviour. In this chapter, then, we will not be searching so much for The One Right Answer as for which of various answers—which cluster of justifications—seems the most plausible in support of human rights.

Do We Need To Justify Human Rights At All?

An influential philosopher, Richard Rorty, has wondered whether we need to justify human rights, or other moral claims, at all.[4] Rorty views the debate over different kinds of justification as one of endless dispute and controversy, a futile quest for The One True Argument about human rights. Rorty believes that we can do very little by way of reasoned argument to change the beliefs and behaviour of a hard-hearted human rights-violator. "(I)t is of no use whatever," he submits, "to say [to such a person] ... (n)otice that what you have in common, your humanity, is more important than these trivial differences," such as race, gender, ethnicity, or national citizenship. Providing philosophical justifications for human rights is far less important than—perhaps even useless in comparison with—developing in people an emotional disposition in favour of respecting people's human rights. Rorty thus extols the virtues of providing "a sentimental education," exposing people to the realities of life of those who are different from them, with the aim of "manipulating their sentiments" in line with respect for human rights. In Rorty's judgment, things like literature and film, along with journalism and television, are much more adept at achieving this aim than the abstract and general arguments of law, political theory and philosophy. An immediate, personal and emotional identification with others is the most effective inducement against violating their human rights, and is much more potent than trying to get someone to follow a chain of reasoning that moves from controversial premises to contentious conclusions. This is not to say that Rorty disapproves of the human rights movement and the prevalence of the human rights culture throughout many parts of the world. He indeed favours the creation of what he calls "an Enlightenment utopia"—i.e., a liberal democracy that is rights-respecting and humane, secure and secular, prosperous and committed to the general welfare in terms of key social goods like education and health care. His point is that a world filled with Enlightenment utopias is more likely to be brought into being through the effects of sentimental education rather than through argumentation and reasoning: "Producing generations of nice, tolerant, well-off, secure, other-respecting students of this sort in all parts of the world is just what is needed—indeed *all* that is needed [his italics]—to achieve an Enlightenment utopia."[5]

Rorty is probably correct to suggest that, often, reasonable argument is not as effective at changing people's beliefs and behaviours as we might wish it to be. We can think of many other motives and drives, other incentives and stimuli, which seem to get people "going" much more readily than a sensible justification. Things like fear, greed, lust, envy, resentment, the desire for power, and so on, clearly play a large role in human behaviour. But what we are seeking here is more a sense of how we *should* act, as opposed to how we *actually* act, sometimes to our regret. Just because we are often moved more immediately, and forcefully, by sensory stimuli and emotional reactions does not imply that we should give in to them utterly, and base our mutual dealings with each other on them, and them alone. *Social institutions cannot be run on sentimentality*: there does need to be a core commitment to human decency and respectful treatment, of course, but needed as well is a lot of rational planning with regard to institutional design, the allocation of resources, measuring the effectiveness of expenditures, devising procedures for reform and change, and so on. It was contended in the last chapter that to leave our status as human rights-holders up to the emotional reactions we just happen to elicit from other people is far too flimsy a foundation for our claims to minimally decent treatment.

Rorty underestimates the degree to which we can be responsive to a reasonable justification and overestimates the degree to which we can be manipulated according to our sentimental dispositions. When we are confronted with a reasonable justification for a claim, whether it be in science, political science, or daily life, our beliefs often do change, albeit usually with further consideration. When they do change as a result of such confrontation, such change is often more enduring in its effect on our behaviour than when we act on the basis of emotion and sentiment. Sentiment shifts, often with shocking and senseless rapidity, whereas the conclusions of a reasonable justification endure. Rorty is right to suggest that we often resist changes in our beliefs much more than we resist changes in our emotions. But change our beliefs we do, especially when confronted time and again with the force of a well-grounded claim made with insight and clarity. Sound systems of education are a standing testimony to this reality. So if we could change the beliefs of someone disrespectful of human rights, it would follow that we could have a much more enduring social shift than if we merely manipulate their passions through tender tutoring in the sensitive arts. And who is to say we will succeed with such emotional manipulation? Some people—especially human rights-violators—are hard-hearted and utterly lack a social conscience. Often, such people are beyond the reach of emotional appeals: they are cold and callous, dissociated from other human beings. They are often openly contemptuous, even hate-filled, toward their victims. Is making them watch *Schindler's List*, or read *The Diary of Anne Frank*, going to move them? Hopefully, yes, but there are no guarantees of that: such a strategy assumes a degree of moral maturity that may not be there. Does reasoning with them offer greater prospects? I believe so, because such people often remain rational in spite of the decrepitude of their character. If they can be persuaded that they act on the basis of incorrect assumptions, or faulty inferences, or in violation of principles they themselves believe in, then they may be more open to reconsider and reform than if they are simply hectored at for not being sensitive enough. An invitation to attend a "pity party," so to speak, can be set aside without regret or affect. It is harder, I suggest, to set aside appeals to consistency, clarity and reasonableness. Often, reformed criminals speak soberly about society's justification for jailing them and subjecting them to force: they speak much more in those terms than in terms of identifying with, and being sensitive to, their victims. But there are, admittedly, no guarantees with reason either: that is why it is ultimately the use of force, and the threat of coercive punishment and rectification, which stands as the most effective and reliable guarantee against human rights violation. When human rights violators fail to respond to other appeals, we respond with force, and rightfully so. Rights, to be real, need to be enforced.

This is not to say, to amend Mao's phrase, that human rights flow from the barrel of a gun. They do not: human rights can be more effectively secured if they are enforced, but such enforcement is *not* what justifies their existence. What justifies the existence of human rights is not force, nor sentimentality, but rather a compelling set of reasons to treat human beings in a minimally decent fashion. Indeed, it is the importance of such reasons, and the principles they stand for, which justify the resort to force in an attempt to secure them from merciless predators, either in the form of individual criminals or unjust social institutions.

The deep irony with Rorty is that, in the final analysis, he too sports a justification for human rights. In spite of all his post-modern protestations regarding the limits of reason, and how we do not need a rational foundation for our human rights claims, it is crystal clear that he offers us an important rationale for supporting human rights: such support contributes to the development of an Enlightenment utopia. This, we will see in greater detail below, is an example of a consequentialist justification for human rights: we should believe human rights exist, and act accordingly, because if we do so society will be improved as a result. We will enjoy the fruits of living in a more pleasant, stable and successful society if we respect human rights than if we fail to do so. Rorty might even offer as evidence a historical comparison, in quality and enjoyment of life, between societies that have respected human rights and those that have not. This is actually a quite compelling and reasonable justification, so it is surprising that Rorty does his level best to suggest there is no need for such justification at all. The reason he does so, upon reflection, becomes clear: since he assumes the superiority of one form of justification all along, he assumes there is no further need to pursue the question. He believes he has the right answer, so he finds the question uninteresting. While we might agree with the strength of his consequentialist form of justification, it seems rather disingenuous for Rorty to pretend that he is not involved in offering a justification at all, or that he is somehow above that, or doing something different altogether. He is not above it: he is in the very thick of the controversy surrounding justification, as any strong defender of human rights must be.

Setting Aside Some Options

As a consequence of things said in the past two chapters, some prominent options regarding human rights justification have already been put aside. These include, most notably, religious justifications and a doctrine known as legal positivism. Religious justifications rest on original premises which, in my judgment, are too controversial and exclusionary, taking us far away from a plausible demonstration of universality and equality with regard to human rights protection. We will not deal with them further.

Legal positivism is the view that it is only those rights that have been effectively codified into law which count as real and legitimate.[6] The reason the positivist offers for respecting human rights is this: respect them, or feel the wrath of the law. The law's majesty demands recognition of rights, and it exacts very real penalties for failure to do so. Positivism draws on powerful resources: it is indeed quite persuasive, to most people, to point out that failure to respect human rights in a particular case can land them in serious trouble with the law. Most us would agree that, from the point of view of personal prudence, that is a great reason to show respect to human rights. The threat of imprisonment or paying burdensome fines, coupled with the stigma of a serious criminal record, combine to concentrate the mind powerfully against violating anyone's human rights. Furthermore, the human rights movement has been successful, in recent decades, in getting human rights codified into both national and international pieces of law: it is fast becoming a real task to keep track of all the bills, charters, treaties and declarations of human rights recently promulgated. In many countries, human rights do form a part of codified and enforced law, and so reference to legal conventions can serve as a powerful and useful first line of defence against would-be rights violators, providing even them with good reason to back off their devious designs and respect other people's vital needs and fundamental interests.

The real issue with legal positivism is whether it can provide more than a first-line defence, or initial justification, of human rights. Many suspect that it cannot. The most obvious weakness in the justification is this: if codification into law is what justifies human rights, then in those places where such rights are not codified, it follows that they are not there justified. This is, of course, inconsistent with both universality and equality. Positivism makes people's rights utterly contingent on whether their society has written such rights into law; it makes human rights utterly dependent on the whims and wishes of the most powerful in that society, who exert strong influence in the legislatures and courts. This, erroneously, takes human rights out of the hands of those who hold them and places them into the preserve of powerful institutions, which may not be sufficiently respectful of the need to treat all human beings in a minimally decent way.

While many countries have codified human rights protections in their domestic legal codes, sadly others have not. And in some countries that have codified elements of human rights, real enforcement of such rights does not always, or even regularly, occur. Such codification gets referred to as "trophy law," or "trophy rights": pretty pieces of paper for display but having no impact on the real world. To those who reply that there is still international law covering such countries, the response is that generally international law only governs those countries that freely accept the terms of rights-respecting treaties, and many of the countries in question do not. And even when one such country has signed an international treaty on human rights, there is little the international community can do to ensure that the country lives up to its own commitments on a reliable basis. What legal positivism implies in these hard cases is this: those people unfortunate enough to suffer under such decrepit regimes have no human rights. This is so because only human rights that have been effectively codified into law count as genuine under this understanding. This strikes most supporters of human rights as an erroneous conclusion.

Supporters of human rights tend to agree that the law can decide whether or not *to recognize* people's pre-existing human rights, but it does not of itself *grant* such rights. Human rights exist first and foremost as moral rights: high-priority moral reasons demanding decent treatment. It often helps, in the real world, to have such moral rights codified into an effective legal system but such is not what justifies us in respecting these rights in the first place. It is the power of abiding moral principles, not the influence of legal institutions, which justifies human rights. People, therefore, should not be thankful they live in a country that has "given" them their human rights: all human beings are owed the objects of their human rights as a matter of justice. At best, people might be thankful they live in a society that recognizes in its laws that they have human rights. But, even then, such a society is not to be congratulated too heartily: it is, after all, only meeting the *minimal* requirements for political decency and social morality.[7]

Moral Convention

If social morality is more the subject at hand, then perhaps our search for a compelling justification would be improved if we turned to examine our shared moral beliefs. Perhaps the ultimate justification for human rights is not that they exist in the law but, rather, that they exist in our shared beliefs about human rights. They exist as a matter of moral custom, and regular ethical practice. We should respect human rights because we agree they exist and are important. This understanding of social convention might allow us to avoid the distasteful implication of legal positivism, namely, that human rights do not exist in those countries where they are not part of the law. We could, after all, point out that even when the law in those countries is silent, there may yet remain a widespread social commitment amongst the people to respect human rights, and so it is there we should rest our argument. As the old maxim of politics has it, *vox populi, vox Dei*: the voice of the people is the voice of God. It is widespread social consent to, and agreement about, basic principles of human rights that justify our belief in them and our corresponding actions.

One objection to raise at this point is this: there does not seem to be universal consent to human rights and to the basic moral regard they stand for and seek to ensure. Human rights violators, most clearly, do not offer consent to the idea that everyone—their victims included—has human rights. One interesting response to this challenge, comes from Michael Walzer. He says that "[i]ndividual rights (to life and liberty) underlie the most important judgments we make" about how we should treat each other, and how we should shape the society we share. These individual human rights "are somehow entailed by our sense of what it means to be a human being. If they are not natural, then we have invented them, but natural or invented, they are a palpable feature of our moral world."[8] Human rights are obvious and elemental moral commitments we share: this consensus is one reason why talk about human rights has come to be so influential in social life. Walzer suggests that this moral world we share, of which human rights are such a "palpable feature," contains two kinds of morality: thick and thin.

Thick, or "maximal," morality is the sum total of the moral beliefs and ethical practices in a given country or culture. It is identical with what we have been calling a country's "social morality." Thick morality, for Walzer, is utterly relative to time and place, and it thus differs considerably from one setting to another. Beliefs about the ethics of sex and intimate relationships, for example, clearly seem to be part of a culture's thick moral code. Such beliefs and practices are not universally shared and tend to be strongly relative to one's cultural background. The legal system of a country would be another important example of a part of that country's thick moral code.

Walzer, unlike others, suggests that in addition to the world's many maximal moralities, and the attending diversity and relativism, there exists one globally shared "thin" moral code. Thin morality is, in his words, "minimal and universal." This thin morality is basic, elemental, even elementary. Thin morality is "largely negative," consisting of prohibitions *against* "the grossest injustices," like "murder, deception, betrayal, gross cruelty" and "torture, oppression and tyranny." We all agree these things are wrong and should be prohibited. Walzer even refers to these rudimentary prohibitions as "moral facts" that are "immediately available to our understanding." This "minimal and universal moral code ... regulates our conduct with all humanity." Walzer emphasizes that the thin theory of minimal morality is universal *only* in the sense of the scope of those who endorse it. It is *not* The One True Morality; rather, it is nothing more (nor less) than that core set of values we find reiterated in every thick moral and political code. Thin morality is nested somewhere within every thick moral code. Thin morality, in short, consists of those basic moral rules that everyone, everywhere believes in.[9]

This does not, of course, mean that everyone, everywhere always acts in accord with thin morality. Thin morality remains, after all, a set of beliefs normative, or prescriptive, of behaviour: it is not a description of how everyone actually behaves. From the fact that some people fail to act in accord with thin morality is *not* an argument against Walzer's view. He is the first to acknowledge the existence of aggressors and violators. His point is that everyone, or very nearly everyone, *endorses the ideals* contained in thin morality, even if their actions sometimes fall short of such ideals. Even rights-violators, for example, endorse the important idea that murder is wrong: it is just that they have truly bizarre ideas about what counts as murder and what does not, or that some of them, in a bad moment, let their base instincts overpower their ordinary moral convictions.

Human rights to life and liberty must, on Walzer's understanding, correlate with those universal and mainly negative prohibitions—against murder, torture, gross cruelty, oppression, tyranny, and deception—inhering in the thin and minimal code of morality shared by all the world's diverse ethical traditions. Human rights, in the final analysis, are core and primary entitlements we all have that we *not* to be subjected to such treatments. We know we have these entitlements not by appealing to our emotions, or to the law, but, rather, by reflecting on the elemental ethical beliefs and ideals we all, or very nearly all, share. Whether there is literal, genuinely universal endorsement is not crucial on this understanding: there will always be some maladjusted morons, or twisted sociopaths, who refuse to endorse what is reasonable and right. That is their problem, and does not diminish the moral force of what the vast majority agrees as being needed for fundamental human dignity and a minimal level of respectful treatment.[10]

Walzer does believe, importantly, that thin morality constitutes a check on thick morality, even though it is thick morality to which we are first exposed and which thus seems the most natural for us. He insists that any government that violates the dictates of thin morality can only be seen as deficient and unjust. Appeal to thick cultural particularities *cannot* justify violations of the thin moral code. One cannot appeal to the charms of cultural difference to excuse the commission of gross human rights violations. This is not, once more, because the thin code stands as The Truth about morality; rather, it is because of the elemental meaning of the thin code already embedded in every thick one. This meaning contains the information that, for all of us, no grosser injustices exist than violations of the thin prohibitions on murder, tyranny, oppression, gross cruelty, and so on. Minimal morality is "morality close to the bone" and as such is simple, universal and intensely held. Maximal morality, by contrast, is a richly articulated cultural code, complicated, qualified and full of such subtle nuance that non-participants in the culture can find difficulty grasping, much less endorsing, it.[11]

Walzer's defence of moral conventionalism is strong because it seems to avoid a most potent objection, namely, that consent to human rights does not seem to be universal. On the one hand, there is no denying that the thin norms as Walzer describes them appear very broadly endorsed indeed, at least in general outline. This is surely related to the fundamental interests that reasonable people see to be protected by such norms as forbidding murder and torture, oppression and cruelty. At the same time, however, we might wonder whether the thin norms are so abstractly put by Walzer that they leave too much space for different interpretations of the same phenomena. Granted, nobody in their right mind is going to explicitly endorse "murder" and "gross cruelty"—very few people come right out and gladly admit they are massive human rights violators. But can Walzer simply leave it there without acknowledging the residual ambiguity with regard to how people understand such activity? For instance, is the death penalty "gross cruelty," or abortion "murder?" What about breeding and slaughtering animals for human consumption? Or torturing a terrorist to gain needed information about his confederates? Think now of such thin prohibitions on "tyranny," "betrayal," and "oppression" and whether there is a globally shared consensus regarding their meaning. Walzer refers quite breezily, almost off-handedly, to the content of minimal morality, presumably owing to his view that we all know more or less what he is referring to. But do we really? I believe Walzer *does* show that the vast majority of reasonable people do indeed endorse some understanding of human rights, and as such this endorsement might be seen as revealing a kind of thin moral code that most of us share. The devil, though, is in the details:

even if we all endorse some understanding of "human rights," it still seems to matter importantly whether we all endorse the same understanding of that to which "human rights" refers. In other words, Walzer may make a compelling argument that commitment to the ideal of human rights is universally shared, or very nearly so. But an equally important question is whether there is near-universal agreement on the practical side of the commitment, namely, to provide the same set of objects to everyone.

What most reasonable people agree to, I suggest, is usually something quite compelling, something not to be ignored or set aside lightly. Custom and convention, while at times hidebound and in need of reform, often contain deep wisdom based on real experience in life. I do not share the common philosophical tendency to have contempt for the beliefs of the "common man," often articulated in such dismissive terms as "the herd mentality." My own view is that there is probably a strong reason why most people concur with a given belief, and this strong reason is indicated by the fact the belief is so broadly shared. This being said, it needs to be stressed that it is *the underlying reason* that is the thing to focus on, not the consensus surrounding it, as this perspective would have it. The consensus is arrived at, after all, by most people being convinced of the underlying reason. And so it is to that which we must turn. To put the point clearly: sometimes there can be widespread consensus about things that subsequently turn out to be a deep error. Think, for example, of the formerly shared belief about the earth's supposed flatness. Now I do think that moral beliefs are different from scientific beliefs, and so this example is not a perfect analogy. But it indicates that raw consensus may not be enough to justify important moral claims. The reason why the belief attracts such consensus is thus the thing to focus on. So social convention, like legal positivism, might serve as a useful first- or even second-line justification for human rights. But it seems that neither goes all the way down, so to speak, to offering us a satisfying starting point, or foundation, on which to rest our justification of human rights.[12]

Personal Prudence

Personal prudence makes a powerful appeal. People respond, with reliable regularity, to those things that seem in their self-interest. We all want to do well by our own lights, and so as reasonable creatures we tend to pursue those things, and perform those actions, which advance that cause. Most, if not all, people do indeed find as an impeccable reason to do something the fact that it is in their personal interests. Since human rights are designed to protect people's most basic and fundamental interests—in life and liberty, in elemental equality and at least a minimal level of welfare—it follows that each and every human being has a powerful reason to assert his or her human rights, and to insist that others respect such claims. This point reminds us of Gewirth's contentions, discussed in the last chapter, that human rights are designed to protect those elements truly necessary for a purposeful human existence, which he summarized in terms of freedom and well-being. *The objects of human rights are so crucial and vital, so integral to effective human functioning and activity, that they are what we want, no matter what we want.* Whatever else we might be striving for in life—rewarding career, loving relationships, fast car, exotic travel—we need secure access to the objects of human rights to enable our pursuit in the first place. It is thus a foremost axiom, or rule, of personal prudence to claim such objects for oneself as a matter of very high priority indeed. Since this reasoning speaks to everyone, it follows that we all have the most compelling personal grounds to assert our human rights to objects of vital need.

Most people would acknowledge that this line of reasoning is very persuasive when it comes to offering them a reason for thinking they themselves have human rights, should act accordingly by claiming them, and so on. I cannot imagine a reasonable person denying that they themselves have human rights after being apprised of these considerations. Only the most doctrinaire, anti-rights ideologue would be tempted to do so, and that at the cost of their credibility. So this line of reasoning seems to get us this far: we all, personally, have the most powerful reasons of personal interest and practical prudence in claiming the objects of our vital needs as a matter of high-priority human right. One question remains: is this far enough?

Some thinkers, like James Nickel, think not. They see two pressing challenges faced by this prudential perspective on human rights justification. First, can personal prudence give us a compelling account of *the limits* of our own human rights claims? Second, and relatedly, can personal prudence give us compelling reasons to respect the human rights *of other people*?[13] With regard to the first challenge, if it is personal prudence that justifies human rights, then surely the limits of what can justifiably be claimed in the name of human rights stretch far beyond vital human needs. Many things other than our vital needs, after all, can serve our personal interests, and powerfully so. In most of North America, for example, owning a car advances one's interests considerably, but of course a car is not something one vitally needs as a human being. Since the limits of what serves our personal interests reside well outside the small scope of vital human needs, then what, on this prudential account, is to prevent people from laying claim to all sorts of things in the name of human rights? The darkest scenario here would be this: what if, in a particular case, it would advance one's personal interests to do something at odds with the personal interests—maybe even the vital personal interests—of another person? If personal prudence grounds human rights, might it then have the perverse result that one can sometimes have the human right to violate the human rights of another?

The answer to this question that defenders of the prudential justification, such as David Gauthier,[14] put forth rests on a version of the old saying that "what goes around, comes around." Personal prudence itself places outside limits on what a person can and should plausibly claim from others and from social institutions. Since there is a kind of consensus—mentioned in the last section—about human rights, it would not be in one's personal interests to press controversial human rights claims, for instance to a car. One is liable, in such a case, to be dismissed as a self-indulgent crank, and promptly ignored. Likewise, one has substantive self-interested reasons not to violate other people's vital interests. *One should respect the rights of others because one wants other people to respect one's own rights.* Reciprocity is an important feature of human relations, and so if one behaves like a greedy and insensitive pig, or even worse like a vicious rights violator, one can indeed count on being subjected to some rough treatment oneself. If one fails to respect other people's human rights, then one should not expect to have one's own human rights respected. It is this realization—of reciprocity in social relations—that should make reasonable people comprehend how it is consistent with their own personal prudence not to violate the rights of others, and in fact to limit their own human rights claims to a core set of objects that everyone can also plausibly claim.

Critics of Gauthier, like Nickel, argue that this reference to reciprocity assumes a degree of equality of power between people that is at odds with the facts of social existence. They point out that some people are so powerful and well-positioned that they have precious little to fear from retribution by others.[15] History abounds with examples of such people—especially malevolent heads of state—who have violated human rights on a mass scale with impunity. How is one to persuade such people that it is in their enlightened self-interest not to violate other people's human rights, and to moderate their own rights claims to a respectable and plausible level? I suppose that supporters of the prudential idea might respond by saying that if one looks carefully at those historical examples, one can usually see that even those powerful people *did* suffer the retribution of society in the end, for instance by being jailed, executed, or driven to humiliation and suicide. Even the most defiant criminals and tyrants often ultimately receive their comeuppance, and this lesson could be impressed on someone mindful of their own long-term interests. The critics, however, object to this defence. The fact that *maybe* rights-violators will be found and caught, and then fittingly punished, is not enough, for it is not always true. Think of former Soviet dictator Joseph Stalin, for example, who died in power. Even if such violators *are* caught and punished, this is often cold comfort indeed for their victims, and for their families and friends. Surely, the critics say, such victims deserve firmer protections than counting on predators to grasp correctly their own enlightened, long-term self-interest. Our goal, so they say, should be to prevent human rights violations as far as we can, and leaving the matter up to people's personal calculations of self-interested prudence is not sufficiently reliable. We need something more firm and universal in its scope, something like a conception of moral duty binding on us all.

The prudential view, in my judgment, has much to commend it. It seems to succeed entirely to what we might call the half-way point, providing each of us, as individuals, with powerful reasons to see ourselves as holders of human rights. Whether this view can progress beyond the half-way point and give us reason to respect everyone else's human rights, and to limit our own human rights claims to a level playing field with others, depends on how effective and accurate one believes the thesis of "what goes around, comes around" to be. If one is convinced that this is an iron law of human relations, then the prudential perspective may provide complete satisfaction. If not, then one has to search for other reasons to get one from one's own individual human rights to a conception of why one should respect everyone else's.

Rawls' Renowned Method

Acclaimed philosopher John Rawls offers one influential attempt to combine the intuitive strengths of a prudential approach to human rights justification with a moral appeal to fairness. His renowned method for justifying political claims, such as those insisting on respect for human rights, invites us to consider ourselves as self-interested rational agents, coming together to negotiate the terms of social cooperation "in the original position behind the veil of ignorance." The original position refers to a hypothetical pre-political situation when all agents come together to bargain, as prudent and self-interested parties, on the rules that will shape basic social institutions, in particular government. All such agents are, by stipulation, behind a veil of ignorance, which deprives them of information that Rawls believes would poison the bargaining session and generate slanted, unfair results. The agents are to negotiate on principles of justice not knowing what their social standing, gender, race, intelligence, natural endowments, religion, income, partisan political attachments, etc., will be once the veil is lifted and they find themselves in society. In stark contrast to the prudential view, agents are deprived of knowledge of their own relative social power. Rawls believes that agents situated as he describes would agree on two core principles of justice, according to which social institutions should be shaped: the liberty principle, allowing for the maximum amount of freedom for each that is compatible with the same degree of liberty for all; and the difference principle, allowing only those social inequalities which benefit all, including especially the least advantaged member of society, and which occur in a context of equality of opportunity.[16]

Now what exactly does this procedure have to do with human rights and their justification? Rawls calls our attention to the worst-off position in society, and to the fact that the agents negotiating the terms of social cooperation do not know where they, and those whom they represent, will end up in society once the veil is lifted. Rawls asserts that it is a rule of rational choice under these conditions to insist on certain bedrock guarantees for the worst position in society. After all, for all they know they, or those they represent, may find themselves in precisely that position once the veil is lifted. They would therefore insist, as a matter of self-interest, on making the minimum position at least minimally decent. What would this involve, exactly? Two things. The first we have already seen: society should be so structured so that any inequalities ultimately benefit even the worst-off. It is often said, for example, that having some kind of competitive economic structure, which allows for some to earn considerably more than others, is beneficial even to the worst-off because the incentive of greater reward calls forth greater effort, leading to more goods and services being produced in society, which should improve the lot of the worst-off, for instance through more tax dollars being generated to secure their welfare benefits.

It is the second element in securing the minimum position that is most relevant for our purposes. Rawls argues that there are things he calls "social primary goods," which he defines as those "all-purpose means" to which members of modern societies need to have secure access if they are to pursue any other ends of action at all. These "all-purpose means" are very much akin to Gewirth's necessary conditions for purposive human action. Rawls includes on his list of primary goods some liberty and opportunity, a subsistence amount of income and wealth, living in a stable and secure social context, and enjoying a vaguely-defined set of "social bases of self-respect." Commentators suggest that, by this last reference, Rawls means something like access to at least a basic level of education and to some kind of social recognition, for instance in the form of equality before the law as a person. In claiming that these items are primary goods, Rawls is suggesting that they are needed to pursue other things of value in life—needed to live a minimally decent life in the modern world. Serious reflection on a life without liberty, without physical security, without any education and without even a subsistence income appears to bear this contention out. Owing to the vital necessity attaching to primary goods, Rawls argues, all the agents negotiating the terms of social cooperation behind the veil of ignorance would insist that society, at the very least, guarantee that everyone have primary goods. There is no way, Rawls insists, that any reasonable agent would run the risk of not having primary goods, not having the all-purpose means needed to pursue other things in life. A life without primary goods is no life at all—no life worth living, anyway. Rawls concludes that the agents would agree to structure society so that everyone, including the worst-off, gets primary goods. It follows that we can think of primary goods as the objects of human rights—i.e., as those things we all have high-priority reasons to claim, and to demand that others respect such claims. In later works, Rawls makes just such a link, thereby defending standard human rights to liberty, security, subsistence welfare, basic education, and equality of recognition as a person before the law.[17]

Rawls stands out, not only for the magnitude of influence his work has had, but also for how he blends the strengths of the prudential approach with genuine moral concern, which as we saw in the last section may provide more readily the universality and equality we are looking for. We witness in his argument a clear-cut and compelling case for each person to claim primary goods as a matter of human right. But what reason does he give us for supporting the similar claims of others? The answer: such respect would be given by all agents in the original position behind the veil of ignorance. Why should we care about that? We should care because such agents *are like us* in being reasonable and self-interested. But such agents are *unlike* us in that they negotiate the terms of social cooperation *under conditions that are free and fair.* There is no coercion or desperation in the original position, just rational agents negotiating prudently and seeking consensus. There are no crude assertions of socio-economic superiority, or perceived biases of gender or race, for such information cannot be accessed behind the veil of ignorance. The agents in the original position have no choice but to bargain solely on the basis of ensuring their own interests as human beings, and they must come to a consensus or there will be no functioning society to result. They can, and would, come to an agreement, and this agreement would involve everyone being provided with human rights and their objects. In sum, we all should agree—here and now, in the post-veil world—to the terms of Rawls's social contract because it was a contract negotiated by agents sufficiently like us in being self-interested and reasonable, but with the added advantage of having been negotiated under conditions of freedom and fairness. Unlike many real-world negotiations, wherein there are serious power imbalances, differences in wealth and access to information, and perhaps even prejudices rooted in differences in religion, language, race or gender, Rawls's hypothetical negotiation should command our attention and adherence since such differences are not allowed to play a role. This is what makes the terms of Rawls's contract fair. So why should we believe that we ourselves have human rights? Because we have the most powerful reasons of self-interested prudence to do so. Why should we believe everyone else also has human rights and, moreover, actually respect them? Because that is the fair thing to do, since self-interested rational agents would all agree to do so under free and fair conditions of social cooperation. Prudence gets us half-way there, so to speak, and then an appeal to fairness picks up the ball and carries it home. A twin commitment to elemental prudence and fundamental fairness gets us to where we want to be: acknowledging that we all have the same human rights.

Some critics of Rawls, like Robert Nozick, allege that agents in the original position would not extend minimal guarantees to the worst-off, preferring instead to free up those rights-respecting resources for competition.[18] As rational agents, they would, so the critics say, trade off the small risk that they would be at the very bottom in exchange for the prospect of getting more in general competition over resources and rewards. There may be some room to dispute what exactly counts as a reasonable risk to take, but Rawls's retort here is that it is manifestly unreasonable to risk being the occupant of a social position that has no guarantees of access to primary goods. Such a risk ignores the real meaning of primary goods and the utterly disastrous position one would be in without them, these necessary conditions for effective and purposeful action in the contemporary world. So the magnitude of the risk, in terms of the dangers faced while in the worst-off position, is not small. Plus, in the original position behind the veil of ignorance, one has no information as to the number of worst-off positions there are in society. The critics seem to presuppose there will be only a small number at the bottom, but it could just as well be that there will only be a few well-off positions in society amidst the degraded and desperate masses. Therefore, Rawls would conclude that it is, in fact, unreasonable to risk living without the objects of one's human rights.

Critics also suggest that Rawls's attempt to get us to set aside our palpable differences—of wealth, power, gender, race, etc.—is simply not realistic. Their question is this: given that we do not really live in the original position, behind the veil of ignorance, how can we realistically expect people to abide by the terms of a purely hypothetical and ideal social contract? The answer involves reminding these critics that Rawls is offering us normative justification—a prescription—for understanding social justice. He is not offering a description, or prediction, of how fallible human beings go about their business. Rawls's perspective is this: yes, we must be realistic in moral theory, but not to the point where we cave in utterly to how people actually behave. The very point of morality and justice, after all, is to improve people's behaviour, and that cannot be done if one assumes from the start that there is nothing really wrong with the way people actually behave. Rawls would suggest that in politics people often fail to behave as well as they should. They do so because they fail to act on the basis of fairness and instead act by caving in to their groundless instincts and prejudices, by trying to lord it over others with their power, by attempting to gouge disproportionate shares of wealth for themselves, and so on. I suggest that history shows Rawls more in the right with this observation. He would draw the inference, then, that we need a theory of justice to establish a set of ideals to aim at to improve our behaviour, and that his theory offers one such set, which among other things demands that we respect human rights. Is that too unrealistic? Is it unrealistic to hold everyone accountable to basic principles of fairness? Of course some people will not adhere, but that is *not* the point; the point is whether there are plausible principles to which we are justified in holding people responsible and subjecting them to punishment for violation. All Rawls is talking about, for our purposes, is ensuring that everyone has primary goods. He is talking about universal respect for a minimum level of freedom and subsistence below which no one is left to fall; he is not talking about massive government spending and coercive intervention in our lives. Is it utterly naïve to expect reasonable persons to arrive by consensus at the judgment that everyone should have secure access to primary goods, i.e., the objects of human rights? I join Rawls in saying that it is not naïve, that most people realize that it is only fair for everyone to have that handful of all-purpose means genuinely needed to live a minimally good life.

Dignity

References to "human dignity," "the dignity of the human person," and "the essential worth of the human person" abound in human rights documents, as do prohibitions on "inhumane and undignified treatment" of one's fellow human beings. Many in the human rights field cite a concept of human dignity as the ultimate justification for human rights.[19] Why respect human rights? Because to fail to do so violates human dignity. There is no denying the rhetorical force of this appeal to human dignity: the fact that so many in the field subscribe to this view is evidence of a kind in favour of its persuasiveness. Furthermore, it is no doubt meaningful to say things like "That is no way to treat a human being" when one is confronted with instances of human rights violation. All of us recognize a resilient moral appeal to human dignity contained within such a proposition.

The difficulty with dignity has to do with what it refers to, with what it itself rests on. Some supporters of the dignity view, referring back to a point made in the earlier section discussing the elements of a good justification, might suggest that for their purposes it rests on nothing. The appeal to human dignity is itself the resting point—is itself the foundation for the justification of human rights. So the concept of human dignity refers to nothing outside of itself; here is where the chain of reasoning showing human rights justification must end. Such a chain would run like this:

1. All human beings should be treated in accord with human dignity.

2. Human rights protect human dignity.

3. *Therefore*, all human beings should have their human rights respected.

The problem with this chain of justification, in my view, revolves around the substantial vagueness surrounding the concept of human dignity. For example, I agree wholeheartedly with each of the three sentences in the above justification yet deny that such is a satisfying justification. I am not satisfied because human dignity is too large, vague and contested a concept to serve as a solid starting point for justifying human rights. For what is "human dignity"? Do we just know it when we see it, so that ultimately this view rests on a controversial appeal to self-evidence? But dignity cannot be self-evident, for how then to explain the "blindness" of human rights violators? If dignity is not just evident but self-evident, how to explain the fact that not all of us see it the same way? All too often, people appeal to self-evidence when they have run out of good reasons for us to agree with them.[20]

Human dignity simply means too many things to too many people. While I agree that every human rights violation involves a violation of human dignity, I do not agree that every violation of human dignity involves a violation of human rights. For example, one is subjected to undignified treatment when one is standing on the corner of a sidewalk on a rainy day, waiting for the light to change, and a car speeds by, subjecting one to a humiliating splash of puddle water. One is also dealt an indignity when one trips on a stairway and is greeted by the ridiculing laughter of nearby children. Many also maintain that wearing those silly hospital gowns, with the breezy split down the back, violates their dignity. More seriously, many view being subjected to any invasive medical procedure as being subjected to an indignity, a kind of necessary evil. But none of these things involve a human rights violation. Examples of indignities abound, and they go some way toward showing that the concept of human dignity is subjectively understood in a way that makes for an unfirm and shifting foundation for human rights claims, at least in comparison to a clearer reference to primary goods or to the objects of vital human need. Attempts to diminish the subjectivity by insisting that the concept of human dignity is self-evident runs afoul of its own problems with plausibility, as shown above, or else transfers the weight of justification onto a concept or value different from dignity. For example, many religious traditions, especially Christian ones, make use of the concept of human dignity when discussing human rights. They then mitigate the subjectivity of the appeal to human dignity by claiming that the demand for human dignity is, in fact, rooted in a command of God. One should treat human beings with dignity and worth because they are all owed such treatment and regard as children of God. This kind of move shows two things: first, that even strong defenders of the dignity approach recognize that more is ultimately needed to back up human rights claims; second, that as soon as that something more is introduced, the focus of the debate switches away from dignity and towards the thing it is now hooked into, in this case a conception of God's commands.

Either way, the dignity approach is revealed as being too rickety to stand on its own two feet.

Consequentialism

We have already seen an example of a consequentialist justification for human rights in connection with our look at Richard Rorty. Consequentialism is the theory that what is most important, from a moral point of view, is considering how one's actions are likely to affect others. It is the consequences of one's actions, not the intentions behind them, which form the most relevant benchmark for measuring the moral worth of an action. When transposed to the realm of justice, consequentialism counsels that what is most important about social institutions is the consequences they actually produce: not the ones they tell us they produce, or the ones their managers sincerely want to produce but cannot. Consequentialism, as the very name indicates, is a results-driven understanding of personal ethics and social organization. Which results does consequentialism most seek to generate? Though the answer varies somewhat among consequentialists, the general response is happiness and well-being. The point and purpose of ethics and justice is to advance overall happiness and well-being among people. Consequentialists tend to be quite dismissive of abstract appeals to God, intrinsic dignity, or rational duty as the ultimate justification for propositions about morality and justice. They prefer, instead, to point toward the need for concrete improvements in people's lives as a more sober and compelling rationale on which all of us can agree. There is no better reason for doing something, consequentialists maintain, than that it advances human happiness—that it forwards genuine pleasure in life and promotes human well-being. The consequentialist justification for human rights, probably first stated by John Stuart Mill,[21] runs like this:

1. We should, through our actions and institutions, advance and not detract from human happiness and general well-being.

2. Human rights promote human happiness and well-being because they protect people's vital needs and fundamental interests, allowing them to pursue those things they find enjoyable and worthwhile.

3. Disrespecting, or violating, human rights, causes serious pain, both to those victimized and to those close to the victims. It also more

generally undermines everyone else's confidence that they can count on having their human rights respected. Human rights violations cause particular pain and general insecurity.

4. *Therefore*, we should, through our actions and institutions, respect people's human rights.

In support of this line of reasoning, consequentialists could refer to the historical record and argue compellingly that those societies that respect human rights are societies where human happiness is more in evidence than in societies disrespectful of them. People who live in rights-respecting societies are certainly better off, and generally happier, than those suffering under conditions of rights violation. Compare, for example, the quality and enjoyment of life of the average citizen in the United States, Australia, Canada, or Western Europe with, say, that of the average citizen in China, Cuba, Iraq, or North Korea. Consequentialists are inclined to suggest that here the facts speak for themselves: if people in a society care about their own overall happiness and well-being, they ought to ensure that their own behaviour, and the social institutions they share, respect human rights. In general, we are all better off—have a better and more consistent shot at enjoying life—if we live in a society that respects human rights.

There is much to be said in favour of this view: it makes a frank and compelling case, indeed. Some might dispute the quality-of-life comparison, noting in particular the far-from-perfect record of rights-respect in the first set of countries. That is fine, but the general point that respect for rights *on the whole* generates a happier and more enjoyable society than the alternative is, in my judgment, decisively supported by the facts of history. It should be noted, though, that many philosophical critics have thought that there is a necessary inconsistency between consequentialism and human rights.

The idea of the critics is that human rights command firm respect—stand as steadfast rules—whereas consequentialism, with its results-oriented focus, might recommend that we be more flexible with our treatment of people. More sharply, critics worry that, as soon as respecting human rights seems to hinder the general welfare, consequentialism will recommend that we set them aside in our pursuit of the most pleasant society. The problem with this criticism is that it ignores the fact that this consequentialist justification of human rights is just that: an explanation of the normative grounds of human rights from a results-oriented viewpoint. In other words, this viewpoint *accepts* human rights, and seeks to offer a compelling and graspable reason for us to respect such rights. In doing so, it shows us clearly that there is no *necessary* inconsistency between consequentialism and human rights. I grant that there have been forms of consequentialism that reject human rights: we will discuss Jeremy Bentham's form of classical utilitarianism, and his fierce attacks on human rights, in a later chapter. But from the fact that *one* prominent form of consequentialism rejects human rights, it does *not* follow that *all other* forms of consequentialism must follow suit. Indeed, we have just shown that this is not the case.

A more enduring criticism is whether a consequentialist justification of human rights can effectively deliver on the equality and universality of human rights. If the justification for them is ultimately about pleasure and happiness, then how can we ground the equality of human rights claims, when the causes of happiness are so variable from person to person? Moreover, what is to limit human rights claims to a finite set of plausible objects—such as those of vital need—if their ultimate purpose is to advance pleasure? We can get much pleasure out of non-necessary things, after all. Critics of consequentialism here use a famous thought experiment. If morality and justice are all about happiness and pleasure, then why not have the government provide everyone with a weekly orgasm pill, and call it a just society? Why not hook everyone up to a pleasure machine that regularly releases endorphins, and call it utopia?[22] If the point of human rights is happiness, does it follow that we have a human right to whatever makes us happy? If not—and presumably the answer must be negative—then what resources can consequentialism draw on to ensure us that its principles do not end up justifying an enormous, and excessively large, number of human rights claims? In my view, it is only a more focussed approach, based on a slim set of primary goods, or genuine vital needs, that can prevent such unsustainable "rights inflation."

Inference

One of the most slick and crafty justifications for human rights is that offered by H.L.A. Hart, with amendments attached by Henry Shue.[23] Theirs is a strategy of indirection and inference. The argument, inspired by Hart's legal training, goes like this: if we have any rights at all, then it follows we must have human rights. We do well here to recall Chapter 1's distinction between general and special rights. Special rights are particular entitlements that certain people enjoy in certain places and times, according to certain criteria. Special rights can be legal or moral. An example of a special legal right, at least in countries with a free market economy, would be one's ownership of a car. This is a particular and concrete right *one* person has to *that* car, as acknowledged by property laws in such countries. The same relationship is also a special moral right in most countries with free markets: one's right of private property ownership to the car is, generally, respected by other people. They see one as not only legally but also morally entitled to be recognized as owner of that car. Another example of special rights, both legal and moral, would be those in the context of a parent-child relation: the rights and correlative duties hold only between *those* people, and only until the child comes of age. General rights, by contrast, hold not just between particular persons with a special relationship between them but between all persons. Unlike special rights, general rights are thought to have no relativity to time or place. We have seen that human rights are general rights; indeed they are probably the only kind of general rights.

The heart of Hart's ingenious argument is this: if one has any special right whatsoever, then one must be seen as having at least one general right, namely, to liberty. What justifies his insistence on the "must," on the necessity of the inference? Hart urges us to think about it: it makes no sense whatsoever to say that John has the special right as owner of his car to, say, drive it where he wants, unless one also presupposes that John has the more general entitlement to that degree of personal liberty required to do so. Likewise for various special rights with regard to marriage, to home ownership, to turn right at the next lights, to sue somebody, to get a tax refund, to get what you paid for, and so on. For just about any special right we can think of—and there are oodles of them in contemporary life—we see that it makes no sense to speak of one as a special right-holder without also acknowledging that one must possess the general right to liberty. For anyone to make use of a specific entitlement to do, or have, something, that person must at least have a general background entitlement to the very freedom required to do that something, or come to have it as the case may be. All special rights presuppose the general, or human, right to liberty. Thus, if someone has any special rights at all, be they moral or legal, then that person must also have the human right to liberty. And surely everyone has at least one special right, either as the owner of something, or as the citizen of some country, or as a participant in some kind of moral relationship with at least one other person. Therefore, we all have the human right to liberty.

It is hard not to be impressed with this argument. Some shortfalls might, however, be discerned. First, this argument seems to make human rights contingent on other rights. Second, it delivers only a human right to liberty, when most rights advocates are looking for more. The concern in connection with the first criticism is that it is human

rights that should be seen as the most important and utterly foundational. But Hart's argument seems to make human rights derivative from
other, less important kinds of rights. Most people are inclined to say that
human rights arise necessarily out of something about the human person, or at least some foremost moral principle regarding the treatment
of such a person. But Hart appears to make human rights utterly contingent upon whether or not the person in question just happens to hold
a special right. Hart's response, I think, would suggest that this concern
is mostly a matter of approach, or ways of thinking about human rights.
From the fact that his strategy for *justifying* human rights involves an
inference, or derivation, from special rights, it does not follow that
human rights must be seen as being less important than such particular
rights. Indeed, on Hart's account, one observes that respect for human
rights is in fact necessary for respect for special rights. Without one's liberty, all the special rights in the world stand as useless and empty. While
it is true, and perhaps disturbing, that a person utterly devoid of special
rights could not be shown by this strategy to have human rights, Hart
insists that, as an empirical matter, everyone does in fact have at least
one special right, and thus also has human rights. We know all citizens
in rights-respecting countries have scores of special rights, so there is no
problem there. Even in countries where human rights are not officially
recognized, and perhaps are actively violated, everyone can still be seen
as a special right-holder. People in such sub-optimal societies often still
own things, often have legal rights detailed by that state's constitution,
and moreover engage in personal relationships, especially family ones,
that bring with them special moral rights, for example to recognition, to
fidelity, to responsiveness and care, etc. All we need is one (measly) special right, either moral or legal, and we have what we need to show the
existence of human rights. So even in countries like Cuba or North
Korea, where citizens perhaps cannot own things privately and perhaps
have very few substantive legal guarantees and entitlements, the people
there still presumably engage in private relationships that have special
moral rights woven into their very fabric.

The concern with the second criticism is that while Hart's argument
may succeed on its own terms, these terms are too narrow to give us the
full set of human rights we are looking for. Hart would probably reply
that there is room for legitimate disagreement, even among those who
support human rights, regarding the exact set of objects of human
rights. Hart views the scope of such objects very traditionally, essentially limited to standard legal and political entitlements designed to protect
human liberty. Shue has adopted Hart's strategy for human rights justi-

fication, but in defence of a more robust set of claimed objects. He lays out his version of Hart's inference in this way:

1. Everyone has the right to something.

2. Some other things are necessary for enjoying the first thing as a right, whatever the first thing is.

3. *Therefore*, everyone also has rights to the other things that are necessary for enjoying the first as a right.[24]

Shue stipulates that security, subsistence and liberty are the three necessary conditions for any subsequent exercise of special rights and thus form what he calls "the basic rights." Rights to security, subsistence and liberty are basic and general, the objects one must enjoy if one is to make any use of one's non-basic, or special, rights. So if one has at least one special right, one has human rights to security, subsistence and liberty. Liberty alone, Shue submits, is not enough to make exercise of one's special rights meaningful. One must be entitled not only to the freedom needed to exercise one's special rights, but also to the state of security and subsistence equally needed. Shue believes, much as Gewirth does, that we cannot act meaningfully, or perhaps even act at all, unless we enjoy not only some liberty but also some security from violence and the material wherewithal to survive and to have the energy to exercise special rights. We are not only moral creatures who need freedom to act voluntarily and purposefully but also material creatures requiring food and water and assurances against devastating physical assaults. So special rights, according to Shue, imply more than freedom. But such is the elasticity of these concepts that many could agree with Shue but prefer to view such further objects as themselves kinds of freedom, as opposed to separate and new objects of human rights. Think, for example, of former American president Franklin Roosevelt's articulation of "The Four Freedoms": freedom of speech and belief, and freedom from fear and want.[25] This dispute, however, turns our attention nicely to the important issue of which exact set of objects we have human rights to claim. This topic, of the specification of the objects of human rights, is the subject of the next chapter.

Vital Needs and The Duty Not to Harm

Many of the preceding justifications of human rights—e.g., those of Gewirth, Walzer, Rawls, Hart and Shue—have been rooted in a concern to protect everyone's access to a set of objects seen as necessary for acting purposefully and meaningfully in life. This concern was also evident at the end of last chapter, when the characteristic of having fundamental interests in living a life of minimal value was added to our set of characteristics defining those who hold human rights.

It is obvious to any reasonable observer that all human beings have vital needs in life and fundamental interests in living a life of at least minimal value to themselves and the world. To make such an assertion is not at all to ignore or downplay the wondrous diversity of human experience. It is merely an accurate observation regarding the necessary conditions of our survival—not only as biological human beings but also as creatures with desires and aspirations, both personal and social. For all our achievements and potential, we remain finite and needy creatures desirous of living a life we ourselves see as at least minimally worthwhile. We want both life and the good life. But the good life must be understood as composed of elements that we might call, after Walzer, thick and thin.

A thick vision of the good life is highly personal, diverse, relative and subjective. A thin vision, by contrast, is of those objects genuinely needed to survive and to be able to pursue one's thick vision at all. No one has the human right to succeed in securing her thick vision of the good life. Someone may very much want to be a movie star, or a head of state, or mega-wealthy, but that person has no human right to claim that the rest of us are duty-bound to do our part in realizing his aspirations. The first reason is that such a claim is inconsistent with the universality and equality residing at the heart of human rights. If there are human rights, they exist equally for everyone fulfilling the characteristics of a human rights-holder. Since we cannot all become movie stars, or heads of state, such objects, positions and lifestyles cannot be claimed as a matter of human right. The second reason has to do with the burden that would fall on the rest of us if we were duty-bound to aid someone's political or film career. The burden, clearly, would be unreasonable: we have our own lives to lead, thanks very much, and have better things to do than to see how we can play a role as props in another person's thick projects. Human rights claims, therefore, must be confined to the essential ingredients of a *thin* vision of the good life: the objects of vital need, which James Nickel has referred to as those needed to both *have* and *lead* a life.[26] If we want to survive and begin to pursue our personal goals at all, we must have the objects of our vital needs and fundamental interests. It was contended, at last chapter's end, that there are five such objects, claimable by everyone: physical security, material subsistence, personal freedom, elemental equality, and social recognition.

The reference to reasonable burdens needs to be applied not only to the thick, but also to the thin, vision of the good life. Much has been made thus far of the connection between human rights and vital human needs. But it must be stressed that this connection is not one of straightforward equivalence. In particular, one does not have the human right to claim absolutely everything in which one might come to have a vital need. Judith Thomson illustrates this point vividly with her thought experiment regarding the dying violinist.[27] Suppose a world-famous violinist is dying and, for whatever reason, he can survive only by being hooked up to you by machine, for twenty-four hours a day, nine months in a row. During this time, your kidneys and liver will cleanse his blood of the poison that is killing him. There is no denying that, in this hypothetical case, the dying violinist vitally needs to be hooked up to you: without such action, he will die. But it seems wrong to suggest that he has the human right to be so hooked up, since the burdens that would impose on you would be very heavy and unreasonable. The hooking up would directly interfere with your ability to lead your life in a manner of your choosing, at least for nine months; and this is supposing that the procedure would pose no physical danger to your own life, which is not on the face of it obvious. Here, then, we have at least a hypothetical case where there is genuine vital need for something, but no corresponding human right to that something.

What the case of the dying violinist illustrates is that what we have human rights to is *not* simply the objects of all our vital needs and fundamental interests but, rather, that others and social institutions *do their fair share* in enabling us to have the objects of our vital needs and fundamental interests. We will talk in greater detail, in a forthcoming chapter, about fair shares and the full nature of the duties correlative to human rights. For now, doing one's fair share means that, on the one hand, if someone already has an object of her vital needs, one ought not to take it away from her. If the person, on the other hand, does not yet have the object, a fair share means doing one's part in providing that object to the person *provided that one's part in the provision comes with a readily absorbable cost to oneself.* In particular, one's part in the provision cannot come at the price of one's own vital needs and fundamental interests in both *having* and *leading* a life. It would, after all, be unfair and unreasonable to require one person to sacrifice his own vital needs so that the needs of another could be met.

To fail to do one's fair share in enabling others to have the objects of their vital needs is to do them grievous harm. Such failure amounts *either* to positively thwarting and hindering their possession of their vital needs *or else* to negatively and negligently ignoring their serious suffering when one could do something about it at readily absorbable cost. Such failure denies to others their capacity to live minimally good lives and may actually attack their very ability to survive at all. The core principle on which this reasoning rests is that it is fundamentally wrong to do grievous harm to people without just cause. The only just cause for doing such harm would be that the harm is being done to a human rights-violator in the name of protecting the human rights of another person. So the ultimate principle here is this: *it is morally wrong to do grievous harm to human beings.* As stated in the famous Hippocratic Oath, sworn to by all medical doctors, one should *"do no harm."* We should add here that the harm one must avoid doing is neither trivial nor fleeting, like hurting someone's feelings; rather, the harm in view here has to do with the direct and material hindrance and crippling of another person's ability to live a minimally good life.

The duty not to do grievous harm is one of the most widely shared, and deeply moving, conceptions of universal moral duty. The only thing capable of dislodging this duty is if those in question have forfeited their right not to be grievously harmed by performing acts of human rights violation. Otherwise, we ought not to do them grievous harm, and that means doing our fair share in enabling all people to have the objects of their vital needs and fundamental interests. Thus, the reason each of us has to respect the human rights of others—in addition to demanding respect for our own—is that failure to show such respect is to cause them grievous harm. And causing grievous harm to a human being without just cause violates a primary and powerful moral duty whose vital importance we all acknowledge.

Conclusion

We have to justify our human rights claims. We must be able to offer people good reasons why we think we have human rights—why we think all of us are owed a minimum standard of decent treatment. Any such justification must rest somewhere, and usually it is the selection of the resting point, or foundation, that is decisive regarding whether or not we find the justification persuasive. In this chapter, we canvassed a number of influential and important strategies for justifying human rights, finding some more persuasive than others. Among the unpersuasive accounts, we enumerated legal positivism, appeal to religious faith, and abstract appeals to human dignity. Among the more "middling" accounts—subsisting somewhere between unpersuasive and persuasive, depending on one's interpretation—we discussed Walzer's citation of a large social consensus in favour of respecting human rights, alongside prudence-based appeals to everyone's self-interest in respecting human rights. Among the more clearly persuasive accounts, we listed consequentialism, the strategy of inferring human rights from special rights, and Rawls's mixture of both prudence and fairness. The final section commended a justification rooted in the "positive" value of protecting people's vital need to both have and lead a minimally good life, coupled with the "negative" value of not violating a foremost duty we all have, namely, not to inflict grievous harm on our fellow human beings. In other words, there are a number of very good reasons to believe that we all have human rights, and that we each ought to respect everyone else's.

Notes

1 Aristotle, *Nicomachean Ethics*, trans. W.D. Ross (Oxford: Oxford University Press, 1998), Book 1, sections 1-3.

2 No one made this point better than Bertrand Russell. See, e.g., his *Wisdom of the West* (London: Bloomsbury, 1989).

3 An argument probably made first by J.S. Mill, in his *On Liberty* (Indianapolis: Hackett, 1978).

4 R. Rorty, "Human Rights, Rationality and Sentimentality," in S. Shute and S. Hurley, eds., *On Human Rights* (New York: Basic Books, 1993).

5 Rorty, "Sentimentality," 142-48; R. Rorty, *Contingency, Irony and Solidarity* (Cambridge: Cambridge University Press, 1989).

6 H.L.A. Hart, *The Concept of Law* (Oxford: Clarendon, 1961). Hobbes, Bentham and Austin also articulate versions of legal positivism.

7 J. Feinberg, "The Nature and Value of Rights," *Journal of Value Inquiry* 1 (1970/71): 243-57.

8 M. Walzer, *Just and Unjust Wars* (New York: Basic Books, 1977), 54 and xxx.

9 M. Walzer, *Thick and Thin: Moral Argument at Home and Abroad* (Notre Dame: University of Notre Dame Press, 1999) 7, 15, 42-52; M. Walzer,

Interpretation and Social Criticism (Cambridge: Harvard University Press, 1987), 23-29.

10 With regard to the universality of human rights, Walzer says that "the language of rights ... is translatable" from one culture into the language of any other, at *Thick and Thin*, 10.

11 Walzer, *Thick and Thin*, 5.

12 For more on Walzer and conventionalism, see my *Michael Walzer on War and Justice* (Cardiff: University of Wales Press, 2000).

13 J. Nickel, *Making Sense of Human Rights* (Berkeley: University of California Press), 84-90.

14 D. Gauthier, *Morals by Agreement* (Oxford: Clarendon, 1986).

15 Nickel, *Making Sense*, 84-90.

16 J. Rawls, *A Theory of Justice* (Cambridge, MA: Harvard University Press, 1971).

17 Rawls, *Theory of Justice, passim*; J. Rawls, *The Law of Peoples* (Cambridge, MA: Harvard University Press, 1999), especially pp. 78-82; R. Martin, *Rawls and Rights* (Lawrence: University of Kansas Press, 1985); T. Pogge, *Realizing Rawls* (Ithaca, NY: Cornell University Press, 1989).

18 R. Nozick, *Anarchy, State and Utopia* (New York: Basic Books, 1974).

19 G. Vlastos, "Justice and Equality," in J. Waldron, ed., *Theories of Rights* (Oxford: Oxford University Press, 1984), 41-76; J. Maritain, *The Rights of Man and Natural Law* (London: Centenary, 1944); J. Finnis, *Natural Law and Natural Rights* (Oxford: Clarendon, 1980).

20 I owe this argument to P. Jones, *Rights* (New York: St. Martin's, 1994), 94-98.

21 Mill, *On Liberty, passim*. See also D. Lyons, "Human Rights and The General Welfare," *Philosophy and Public Affairs* 2 (1976/77): 113-29; R.B. Brandt, "Utilitarianism and Moral Rights," *Canadian Journal of Philosophy* 34 (1984): 1-19; R.M. Hare, *Moral Thinking* (Oxford: Clarendon, 1981); R.G. Frey, ed., *Utility and Rights* (Oxford: Blackwell, 1985).

22 J.C. Smart and B. Williams, eds., *Utilitarianism: For and Against* (Cambridge: Cambridge University Press, 1973); A. Sen and B. Williams, eds., *Utilitarianism and Beyond* (Cambridge: Cambridge University Press, 1982).

23 H.L.A. Hart, "Are There Any Natural Rights?" *The Philosophical Review* (1955): 175-92; H.L.A. Hart, *Essays on Bentham* (Oxford: Clarendon, 1982), 79-104; H. Shue, *Basic Rights: Subsistence, Affluence and U.S. Foreign Policy*, 2nd ed. (Princeton, NJ: Princeton University Press, 1996).

24 Shue, *Basic Rights*, 16-18.

25 These four freedoms subsequently made their way into the preamble of the UN's *Universal Declaration of Human Rights*.

26 Nickel, *Making Sense*, 51-52.

27 J. Thomson, "A Defence of Abortion," *Philosophy and Public Affairs* 1 (1976): 47-66.

Chapter 4

What are the Objects
of Our Human Rights?

As noted in Chapter 1, what we care about most is not our human rights
but, rather, the objects of such rights. We now know who the right-holders are, and of various powerful reasons that justify human rights. We
now need to know more about those things to which we have human
rights. Human rights are always rights *to* something, and in the final
analysis we most want our hands firmly *on* that something. There used
to be a famous hamburger commercial on television that asked the
memorable question, "Where's the beef?"[1] The real beef in the human
rights debate can be found in the debate over the objects of such rights.
The objects are what we really want—the substantive stuff, so to speak—
and so are the source of much of the controversy surrounding human
rights, and especially the duties correlative to them. I have already suggested that we have human rights to, most centrally, five abstractly-
defined items. I label these items "the foundational five," for reasons to
be detailed below. To recap, the foundational five are physical security,
material subsistence, personal liberty, elemental equality, and social
recognition. I believe these five items fully capture the set of those things
we can sincerely and legitimately claim as the necessary ingredients for
a life of minimal value in the modern world. But we can imagine someone asking, what do each of these five abstract items imply in terms of
concrete goods and benefits, in terms of actual social arrangements?
Furthermore, what do other solid sources say about the objects of
human rights?

A compelling course of procedure, by way of response, is to examine
some of the most prominent human rights documents in chronological
order, discerning the evolution of thought about the objects of human
rights. This contextualizes the important debate over objects within the
flow of real-world history and political struggle. After such a tour of
some human rights history, we can return to more abstract theoretical
considerations as we pursue a compact and accessible account of what
set of objects we can legitimately claim as the objects of our human
rights. The reader should note that, of the documents mentioned below,
four are included in Appendix A. The reader is invited to read these documents in their entirety.

Magna Carta

In 1215, King John of England was broke. He had exhausted the national treasury fighting wars, particularly the Crusades against Islam in the Middle East. He needed cash badly. Large land-owners in the English countryside—self-styled barons and earls, lords and dukes—were flush. King John, accordingly, hit them up for money. The nobles agreed but only in exchange for John's signing the Great Charter, a document that recognized various rights they had been claiming. Which rights? First and foremost, recognition of their property rights as owners of vast tracts of land. Essentially, the king promised to keep his greedy hands off their holdings. Second, rights to their freedom of movement throughout England for the purpose of trade and commerce. Third, and most famously, the Magna Carta lists a whole series of entitlements to due process in any legal proceeding, such as the right not to be arrested for an alleged crime "without a credible witness"; the right not to be detained in jail without being informed of the charge against oneself; the right never to be "molested" while in prison awaiting trial; the right to trial by an impartial jury of peers (i.e., fellow property-owners); and the right, if found guilty of a crime, to be subjected only to punishment "of the same degree as the offence." Rights to such objects, of course, were claimed by these land-owning nobles only for themselves: there was no sense whatsoever, at the time, that all humanity could lay claim to these privileges. They have all, however, made their way into nearly every major human rights document since that far-away time.[2]

The English Bill of Rights

England underwent a "Glorious Revolution" in 1688-89. The Catholic King James II was overthrown, and the Protestant monarchs King William and Queen Mary, both from the province of Orange in Holland, took his place on the throne of the United Kingdom. They then issued a bill of rights, as a kind of political proclamation, to show they intended to be constitutional monarchs—rulers bound by a firm set of principled laws, as opposed to absolute monarchs, legally unbound and governing on the basis of personal taste and impulse. The Protestants portrayed James II as having been an absolute monarch and thus declared their overthrow of him "glorious." The English Bill of Rights declared that absolute monarchy was "illegal" and that there should be an elected parliament to advise the monarch: "The subjects ... have the right to petition the King" through their elected members of parliament, and election to parliament must be "free and fair." Of course, by "free and fair" they meant that no law-abiding and property-owning man, of a certain age and lineage, should be prevented from running for a seat in parliament. Wealthy nobles should not be prevented by any king, or other nobles for that matter, from running for public office. More significantly, the Bill proclaimed a right "to freedom of speech and debates" within parliament. This right, we saw in Chapter 1, has since evolved into a standard immunity-right in most modern Western democracies: elected legislators may not be prosecuted for anything they say while in the legislature. Affirming the right of trial by jury, the English Bill also declared that those convicted of a crime have the right not to be inflicted with "cruel and unusual punishment." The Bill also entitled Protestant subjects with the right to bear arms for their own defence against a feared Catholic backlash against the Glorious Revolution. This last right, so clearly the source of the right to bear arms in the American Constitution, underlines how far from being universal these older rights were: Catholics had no such right to bear arms for their own defence.

The significance of these rights in the English Bill is that they widened the scope and number of objects claimed as a matter of justice: in addition to property rights and due process rights during legal proceedings, there now appeared certain rights to self-defence, political participation, free political speech, and even some personal security from cruelty and torture.[3]

The American Rights Documents

The American Declaration of Independence from England, signed in 1776, famously proclaimed, "We hold these truths to be self-evident, that all men are created equal, that they are endowed by their Creator with certain unalienable Rights, that among these are Life, Liberty and the pursuit of Happiness. That to secure these rights, Governments are instituted among Men, deriving their just powers from the consent of the governed." When a government fails to respect the people's rights, they have the right to revoke their consent, and establish a new and better government. The Declaration *of* is thus also a justification *for* independence.

This ringing declaration seems, at first glance, to be a radical break from the first few rights documents produced in England. The American Declaration rejects the class structure of English society, where all the rights were reserved for high-born and propertied nobles. The

Americans declared that all men are created equal and are thus entitled to whatever objects they have got coming to them as a matter of right. Americans thought it "self-evident" that, since all men are children of God, they must possess equal intrinsic worth by their very nature: intrinsic worth because created by God Himself, and equal worth because no one is more a child of God than the next man. It is important to note, of course, that the drafters of the American Declaration did not follow through successfully on this lofty sentiment about equality, at least in the short term. As in England, only property-owning men were at first allowed to vote and to participate in the politics of the new republic. In addition, the continuation of slavery in the American South until the 1860s blighted all such pretence toward equality. It is rather ironic, indeed, that the first explicit declaration of universal equality in a rights document came out of such a decidedly unequal society.

What rights did the American revolutionaries believe all men have by their nature as children of God? The reply is well known: rights to life, liberty and the pursuit of happiness. The American right to life is an extension of the earlier English right to security of the person: a right to basic and reliable protection against serious and standard physical threats to one's life, notably the violence of other people. It is, most centrally, a right not to be assaulted and murdered, and it probably implies a further right to a functioning system of law and order designed to provide reliable protection from just such transgressions. The right to liberty is more tricky and complex, and perhaps better left for our look at the subsequent U.S. Bill of Rights, but here it seems philosophically connected with the pursuit of happiness. Provided that citizens refrain from violating the rights of others, they ought to be free to pursue whatever they believe will make them happy. Government, the revolutionaries believed, ought not to privilege and protect one way of life through legislation—in particular, the way of life of an aristocratic and Anglican British landlord. Government should, rather, merely enforce for all the basic ground-rules established by these fundamental rights, and then stand aside and let people live their lives.

The Declaration of Independence was, and remains, a political proclamation, and as such carries no legal weight in American courts. What does carry legal weight is the American Bill of Rights, which refers to the first ten amendments to the American Constitution, which was brought into force between 1787 and 1789. The American Bill of Rights is reprinted in Appendix A. The vast majority of the rights contained in this Bill are rights to due process, much as witnessed above in the English documents. Amendments Five through Eight contain some American additions to due process, such as the rights not to be put in double jeopardy and not to be compelled to testify in a case against oneself. In the Fifth Amendment, reference is also made most generally to the right not to "be deprived of life, liberty or property without due process of law" and, even if property should be seized legally, one is still owed "just compensation." The Second Amendment contains the controversial right to "keep and bear arms." The Fourth Amendment contains further due process measures, specifically focusing on police powers during arrest and how they need probable cause before they can search or seize anything during a criminal investigation.

The First Amendment to the Bill of Rights contains the right to liberty, which is probably the hallmark of the American contribution to contemporary human rights theory. This storied amendment declares that people have rights to the free exercise of the religion of their own choice, as well as to freedom of speech and of the press more generally. Furthermore, people have the right to assemble peaceably and to petition government. This right of freedom is certainly more extensive than the older British right, since the freedom of speech defended above was narrowly in connection with speech in parliament. There is no such restriction of scope in the American document, and in fact the press's right to speak out is also explicitly included. The right to peaceably assemble is also new, and most probably intended as a protection both for religious worship and for partisan political rallies.

It is important to remind ourselves of the precise historical origin of the American obsession with freedom: it resides in the quest for religious liberty, which is the very first right enumerated in the Bill. People often forget that America, in its modern form, was founded not for the sake of open spaces and abstract freedom but rather quite specifically for the sake of religious freedom. Of particular concern was the freedom of sectarian Protestants, such as the Pilgrims, from the Anglican Church back in England. The quest for religious freedom clearly connects with that other uniquely American piece of rights-talk: the pursuit of happiness. People ought to be free to pursue their own vision of righteousness, of godly behaviour and salvation, provided only they respect the rights of others in doing so. This is, in comparative terms, a tolerant and liberal political position, and was clearly the product of, and reaction to, the intolerance and murderous violence between Catholic and Protestant that had been tearing Europe apart at the time. There is nothing like this idea of "live-and-let-live" tolerance in the prior English documents, and this core value commitment—to pluralism and the pursuit of personal meaning—is very much at the heart of the contemporary human rights movement.[4]

French Declaration

Inspired by the success of the American Revolution, dissidents and activists in Paris began the French Revolution against the monarchical regime of Louis XVI in 1789. Though the Revolution was soon to spin out of control into chaos and terror—events which paved the way for Napoleon to re-establish control through military dictatorship, in the early days of 1789 the revolutionaries issued the Declaration of the Rights of Man and Citizen. The French Declaration is reprinted in Appendix A. This document has probably been the most influential rights document throughout Europe, and is often copied. Not surprisingly, the French Declaration itself copied much of the content of the prior English and American documents. It offers the same due process protections and the same respect for the rights to "liberty, property, security and resistance to oppression." Of property and security, there is little new added. The liberty provisions are for freedom of conscience and religion as well as freedom of communication, including especially freedom of the press. The Declaration also suggests that a *maximal* amount of liberty ought to be the goal of any society, stipulating that all actions should be permitted except only those that are "injurious to others." The French Declaration's distinctive contribution to human rights history rests in two fields: the right to political participation and the right to equality.

Not only does the Declaration maintain a right to resist oppression, it also states explicitly that "all citizens have the right to concur personally, or through their representatives, in the formation of the law." Law must express "the general will" of the citizens in this way: the right to govern resides with the whole of the nation, and not with a small set of self-styled elites. These were the widest and deepest declarations of popular sovereignty, and of the right to participate in one's own governance, until that point. The French Declaration is perhaps most notable, though, for its bold, repeated and approving references to the right of equality. The very first article declares that "men are born free and equal in rights; social distinctions may be based only upon general usefulness." Subsequent articles swear that all citizens are equal before the law, should be taxed "equally ... in proportion to their means" and have the equal right to seek public office, which should be distributed solely on the basis of merit, not heredity or privilege. One of the main forces animating the French Revolution, at least during this first moderate phase, was to abolish all exclusionary social privileges, offices and distinctions, and to replace them with a universally accessible system of social recognition and reward, wherein participation and talent counted for everything. The revolutionaries thus took great delight in referring to everyone as "Citizen," instead of "Mister," "Missus," "Doctor," "Mayor," up to, and including especially, "King."[5]

United Nations Universal Declaration

The United Nations (UN) was created at the end of World War II to increase peace and security in the international system following two devastating global conflicts. In 1948, the UN proclaimed a Universal Declaration of Human Rights, which is reprinted in Appendix A. This rights document is probably the most influential contemporary human rights document. Love it or hate it—and the Universal Declaration has attracted its share of both emotions—it sets the tone for all current debates about the objects of human rights. It thus merits detailed treatment.[6]

Since there are such a large number of rights contained in the Universal Declaration, I propose to ease our examination of it by grouping them all together under the headings of the foundational five objects I have already argued for: personal security, material subsistence, personal freedom, elemental equality, and social recognition.

Consider first personal security. A number of articles in the Universal Declaration, particularly 3-5, 9-11 and 14-15, express this vital human need. Article 3 stipulates that everyone has the right to "*life*, liberty and *security of the person*" [my emphasis]. Articles 4 and 5 posit, respectively, a human right not to be enslaved or held in slavery, and not to be subjected to torture, or to cruel and unusual punishment. Article 9 maintains that no one shall be subjected to arbitrary arrest, detention or exile; Articles 10 and 11 guarantee fair trial and due process, notably the presumption of innocence and the constitution of a competent and impartial judiciary. Articles 14 and 15 concern one's right to seek asylum in a foreign country if one faces groundless persecution in one's own country, as well as a right not to be deprived arbitrarily of one's nationality, which in the modern world is an important aspect of personal security: stateless or nationless people, such as refugees, face very insecure conditions in a world dominated by nation-states.

This brings us to material subsistence. Articles 17 and 22-26 seem to be the most relevant. Article 17 is the human right to own property and the right not to be arbitrarily deprived of one's property. Article 22 is the right to social security; Article 23 is the right to work, to fair pay, to equal pay for equal value, to form trade unions, and to social assistance in the event of prolonged unemployment; Article 24 is the right to rest from work and to enjoy leisure (including a right to "periodic holidays with pay"); Article 25 is the right to a minimal level of satisfaction of one's vital physical needs, notably to food, clothing, housing, medical care and "necessary social services"; and Article 26 is the right to education, at least in its basic primary and secondary forms. These are among the most controversial objects contained in the Universal Declaration.

To the extent to which every single right listed in the Universal Declaration is affirmed as a human right claimable by all, the entire document is a resounding endorsement of human equality with regard to basic, dignified treatment by others and by social and political systems. More specifically, Article 1 declares that "all human beings are born free and *equal* in dignity and rights" [my emphasis]. Article 2 mandates that everyone is entitled to all the objects listed in the Universal Declaration "without distinction of any kind, such as race, colour, sex, language, religion, political or other opinion, national or social origin, property, birth or other states." Article 6 guarantees everyone's right to be recognized as a person and Article 7 goes on to guarantee equality and non-discrimination before the law. Article 21 affirms that everyone has the right to run for public office, and that everyone has the right to equal access to public service.

To what extent do the human rights listed in the Universal Declaration protect freedom and liberty? A number of articles are relevant here. Article 1, once more, declares that "all human beings are born *free* and equal in dignity and rights" [my emphasis]. Article 3 enshrines the right to "life, *liberty* and security of the person" [my emphasis]. Article 12 stipulates that one has the right to be free from "arbitrary interference" with one's private life. Article 13 protects freedom of movement within borders and the right to emigrate across them. Article 16 says that we all have the right to found a family with a partner of our own choosing, while Articles 18 and 19 protect freedom of thought and conscience, and freedom of expression and belief. Article 20 enshrines the right to freedom of association with others, and freedom from being forced to join an association against one's will. Article 21 mandates the right of positive liberty to take part in government, particularly to vote in democratic elections and to run for office.

In terms of social recognition, Article 6 mandates that all have the right to be recognized as persons before the law, and Article 15 stipulates that one has the right to one's nationality and is not to be deprived arbitrarily of it. The right to recognition and membership also seems implied in Article 20's right to freedom of association with others, Article 21's rights to participate in politics, and Article 27's right to participate in "the cultural life of the community."

The only articles in the Universal Declaration that have been left out here are 8 and 28-30. Article 8 seeks to make human rights real by stipulating that anyone who has his human rights violated is entitled to a concrete remedy—such as compensation—for such violation. Article 28 underlines the point by declaring that everyone has the right to "a social and international order in which the rights and freedoms set forth in this Declaration can be fully realized." Article 29 sets out a number of restrictions and qualifications on the human rights listed in the rest of the Universal Declaration. Article 29 stresses that everyone is just as much a duty-bearer as a rights-holder, and that one is duty-bound to respect the human rights of others. Then, controversially, the Article goes on to list reasons why human rights may be ignored, or otherwise put aside: "the just requirements of morality, public order and the general welfare in a democratic society." Depending on how one interprets this very loose clause, it could merely suggest, on the one hand, that human rights are, as Dworkin said, trumps *only* in ordinary conditions in a normal society. While that seems fine, the phrase might, on the other hand, mean that the exemptions are so broad and sweeping as to provide cover for any human rights violator acting in the name of public welfare. That, of course, would not be so fine: indeed, it would largely undermine the rights protections contained elsewhere in the document. The most consistent interpretation thus appears to be the first one. This is borne out by considering that the last Article, 30, reiterates that no one is permitted to aim at the destruction of human rights.

Human Rights Inflation

It should not be thought that the handful of human rights documents referred to above exhausts the list of historically significant rights documents. They are offered as the most enduring, penetrating and influential, but by no means are they alone. By now, there must be hundreds of such documents, whether they be national laws, statutes, bills, charters and declarations of rights, or international treaties and covenants.[7] The number is constantly increasing, not only in terms of laws and treaties dealing with human rights but also in terms of the objects being claimed as a matter of human right. Historically, there is a discernible pattern of what we might call "human rights inflation" over time: the number of objects claimed as a matter of human right is steadily rising. In Chapter 1, we noted the existence of both first-generation and second-generation human rights. First-generation human rights are those to security, property, participation and fair process, much as contained in the English, American and French documents. Second-generation human rights are those socio-economic entitlements to subsistence, welfare, leisure and culture, as contained in some of the articles in the Universal Declaration. Some human rights thinkers are even tempted to speak of a brand-new wave of "third generation" human rights, to such objects as national self-determination, economic development, a clean environment, affirmative action programs, the survival of one's mother tongue as a functioning language, parental leave benefits, various minority group rights, and the list goes on and on from there. The Canadian Charter of Rights and Freedoms is contained as the final document in Appendix A. One of the more recent rights documents, it contains references to rights of all three generations.[8]

What should we make of this process of human rights inflation, this tendency to generate more and more claims as a matter of human right over time? There are both hostile and cynical, as well as welcoming and supportive, interpretations. The hostile and cynical interpretation of human rights inflation views it as bogus—a completely unwarranted extension of the idea of human rights to cover things that it simply cannot be stretched to fit. Defenders of this view, such as Maurice Cranston and Robert Nozick,[9] tend to believe that only first-generation rights are truly deserving of the exalted, yet elemental, status owing to human rights, whereas all subsequent rights claims are merely desirable goals dressed up, by partisan activists, in the more powerful and action-inducing language of human rights. These activists know a good idea when they see it, and have tried to use this one to advance their own narrow agenda, whether it be economic equalization, nationhood, gay rights, or cultural and linguistic protection. Defenders of the hostile view tend to view the United Nations Universal Declaration as a particularly pernicious document, even as a kind of fork in the road where things started to go wrong with human rights theory. The most common argument that defenders of the hostile view employ is that the costs of providing everyone with the objects of second- and third-generation rights claims would be outrageous, assuming it were even possible in the first place, which many are not willing to stipulate. Most notorious, and laughable for them, is the Universal Declaration's inclusion of "holidays with pay" among the objects of human rights. They ask, how is such material connected with vital human needs? Since the correlative duties they would impose would be excessive and destructively burdensome, human rights that are not claims to elemental due process rights and political freedoms do not really count as human rights.

The welcoming and supportive view, however, tends to endorse the Universal Declaration. Defenders of this view, such as Henry Shue, Alan Gewirth and Jack Donnelly,[10] focus not so much on the affordability of the objects of socio-economic and cultural rights as they do on the consistency of the principle behind such entitlements with the principle behind the more traditional civil and political rights. Loosely speaking, their argument is this: if we need due process protections, and the right to vote and speak freely, we also need material subsistence, basic health care and education, and the right to participate in the cultural life of our communities. It is just as elemental, they assert, to access basic health care and education as it is to access a trial by one's peers. In fact, defenders of the supportive view are inclined to think that the need for socio-economic rights is even greater and more obvious than for the standard civil and political rights—with the important exception of the right to life or personal security. In general, though, defenders of the supportive view are not critics of civil and political rights: they simply want to include them in the package of human rights objects but then increase the size of that package to include socio-economic and cultural objects. Besides, supporters insist that sticking to one static, traditional list of human rights objects ignores the clear fact of social change in general and, in particular, our tendency as we become more advanced to believe more and better things are required to ensure minimally decent treatment for all.

The Great Debate

This leads us naturally into the great debate concerning the defenders of first-generation rights and the defenders of subsequent-generation rights. James Nickel has suggested that so entrenched has this divide become that it almost makes sense to view the defenders of first-generation rights as declaring that all objects of legitimate human rights boil down to one kind of thing, freedom, whereas defenders of subsequent-generation rights declare that the objects of human rights all boil down to material benefits. Nickel labels this the debate between the "choice-based" perspective on human rights objects versus the "benefit-based" perspective.[11]

The choice-based perspective, or theory, suggests that the essence of a human rights claim is that it is a claim to a protected personal space within which we are all free to make the most important decisions in our lives. Such decisions include questions of how we should be governed, what career we should pursue, whom we should marry, whether we should have children, what our hobbies should be, where we want to live, and so on. Human rights form, as it were, a normative boundary or moral perimeter around each of us, protecting us from outside interference with our own personal freedom. We are all entitled to a protected personal space: it is not too much to ask from others that they respect such space on pain of being subjected to punishment. And it is not too much to ask of social institutions that they do what is needed to ensure reliable protection of such personal spaces, and then refrain from invading them themselves. Thus, we need human rights to personal security; legal protections and guarantees of fairness in the event of being charged and tried for committing a crime; freedom of religion, thought and expression; freedom of movement and association; and participation in governance through an electoral process. In general, defenders of the choice theory believe that we are all entitled to the largest possible personal space of freedom, provided only (as always) that we respect everyone else's space.

One important and interesting addition to the list here is the right to own private property, one of the most controversial human rights ever claimed. A number of critics of the choice theory have suggested that this is an object quite unlike the others, and does not seem to be a kind of freedom as much as a kind of material benefit, and potentially a very profitable one at that, quite far removed from the minimal baseline of human need that is supposed to loom large in debates over the objects of human rights. It might also be relevant that property was probably the first right ever claimed in formal rights documents, and this may shed light on the ultimate motivation behind the choice theory, such as excessive selfishness or financial greed.

Choice theorists respond in one of several ways to these criticisms of the right to private property ownership. Some view security in possession of one's property as an extension of the right to personal security. Since we are material creatures living in the material world, what personal security would we have in a world where we could not count on our possession of, for instance, our clothes, our shelter, and especially our food? If we cannot claim such things as our own private property, what is to stop others from taking them, and where would that leave us? Their answer: in a desperately insecure condition, forced to scramble for survival. Other choice theorists view private property ownership as an extension of personal freedom. One argument is rooted in a claim about personal identity, suggesting that there is little difference between "me" and "mine": we define our very selves through our material possessions. Thus, we are entitled to claim ownership over our material goods. Another version views property as the necessary condition for the substantive enjoyment of the other freedoms. Since we require some resources to enjoy such other freedoms as freedom of movement or to participate in governance, it follows that we must be allowed to avail ourselves of such resources, and moreover to count on having access to them. A third version suggests that the presumption in favour of allowing for a *maximal* amount of freedom includes within it entitlement to private property ownership. Provided private property ownership does not interfere with the personal space of others, it is to be permitted by default, as a matter of allowing for the greatest possible personal freedom in society.

What about equality under the choice theory? Choice theorists tend not to endorse a separate right to equality so much as to defend everyone's equal right to enjoy each of the above freedoms. Equality is not itself an object, they say; rather, equality is about having *the same entitlement as anyone else* to the real object of human rights claims, namely, a protected space for making personal choices. Any attempt to enforce some substantive kind of equality after everyone has been given their own space is pernicious, because it presupposes a more interventionist government; costly, because the government needs resources to grow and act; and at odds with the maximization of liberty principle, because it establishes a cap on how "different" people are allowed to become in terms of their achievements and possessions.

There is a two-fold foundation for the choice theory, one part focusing on the entitlement side, the other on the duty side, of the human rights equation. On the entitlement side, defenders of the choice theory place foremost value on free choice and self-direction in life. They view human beings as creators of their own lives through the choices they make, the roads down which they travel. We are, most essentially, choice-making beings. We vitally need freedom as the very kind of creatures we are, and we should be permitted the maximal amount of freedom so that we can pursue self-direction to its fullest. A society composed of free and self-directing human beings, with minimal government interference in their lives, is the general picture of an ideal society presupposed here.

Government should provide law and order, enforcing the perimeter of rights around each of us, but beyond that point should avoid interfering and let us lead our lives and take care of ourselves. A society made up of such autonomous beings would be both free and diverse. This choice theory about human rights objects has clear affinities with both the contractarian and rational agency views elucidated in Chapter 2, in connection with the issue of who holds human rights: the image of the self-directing being contains the presumption of rational agency and the ability of such a being to enter into mutually beneficial social contracts. There is also some similarity to the view that moral goodness is what roots human rights-holding, since having free choice is a necessary condition for making morally good choices.

On the cost side, choice theorists suggest that performing the duties needed to provide rights-holders with the objects of civil and political rights is both reasonable and affordable. It is not too costly to require people to refrain from interfering in other people's lives, nor to require social institutions to do no more than provide the law and order needed to secure everyone's personal space. Granted, there should be no illusion that performing these duties is cost-free, as some of the more unsophisticated choice theorists have suggested. Like anything else real in life, these duties come with an expenditure of resources, or at least with opportunity costs in having to forego some actions in exchange for respect and enhancement of others. *Human rights, it must be said, are designed to impose some costs*: notably, by this understanding, the cost of not being able to interfere in the personal space of others. Furthermore, the system of law and order has to be paid for, and an effective one will not come cheap. But, owing to its vital importance in saving us from anarchy, and in providing reliable protection for our personal spaces, it is a price that choice-making beings should be more than willing to pay. The real question and debate here focuses *not* on whether costs should be imposed but, rather, on which costs are reasonable to impose and which are excessive. Choice theorists, as defenders of first-generation rights, suggest that only *they* stick to the former, whereas benefit theorists, as defenders of subsequent generations of rights, slide over into the latter. Requiring people to refrain from interfering with free choice is reasonable whereas requiring them to pay the bills so that everyone can have health care, education, culture and income is not.

Benefit theorists argue that the main object of all our human rights claims is not freedom but, rather, vital material benefit. For them, the main value contained in the human rights idea is not the maximization of liberty for all but, rather, maximizing the satisfaction of everyone's vital material interests: making everyone's life better in a concrete and measurable manner. Benefit theorists concede that personal security is a vital material benefit, indeed the ultimate such benefit, the necessary condition for enjoying all the rest. They may also agree that at least some, and perhaps even all, of the various freedoms defended by the choice theorists are also beneficial, perhaps even vitally so. The unique contribution of the benefit theorists rests on their insistence that the objects of civil and political rights do not exhaust the domain of what we *both* vitally need as the kinds of creatures we are *and* what we can reasonably claim from others and from social institutions.

It is as plain as day, for benefit theorists, that we vitally need certain material objects and resources if we are to survive at all, much less enjoy a minimally decent life in the modern world. Choice theorists may believe that such material neediness can ultimately be satisfied by allowing people to accumulate and use their own property. Benefit theorists retort that such is not a guaranteed assurance that everyone will enjoy access to at least a subsistence level of resources, and thus is at odds with the foundational commitment to equality inherent in the human rights idea. Some people may, through no fault of their own, fail to acquire that minimum of property required to meet their subsistence needs over time. If the choice theorists condemn such people to non-subsistence, then are they not interfering with the ability of those people to make meaningful choices? Far better, benefit theorists submit, to have it be a matter of human right that all be provided such social security, in the event that they cannot provide for themselves. It is not too much to ask of people and social institutions that they devise such a system of social security, so that human beings enjoy minimally decent treatment. We ought not, as decent people, to just sit there and watch our fellow human beings starve to death, or suffer through homelessness, when we can do something about it. Benefit theorists insist that such a system of social security is readily affordable, that it would not require an excessively burdensome taxation system. They point out that such a system does not mean direct provision of clothes, food, water, and shelter to everyone on the planet, which would indeed require vast sums of taxes and elaborate social engineering. The system would mean, rather, that there be an adequately funded policy of social security that can provide a subsistence income *to those who cannot provide it for themselves.*

Benefit theorists also want to say that the provision of at least "basic" education and health care, alongside social efforts at maintaining a reasonably clean environment (especially water), are also affordable. They need not make the implausible claim that such provision is cheap, any more than choice theorists have to argue implausibly that a well-functioning system of law and order can be had for a song. Unlike the choice theorists, though, benefit theorists need to claim that access to basic education, preventative health care and a clean environment is as much a vital need to us as law and order. The arguments they trot out are not unreasonable. Basic preventative health care—like inoculations against standard life-threatening illnesses, education about nutrition and exercise—is designed to avert some of the most standard and serious threats to preventable, premature death. Such health care is, in its own way, as much an aspect of personal security as a system of law and order. After all, everyone gets assaulted as children with dangerous bacterial infections and viruses, whereas not all of us—indeed, only a minority—ever get assaulted by criminals. While the benefit principle here seems powerful, it must be admitted that so much depends, regarding the issue of affordability, on how "basic" preventative health care gets defined. The same applies to "reasonably clean" water—an irrefutably vital need of ours—as well as to "basic" education. The difficulties are truly in the details.

Education seems more controversial than either basic social security, preventative health care, or clean water. It is, no doubt, a benefit to those who receive it, but is it a *vital* material benefit, something without which we cannot live minimally decent lives in the modern world? Once more, it depends crucially on what one means by "basic." The Universal Declaration declares that "education shall be free, at least in the elementary and fundamental stages." Presumably this means something like core literacy and numeracy, alongside fundamental life skills like nutrition and personal finance. The human mind does need at least some prodding to develop, and presumably choice theorists, with their emphasis on free choice, would approve heartily of at least developing that amount of intelligence required to know how to go about making free choices that are sensible. *How much*, though, is that amount? And is that minimum enough, or is a more extensive system of education defensible, on grounds for instance that it enables one to make a sensible choice when one is voting and participating in governance? The controversies are evident, and not solvable at this point, beyond the general observation that some provision of education may be claimable as a matter of human right, subject to more extensive research into the level that is truly needed to make for oneself a minimally decent way in this world.

Controversies explode in number and complexity when one considers further aspects of the Universal Declaration, such as the so-called human rights to "fair pay," to "equal pay for equal value," and of course the right to "holidays with pay." These are all clearly material benefits but it does seem a stretch to pretend that they are vitally needed if we are to live minimally decent lives in the modern world. Having a paid holiday does not seem needed as protection against a serious and standard threat to one's existence, nor does fair pay. Fair pay would be great, of course, but seems so abstractly defined as to be of little value in helping us determine in practical terms the true objects of our human rights. There are some objects contained in the Universal Declaration which benefit theorists either do not, or at least should not, claim as the genuine objects of human rights.

The obvious question to ask at this point is this: *are these two theories really so different?* Especially when we consider that they both endorse such core objects as personal security and access to material resources? Granted, some of their defenders definitely *act as if* they are as different as night and day, but need we buy into the idea of such a sharp split between the two theories? There are compelling reasons to refuse to respect the so-called split, and seek instead a unified theory of human rights.

A Unified Theory of Human Rights Objects

We need some tightening up, some theoretical elegance, at this point. Consider the following simple diagram of how the specification of human rights objects occurs:

Fig. 4.1

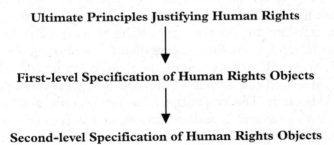

At the level of ultimate principles, we discuss and defend the kinds of issues dealt with in the past two chapters: identifying rights-holders and offering arguments justifying the very existence and nature of human rights. Then, at the first-level specification, we take the ultimate principles and deduce from them what abstractly-defined items we can claim. Since in my own justification I made much of the having of vital needs, and of the duty not to inflict grievous harm in connection with a person's vital needs, my own first-level specification consists of a list of vital needs and fundamental interests we all have. Hence "the foundational five" objects of security, subsistence, liberty, equality and recognition. Second-level specification occurs when one takes the abstract objects in the first-level specification and then spells out, in much fuller detail, what each of them implies in terms of concrete goods and benefits. This is the logically final stage of specification, completing the transition from the most abstract issues of justification down through the first-level derivation and, lastly, second-level application to actual concrete objects and social arrangements.

My own understanding of second-level specification was suggested in the last section. In general, I find that the existing human rights documents, especially the United Nations Universal Declaration, provide excellent guidance. The one exception would be the excessively robust enumeration of second-level subsistence rights in the Universal Declaration. Subsistence, for me, implies the right to be secure in the possession of one's property, should one already have the means of one's own subsistence. It also implies that those not in possession of such means be provided them by society, usually with some form of social welfare transfer payment. There is a material minimum below which no human being ought to be allowed to fall. But beyond that, such objects as paid holidays cannot plausibly be claimed as matters of vital human need, and thus as fitting human rights objects. Otherwise, I would stand by the Universal Declaration's second-level specifications: how *security* means not just freedom from widespread violence and torture but also access to standard due process rights, rights to emigrate and seek asylum, and the right to sue for compensation for serious injuries wrongly suffered. Above all, security implies the right to live in a social system that provides a reliable system of law and order, the framework of a decent civilization. The conjunction of both security and *subsistence* implies rights to at least a basic education, to a level of environmental assurance regarding clean food, water and air, and to elemental measures of health care, notably health education, inoculations and some forms of emergency care. *Equality* implies that everyone has the same human rights, in the first-level sense of the foundational five. It also entails equality before the law as a person, and freedom from vicious discrimination which demonstrably hinders one's ability to live a minimally good life in the modern world. It enshrines a right of equal access to those social institutions which affect vital human need, especially with regard to the right to seek public office. *Freedom* likewise implies rights of political participation, as well as standard items like speech and expression, conscience and religion, and association and movement. Freedom, above all, implies the right to make for oneself the most important choices in one's life, subject of course to one's own reciprocity. Much of social *recognition*, in terms of second-level specification, gets captured by those things that equality and freedom provide: the added idea is that there is not just a right to things like equality and freedom but also a right to be recognized *as* a right-holder, with all the moral standing we associate with such status. So standing as a person before the law is crucial here.

Crucial to both levels of specification is this set of steps:

1. Reflection on the meaning of the object in question (be it a freedom, concrete good or benefit) and its demonstrable connection to the ultimate principles of justification;

2. Reflection on the identity of the right-holder;

3. Reflection on the social context within which the right-holder will possess the object; and, finally,

4. Reflection on what is a reasonable correlative duty to mandate others—and indeed, oneself—to bear.

Each and every step must be undertaken in each level of specification. At the first level, for instance, we reflect on what abstract objects every human being vitally needs to both have and lead a minimally good life in the modern world. For this, we appeal to an understanding of human nature and needs, we reflect on the necessary conditions for survival and purposive action, and we generalize from our own most fundamental interests in personal prudence. This must, however, be complemented by reflection on what burdens we can reasonably expect others, and ourselves, to shoulder as duty-bearers. The result can only be a list of abstract objects which is thin, minimal, affordable and universally enjoyable—yet still vital, valued and substantive. Hence the foundational five.

There is more room for legitimate, well-intentioned disagreement about human rights objects between the first- and second-level specification than there is between the justifying principles and the first-level specification. The major dispute, at the transition from principles to the first level, is between choice and benefit theorists. Essentially, the dispute boils down to whether the first level includes anything more than liberty. The answer, I suggest, is that yes, it clearly does, and that ultimately the split between the choice and benefit accounts cannot be sustained. Both accounts are more properly integrated into something like a primary goods, or a vital needs, understanding.

Even the choice theorists, like Nozick, concede that more than freedom is required to achieve the autonomy they enshrine as their ultimate justifying principle. Obviously, one needs to be around if one is to be autonomous, so of course a claim to one's own life, or more properly to one's own personal security, must be made. Additionally, choice theorists celebrate the fruits of freedom for everyone, believing that all people should be allowed to pursue their own vision of the good life. Thus, they embrace a form of elemental equality between persons. Compelling contention can also be made that insistence on such equality—regarding the right to autonomy—comes hand-in-hand with a claim to social recognition. Why is one entitled to pursue one's own course in life? The answer: because it is one's own life, after all, and other people ought to recognize and respect that fact. The real dispute, then, between choice and benefit theorists is over claims to material subsistence. Choice theorists recoil in horror, gasping at the perceived costs of such provision. But this is a mistake at the first level of specification, for it is only when we get to the second level that a full and accurate tally of the costs can be had. Moreover, it seems obvious that, if we are to survive, and have enough energy and stamina to pursue our own vision of the good life, we must each have at least a subsistence level of material resources. Subsistence is truly an empirical, or factual, necessity for material creatures like us living in the material world. Admitting this is to admit nothing more than the truth: it is not to admit the permissibility of a massive and destructively burdensome system of widespread redistribution and lavish state-sponsored welfarism. Arguments over *the extent* of the subsistence minimum can be made at the second-level specification but the principle *that a* subsistence minimum is required at the first level by the ultimate justifying principles is solid. Indeed, even a classical choice theorist like Hart wrote, late in his career, about the need not just for freedom but also for vital material benefits. Rawls is another prominent figure who, prompted by Shue, broadened his horizons beyond freedom: "[T]he sensible and rational exercise of all liberties, of whatever kind, as well as the intelligent use of property, always implies having general all-purpose economic means."[12] Indeed, Rawls's reference to property inclines one to point out that the insistence on property rights by choice theorists like Nozick constitutes their own recognition of the need for secure access to the means of material subsistence at the first-level specification of human rights objects.

Equally mistaken is the counter-suggestion, made by such benefit theorists as Shue, that perhaps it is liberty that deserves expulsion from the first-level set of human rights objects.[13] Shue argues, in passing, that we do not seem to *need* freedom as much, for instance, as we do security and subsistence. We can survive without freedom but not without our health and safety, not without food and water. Slaves survive, but the starving and severely beaten do not. The mistake here, in my view, is the flat equation of "vital needs" with the strict requirements of mere biological survival. This is one reason for the insistence, in this text, on the preferred phrase, "vital needs for living a minimally good life." Justice is not just about preserving life: it is also about securing and forwarding the good life. Clearly, we want more out of life than just our lives, more than the simple experience of being around. We also want to pursue things that attract us. As Nickel says, we want to both *have* a life, and to *lead* it as well. For this, we need some freedom and liberty. We are material creatures but that does not exhaust our nature; we are also creative creatures, creatures with personal projects and interests, creatures responsive to the demands of morality and justice. All of these latter characteristics presuppose freedom and require its real-world realization.

These considerations all underline the strength and cogency of my foundational five listing. To live a minimally good life, we all vitally need personal security, material subsistence, personal freedom, elemental equality and social recognition. Moreover, these abstract objects come at absorbable cost: we can easily imagine societies where everyone enjoys such thin and minimal, yet firm and meaningful, objects. Many of us already live in such societies, which have managed to avoid crumbling under the weight of the costs. I conclude that there is very little room to doubt, or debate, the first-level specification of human rights objects *and* still be a supporter of human rights. Of course, one is always free to deny that people have human rights to security, and so on, but then one is much more likely to reject the very idea of human rights. We will deal with such skepticism later. For now, though, the point is that it is difficult to imagine someone believing in human rights but not in rights to security, subsistence, liberty, and so on. If we fail to have human rights to the foundational five, then what do we have human rights to at all?

The Second Level

The story changes slightly when it comes to the move from first- to second-level specification of human rights objects. There is more room for principled disagreement here. Most of the differences between various contemporary human rights documents are differences regarding the scope of second-level specification. For instance, does the first-level object of personal security also include within its scope the right of a person to own and carry a gun for her private protection? Does social recognition include within its scope the right to claim from the state funding for programs on bilingualism or multiculturalism? Does elemental equality also call for affirmative-action hiring programs, or for the legalization of same-sex marriages, or for development aid transfers from rich countries to poor ones? Does liberty include the right of members of a community to separate themselves from existing political arrangements, forming a brand new country of their own? Does material subsistence include the right to an actual job and actual living quarters, or merely to a level of income thought to be sufficient to get such things on one's own?

These debates are not going away and are a logical consequence of the residual ambiguity inherent in the abstract first-level list of the foundational five. What the "generations" metaphor captures accurately is that different generations can add plausibly to the list of second-level specifications—*either* by offering compelling new nuances to the meaning of one of the foundational five, *or* by showing that the given meaning now implies new things in a transformed social context, *or* by pointing out that a rise in living standards has now made affordable objects which used to be cost-prohibitive. This is what makes human rights *a continuing project* whose closure is neither to be expected nor to be welcomed: there is nothing contradictory nor threatening about the idea of a basic minimum of decent treatment which tends to rise somewhat over time.

What the "generations" metaphor should *not* be read as conveying is a sense that each "generation"—first, second, third, whatever—represents a difference in kind, the creation of yet another distinct "kind" of human right. That is false: there is only one, unchanging core set of human rights. This core set—the foundational five—forms one coherent whole, unified by the picture of vital human need for, and fundamental interest in, a minimally good life. There is no series of splits and fractures in the set of human rights, pitting one "generation" against the next. Ultimately, there can be no sibling rivalry within the family of human rights.

There is one set of human rights, but that does not mean that the one set implies one, and only one, exact list of fully detailed second-level specifications for everybody. As mentioned in Chapter 2, it is totally consistent with the idea that everyone has the human right to liberty to note that this one human right may imply some different second-level specifications, depending for instance on whether the right-holder is a child or an adult. Reflections on the capabilities of a child, in the face of the complexities of public policy choices, leads us to the sound conclusion that a child ought not to have the full rights of political participation which we acknowledge adults must have as part of their freedom. This does not mean that they have different human rights—again, we all have exactly the same human rights to the same set of the foundational five. What it *does* mean is that, at the second-level specification of objects, there is some space for pluralism, context and application. This is rooted in the fact that material differences, in either the social context or the relative capacities of the right-holders, can make a meaningful difference in our interpretation of the full specification of their human rights.

Human rights, to remain relevant and vital, cannot commit us to a cookie-cutter conception of social organization. One size does not fit all; there is no one exact and rigid mould for a just and rights-respecting society. The ultimate principles endure, yes, as do the first-level objects known as the foundational five. But beyond that there is *some* latitude in the second level to allow, as circumstances and people change, for new claims that are both plausible and affordable. I stress the "some" because many purported second-level claims are patently false: no one, for instance, needs a Porsche to survive. The second-level claim cannot be just any old claim if it is to succeed: it must be consistent with, and plausibly connected to, the meaning of at least one of the foundational five. It must also impose duties and burdens which are fair and readily absorbable. While there are some pluralism, flexibility and contextualization here, they remain limited by the foundational five, by considerations of cost and, ultimately, by the core principles of justification themselves.

So trying to offer the be-all and end-all list of each and every thing to which each and every person has a human right is revealed to be a fool's game. Such ambitions presuppose a kind of rigidity and absolute closure that is not a necessary component of the human rights idea. Far more plausible is the conception offered here: there *is* a timeless and changeless core, composed of both vital human needs and the moral duty not to grievously harm. From this base, we can deduce the finite first-level specification, and call it the foundational five. The foundational five cannot be made too specific, lest we run afoul of the universality and equality residing at the heart of the human rights idea. But the foundational five still have real meaning, and this fact does rule out a number of false and contentious second-level derivations. The foundational five have real substance that allow us to rule certain things out, preventing gratuitous rights inflation, but their meaning is not so rigid and fixed that we can deduce from them alone *everything* that might plausibly be claimed as a matter of human rights by everyone in every circumstance. There is thus room for some additions to the second-level lists around which previous generations, and the present one, have crafted a consensus. In other words, there is a firm foundation at the core of human rights with room for some growth at the edges.

The burden of proof is always on the claimant proposing a brand new second-level specification for human rights. Such a claimant must show that the sought-after object really is implied by the meaning of one of the foundational five. Ultimately, this means that the claimant must paint a persuasive picture that the sought-after object is an integral part of his vital need to both have and lead a life of minimal value in the modern world. The additional burden is for the claimant to show that the correlative duties that would be imposed in order to guarantee secure access to the sought-after object are both affordable and reasonable. The costs cannot ever add up to the point where such provision would interfere with, and undermine, other people's ability to both have and lead their own lives. So there is always going to be some political struggle and argumentation associated with human rights and what they fully imply in detail. Such is the weight of this burden of proof that we can rest content that the flood-gates have not been opened to runaway human rights inflation, and that only genuinely needed and valuable goods, suppliable at affordable cost, will win their way through to widespread acceptance. The existing documents provide an excellent indication of those objects to which we have human rights, but there remains room for more objects that can meet this burden of proof in the future.

There will always be those who abuse the powerful language of human rights to try to get their greedy hands on various luxuries, or benefits, in which they have personal or partisan interest. To them, right-thinking people reply that unless their claims can genuinely satisfy the above burden of proof, they will not be claimable *as human rights*. Of course, some people may be lucky enough to live in a society wealthy enough to provide such luxuries on top of human rights objects. But that would be a local matter of special rights, or of freely offered privileges. It would not, however, be a matter of advancing the cause of human rights and thus could not plausibly be claimed as such. *Human rights are precious things, and they are cheapened when people try to elevate any old claim they have into the status of a struggle over human rights.* We should be suspicious of such attempts, while expecting that there will be a lot of them because human rights status is both coveted and powerful. We should confront all such attempts with the above burden of proof, expecting most to fail to meet its requirements. At the same time, we must acknowledge that there could well be claims made in the future which do indeed satisfy the burden, and which thus come to deserve recognition as fully-fledged objects of human rights.

Conclusion

Dispute over the exact set of human rights objects has been a hallmark of human rights history. Various communities have offered different lists of such objects, and various thinkers have suggested there is a split between those who view the objects as choices, and those who view the objects as goods and benefits. In reply, I have sought in this chapter to craft a unified theory of human rights objects, moving from the ultimate justifying principles down to the most detailed second-level specifications. At the first level, there is the foundational five set of objects: security, subsistence, freedom, equality and recognition. This set is unified because it is rooted in one coherent concept: that of living a minimally good life in the modern world. It must remain abstract and general, lest we violate universality and equality. The foundational five respond to our deepest wants and vital needs, and are affordable to realize. What the foundational five imply in terms of second-level specifications is up for *some* dispute. Second-level specifications can reasonably differ from person to person, but only if such difference is actually called for in terms of the very meaning of the foundational five themselves. The value of liberty, for example, might imply a slightly different list of second-level objects for a child than for an adult. It seems that the Universal Declaration provides about as good a list of second-level specifications as any currently on offer, with a few exceptions regarding the extent of subsistence rights and the clauses dealing with reasons to set human rights aside. We should neither expect nor pursue the development of one be-all and end-all list of human rights objects that will hold true for everybody and for all time. There *is* a broadly shared consensus about human rights objects but that does not mean there is absolutely no room for new claims. There is some space, but such new claims must meet a weighty burden of proof and undergo the same trial-by-fire historical struggle that all other claims had to go through.

Notes

1 The commercial was for Burger King and aired in the early 1980s.

2 A recent, comprehensive collection of prominent human rights documents is M.R. Ishay, ed., *The Human Rights Reader* (New York: Routledge, 1997). The documents are, however, abridged. For the Magna Carta, see pp. 56-58.

3 Ishay, ed., *Reader*, 91-93.

4 Ishay, ed., *Reader*, 127-30.

5 Ishay, ed., *Reader*, 138-40.

6 The Declaration is also analyzed in J. Nickel, *Making Sense of Human Rights* (Berkeley: University of California Press, 1987. It is reprinted there in full, along with the two subsequent covenants which together form the International Bill of Rights. See also Ishay, ed., *Reader*, 407-12, 424-41; J. Morsink, *The Universal Declaration of Human Rights: Origins, Drafting and Intent* (Philadelphia: University of Pennsylvania Press, 2000); and L.J. Macfarlane, *The Theory and Practice of Human Rights* (London: Temple Smith, 1985).

7 For more documents, see Ishay, ed., *Reader*; I. Brownlie, *Basic Documents on Human Rights*, 3rd ed. (Oxford: Oxford University Press, 1992); and *Twenty-Five Human Rights Documents* (New York: Columbia University Center for the Study of Human Rights, 1995).

8 D.D. Raphael, *Political Theory and The Rights of Man* (London: Macmillan, 1967); A. Gutmann, ed., *Multiculturalism and The Politics of Recognition* (Princeton, NJ: Princeton University Press, 1992); F.C. Newman, *International Human Rights: Law, Policy and Process*, 2nd ed. (San Francisco: Anderson Publishing, 1995); and H.J. Steiner and P. Alston, *International Human Rights in Context: Law, Politics, Morals* (Oxford: Oxford University Press, 2000).

9 R. Nozick, *Anarchy, State and Utopia* (New York: Basic Books, 1974); M. Cranston, *What are Human Rights?* (New York: Basic Books, 1973).

10 H. Shue, *Basic Rights: Subsistence, Affluence and U.S. Foreign Policy*, 2nd ed. (Princeton, NJ: Princeton University Press, 1996); A. Gewirth, *Human Rights: Essays on Justification and Application* (Chicago: University of Chicago Press, 1982); J. Donnelly, *International Human Rights* (Boulder, CO: Westview Press, 1993); and J. Donnelly, *The Concept of Human Rights* (London: Croom Helm, 1985).

11 Nickel, *Making Sense*, 82-120, 147-70.

12 H.L.A. Hart, *Essays on Bentham* (Oxford: Clarendon, 1982), 79-104; J. Rawls, *The Law of Peoples* (Cambridge, MA: Harvard University Press, 1999), 65, fn. 1.

13 Shue, *Basic Rights, passim*.

Chapter 5

Who Bears Which Duties?

As we saw in the last chapter, the question of what objects we have human rights to cannot be answered without some reference to the duties, costs and burdens that the provision of such objects would entail. We most certainly do *not* have human rights to anything and everything we want. We have human rights only to those things *both* that we vitally need *and* that can be provided at reasonable cost. We know that a claim is at the core of any right, and that a claim is necessarily a claim *on* someone or something, in connection with some sought-after action or benefit, some good or policy. There is simply no such thing as a right-holder without a correlative duty-bearer. The concern of this chapter, accordingly, is with the identity of those who bear the duties correlative to human rights, as well as with the content of what these duties mandate. Who, or what, bears the duties, and which exact duties do they bear? What, in the end, is it reasonable to require in order to ensure the baseline level of decent treatment that human rights seek to establish and protect?

Identity I: Persons or Institutions?

The first great debate deals with a dichotomy between individual persons and institutional structures. It seems fair to say that when most people are asked, "Who bears the correlative duties?," they will answer: "We all do." Everyone—each and every individual person—bears duties of a kind, has a part to play, with regard to the satisfaction of human rights claims. This view has been the dominant one of recent decades, and moreover seems part-and-parcel of the universality and equality residing at the heart of human rights. We all have human rights, and we all bear part of the burden required to make human rights real, i.e., to ensure that everyone actually possesses the objects of their human rights. We all find ourselves on *both* sides of the correlation between right and duty: as holders of our own human rights claims and as bearers of our own fair share of the duties needed to respect and realize everyone else's human rights.[1] This common view is compelling but we need to examine it thoroughly so as to discern its justification. A sound strategy for this would be to test it in light of rival claims.

The most cogent rival claim to the common view, at least recently, is Thomas Pogge's "institutional" reading of human rights claims.[2] Pogge labels the common view the "interactional" or "individualist" reading. The problem with the individualist reading, in Pogge's eyes, is that individuals are not the ones with the main impact, or real causal influence, on whether or not human rights claims get fulfilled. How social institutions are shaped ends up having the greatest impact, in terms of whether or not people get the objects of their vital needs. Most individuals, Pogge submits, have little or nothing whatsoever to do with whether or not one enjoys physical security, material subsistence, liberty, equality and recognition. Consider the case of you and the villager on the other side of the world. It makes no sense, Pogge submits, to say that the villager bears duties correlative to your human rights. The reason is that the villager has no influence on the calibre of treatment you enjoy and receive. To put the matter bluntly, the villager could not violate your rights even if he tried: he simply bears no substantive causal connection to you and to those things you want to claim as a matter of human right. So, then, to say that "everyone," including the villager on the other side of the world, bears duties correlative to your human rights is to say nothing or, even worse, to say something misleading and inaccurate. It only makes sense to say that someone bears duties in connection with something if that someone's action can have a substantive effect on—can make a material difference to—that something. Since it is false that *everyone* makes a material difference to how you get treated, it must be wrong for the individualists to conclude that everybody is a duty-bearer. But if individual persons fail to make a material difference, what exactly makes the grade?

The grade is met by that set of social institutions that are part of what Pogge, after John Rawls, calls "the basic structure."[3] It is crucial to note this, for it means that not just any old social institution will pass. A local stamp collection society, for instance, may well count as a social institution, but presumably it has very little to do with whether or not one's vital human needs get satisfied. The same cannot be said, though, for the local hospital, the regional system for treating drinking water, or the national system of governance. Those institutions—how they are put together, the resources they have, the principles they are founded on, their effectiveness in achieving their aim—can have material impact on one's vital needs. So which set of social institutions make it into the basic structure? What exactly is the basic structure?

The basic structure, Pogge says, is composed of "largely constitutive ground-rules that shape society." The basic structure contains the most fundamental and influential terms of social cooperation. Usually these constitutive ground-rules call for the construction of certain institutions to guide and shape society. The institutions make real the rules: the abstract values and principles that (are to) govern society are given concrete embodiment, and that embodiment in turn realizes and reinforces the values and principles. How the basic structure is put together produces over time effects on society's members which are "profound, pervasive, inescapable and present from birth." The idea is this: the most important social institutions shape the overall social conditions within which we live our lives. Which social institutions we select and staff, the kind of institutions we allow to take root and operate, end up shaping the significant aggregate features of our shared social landscape. The institutions do not literally determine us, of course, but they do exert profound influence *over the social context in which* we freely make our choices and forge lives for ourselves. Pogge suggests that over time the basic structure comes to establish the parameters around what kinds of freedoms and obligations we might enjoy, the political influence we might have, the level of wealth, health care and education we can reasonably expect, the rate of crime and illness we have to face, the opportunities for work and leisure available to us, our life expectancy, the languages we speak, and so on.[4]

Which specific social institutions count as part of the basic structure of a given society? Which ones exert effects over people which are "profound, pervasive, inescapable and present from birth?" Pogge, in response, offers something like the following list:

1. *The mode of economic organization in the society.* For example, do free markets exist, or is the economy centrally planned? How are goods produced and then distributed? Is money or barter the means of exchange? What is the level of taxation, and how is the tax burden distributed? Are people allowed to hold private property?

2. *The mode of political organization in the society.* How is government established and operated? Is it a democracy or not? Who decides who rules, and what powers are the rulers given? How do public policy choices get made and executed? How is the civil service staffed: through patronage or merit? Is there a division of power? Into which fields of human endeavour does government intervene?

3. *The mode of legal organization in the society.* Is there an effective written constitution or not? Is the judiciary separate and independent from other branches of government? Are judges appointed or elected? Do judges or juries of peers try cases? What legal rights do citizens have? Can people appeal legal decisions to a different level of court?

4. *The mode of deploying armed force in the society.* How are law and order secured? How are police officers recruited and trained? When are they allowed to use force? When are people thrown, and kept, in jail? Do civilian authorities exercise ultimate control of the police? How does the society defend itself? What level of defence spending is present? When does the society deploy its army, navy or air force?

5. *The mode of delivering health care and education in the society.* Are basic levels of health care and education guaranteed to everyone? What is the mixture between public- and private-sector provisions of health care and education? What gets taught at school? Who gets into college or university? How are hospitals funded? How are drugs and medicines produced and distributed?

6. *The mode of family association acknowledged in the society.* Is marriage encouraged and divorce allowed? What rights do parents have over their children? What claims do the spouses have on each other? Are same-sex marriages permitted? How are family groupings treated by the law, systems of taxation and education?

How a society answers the questions under each of the above six headings will, obviously, come to exert over time a "profound, pervasive and inescapable influence" over its members, and indeed from the very moment they are born. How a society shapes the six kinds of institution will come to have an enormous effect over who gets the objects of their human rights claims. Thus, Pogge says, it is to these institutions, and not to individuals, that we ought to turn when levying obligations needed to ensure respect for, and realization of, human rights.

Another consideration that Pogge appeals to, in support of his institutional understanding, is the idea that human rights violations have to be, in some sense, "official." For Pogge, it makes little sense to say that, when private citizen Joe stabs private citizen Bob, Joe thereby violates Bob's human rights. Joe has committed a crime, of course; he has still performed a grossly immoral act. But Joe has not violated Bob's human rights, because to say that is inappropriate. We should reserve talk of human rights violations for those cases when it is owing to institutional actions and public choices that people come to have the objects of their human rights unjustly taken away from them, or not provided to them in the first place. Thus, the Holocaust counts as an act of (massive) human rights violation, whereas isolated acts of private murder or assault, etc. do not. In court, for example, most criminals are not charged with human rights violations: they are charged with various and sundry crimes. It is only government officials—malign heads of state, rogue police officers, war criminals—who get charged with human rights violations or other crimes against humanity. Pogge believes that this fact underlines his institutional reading: most national bills, charters and declarations of rights enumerate rights claimable *only* against institutions, especially government, and not also against private individuals. The ensuring of human rights is the responsibility of only institutional structures and depends on how they are shaped.[5]

Pogge makes an important contribution to human rights theory with his institutional perspective. Institutions are indeed vital parts of the picture of who or what bears duties correlative to human rights: they exert a powerful influence over the context within which the objects of our human rights get created and distributed. But do institutions exhaust that context? Do they dominate that picture entirely? Consider the clear fact that individuals can also take away the objects of one's human rights, though perhaps not as readily or as thoroughly as malign institutions might. When a criminal abducts some people, confining them against their will, then he has obviously robbed them of their liberty. The same applies to their personal security when the criminal subjects them to assault or other forms of serious violence. If we define human rights violations as we did in previous chapters—so that it includes any unjust taking of the objects of human rights claims—then it is crystal clear that individuals, alongside institutions, can violate human rights. And if individuals can violate human rights, then they should bear duties that inform them that they should not do so. The correlative duties, I suggest, must logically fall on all those persons who, or associations and institutions which, can violate human rights.

These contentions imply that there is no compelling reason to insist that only "official" misdeeds count as genuine human rights violations. I grant that many legal documents—such as Canada's Charter of Rights and Freedoms (Section 32)—declare that the rights they enumerate are claims against governing institutions only. My reply is that, as with the topic of justification, we can only take the legal realities at face value, and must dig further into the deep moral reasons supportive of human rights. A prime moral reason for thinking that we have human rights is concern that we not be grievously harmed in connection with our vital human needs. Since both individuals and institutions can deal us such unjustified grievous harm, it is only reasonable to conclude that they must both bear duties of a kind correlative to human rights.

Another flaw in Pogge's institutional conception is that it actually seems to unburden individuals from the duties associated with human rights fulfilment. Concrete persons are replaced by abstract institutions as the focus of concern. The faces of our fellow citizens are replaced by faceless social structures, a transfer that appears to lessen the interpersonal bonds of our shared social existence. If institutions are the sole duty-bearers, then it follows that individuals are utterly unburdened in this regard. I suggest this conclusion is counter-intuitive. Pogge actually agrees, and his concurrence is revealing. In spite of the purported "institutionalism" of his account, he stresses that individuals do *not* get off scot-free when it comes to realizing human rights. Two kinds of individual, on his understanding, possess two different kinds of personal burden. First, those individuals who occupy important institutional roles themselves bear duties correlative to human rights. Institutions are not, strictly speaking, faceless structures: they are staffed and run by individual persons, and so it must follow on Pogge's account that such persons bear duties in connection with rights-claims. So police officers, judges, bureaucrats, elected politicians, and so on, all bear individual burdens: they must do their fair share ensuring that the institution they help run does not violate human rights and, equally, plays its own role in the provision of the objects of human rights claims. What counts as "their fair share" will vary according to their own office's function, but in general will increase the greater the power of their position. Thus, the person who at any time occupies the office of President of the United States turns out, on the institutionalist reading, to bear considerable duties indeed relative to the fulfilment of human rights claims. But the reason he does so, Pogge insists, has got nothing to do with the fact that he is an individual human being; it has everything to do with the fact that he temporarily occupies a public office that gives him great causal impact on those goods and benefits we believe are the object of our human rights claims.

The second kind of individual who bears duties, on Pogge's account, refers to the rest of us: ordinary citizens who do not occupy those special roles and public offices that exert enormous effect on other people's lives. Pogge claims that his institutional account, in spite of appearances, implies that everyone "bears responsibility" in connection with human rights.[6] How is this the case? Social institutions are not naturally occurring phenomena: they are all man-made institutions with histories and consequences. They are staffed by individuals and are shaped not only by the decisions and actions of their officers but also by the public more generally. People, for instance, vote politicians into public office. People interact with bureaucrats, can appeal a judge's decision, can protest a politician's vote, can file a law suit alleging police brutality, and so on. People can do something about how social institutions get shaped and how they treat people. So ordinary people must also bear duties of a kind in connection with the fulfilment of human rights. The nature of this kind of duty is described in very general terms by Pogge: he calls it the duty to shape social institutions in a just fashion. What are we, as ordinary individuals, to do? The answer: our own fair share in ensuring that the social institutions that shape all our lives do so in a way that respects all our human rights. What counts as "our own fair share"? Here, too, the answer will naturally vary but will include the idea that *the more one can do, the more one has to do*. The better placed an individual is to affect the shape of the basic structure, the greater his correlative duty to do so. For most people in a decent society, this will mean little more than being a decent citizen: obeying the law, paying one's taxes, giving a damn about one's community, paying some attention to political debates, and supporting appropriate policies at the ballot box on election day. For other people living in more decrepit societies, it may call for something more demanding, like organizing a political opposition, withholding taxes in protest, being a conscientious objector, holding mass rallies in support of a change in government, and so on.

There is little to disagree with here, except the one big point concerning the very concept behind it. Pogge's admissions here show that he cannot sustain his original idea, namely, that there is a sharp split between the individual and institutional understanding and that only the latter understanding "works." His admissions reveal that there need be no difference in kind between the two understandings and that, moreover, the most plausible understanding combines elements of both accounts. Thus the title of our present section, "Persons or institutions?," contains a false dichotomy: the answer is "both." Both individuals and institutions bear duties correlative to human rights. These duties will vary in accordance with the power or affect that the individual or institution has on the objects of vital human need. But this variation implies no split: all of us do bear duties in connection with human rights, most centrally a *personal* duty not to deprive others of the objects of their human rights, and a *political* duty to do our part ensuring that social institutions do not so deprive as well. Since this understanding combines aspects of the individual and institutional account, I suggest we call it the "integrative account."

Identity II: National or International?

Even if we concur with the integrative account, a further issue remains unresolved. Are the institutions that are included in the integrative understanding seen as national or international? Are the duties correlative to human rights local or fully global? Even if we all bear duties of a kind—be we individuals or institutions—do we bear them only in connection with our fellow citizens, or rather across the globe with our fellow human beings? This is an important issue, for it traces the very limits, or borders, of moral responsibility for the fulfilment of human rights. In the history of the struggle for human rights, the consensus answer has been the local, or national, one. Human rights claims were made on national governments in the name of the people composing the nation. Most centrally, human rights were claims to reform local or national institutions so that they treated citizens decently, so that they did their part fulfilling the vital human needs of all instead of filling further the bulging pockets of a privileged few. The dynamic of the French Revolution, for example, illustrates this past reality vividly.[7]

One hears this traditional attitude still today, especially amongst citizens of affluent and powerful countries. Many Americans, for example, express the idea that they have few, if any, responsibilities in connection with the human rights of those on the other side of the world. If the people of, say, Bangladesh are oppressed or starving, then that is the responsibility of the national government of Bangladesh. We can hear the people who express such ideas exclaim, "It has got nothing to do with me, or my country, on this side of the planet." But if we accept the integrative account commended above, we will see that we cannot concur with this exclamation and should therefore reject the traditional, nationalist understanding.[8]

The following two reasons lead to this conclusion. First, the nationalist view assumes that there are very few, if any, causal connections between different nations. Michael Walzer, for one, calls this the "relative self-enclosure" thesis.[9] Since nations are relatively self-enclosed, having little causal impact on each other, it follows that little can be demanded from foreign nations by way of helping to realize the human rights of one's own citizens. This thesis may have been defensible in the past but is so no longer, owing to the onset of globalization. We now know that foreign countries—especially affluent and powerful ones—can and usually do exert real causal impact on domestic societies nearby, and at times even across the globe. The international impacts and interconnections are manifold, ranging from surface ties of diplomatic contact and educational exchanges to forceful undercurrents of trade and investment. The most obvious and serious case of international impact deals with the use of armed force: there can be no denying that a decision to go to war with another country will have an impact on the vital human needs of the people in that country, particularly in connection with their physical security and liberty. We may not yet be living in a full-blown "global village," in Marshall McLuhan's phrase, but there are obvious interconnections between nations.[10] These interconnections can affect whether, and to what degree, people possess the objects of their human rights. If our actions over here on this side of the world *can* violate the human rights of people on the other side, then the integrative understanding tells us that we *should* bear duties correlative to such rights. Saying this is completely consistent with the compelling idea that there remain real differences regarding who or what bears the duties *most heavily*. One can point out that the main burden for ensuring human rights satisfaction in a country lies with that country's national government without thereby concluding that that is the only entity bearing duties. To have the main burden is not to have the only burden. We can see this most clearly in those horrible instances when a country's national government unleashes unjustified violence and massacre upon its own people. Even though that rogue regime bears the primary responsibility for such human rights violations, need it follow that the rest of us have no moral obligations whatsoever? That we can just wash our hands of it and sleep easily, knowing the terrible fate of the victims? Our intuitions suggest not, as does our theory here: if we are in a position to stop such massacres, at absorbable cost to ourselves, then we ought to do so, on grounds that the human rights of the victims demand it. This is the best kind of moral justification behind calls for armed humanitarian intervention in a foreign country. Such calls have been very familiar in recent years, from Bosnia to Somalia, from Haiti to Rwanda, ranging all the way to Kosovo and Serbia.[11]

The second reason the nationalist view fails is that it assumes that moral demands alter radically along political borders. There are strong reasons to doubt this assumption. One has just been mentioned: moral demands and duties are inherent in any relationship where there is a causal connection between people that affects someone's vital needs. Since there are such causal connections that cross political borders, it follows that there are moral demands and duties that cross such borders. The unchanging essence of these duties concerns, primarily, the need not to unjustly inflict grievous harm on people and, secondarily, the need to do one's fair share in seeing that people possess the objects of their vital needs. The other reason for doubting the nationalist view has to do with the nature of morality itself, and the nature of human rights defended in this book. There are sound grounds for believing that, whatever the real differences that remain in moral beliefs between people, there exists a core set of elemental moral demands acknowledged by (essentially) every decent person. This refers back to Walzer's remarks, in Chapter 3, regarding a universally shared thin moral code.[12] Essentially every moral code in the world forbids the unjust infliction of grievous harm on others, and the understanding of human rights offered in this text defines human rights as protections from precisely such harms. In other words, the most important and fundamental requirements of morality and justice are subscribed to world-wide, and thus do not alter radically along political borders. Human rights are a central feature of such fundamental requirements. It is as wrong for our government to violate human rights on the other side of the world— e.g., through an unjust war—as it is for our government to violate the human rights of our fellow citizens here at home. Pointing this out in no way affects the idea that citizens may well owe each other *more* than they do foreigners, that they may share additional moral beliefs and commitments that foreigners do not. That is probably true, is morally permissible, and in fact is one of the hallmarks of a genuine community. What is impermissible is the idea that citizens owe foreigners nothing at all. Every citizen, and every institution, owes it to everyone not to violate their human rights. If one is in a position to affect another's human rights, then like it or not one bears duties in connection with that person's rights.

A summary of this section is in order before moving forward. All of us—individuals and institutions—bear duties of a kind in connection with human rights. The limits of such duties stretch beyond our own communities and circle the globe. There is no limit, firmly fixed right at the start, to the duties we each bear in connection with human rights. It all depends on whose human rights we are talking about, and the degree of power and influence we have over whether or not that person gets the objects of their human rights. The general principle is this: *the more power and influence one has over the objects of another's vital needs, the greater the degree of responsibility one has in connection with that person's human rights.* For most of us, that means that the domestic institutions of our own society are the major focus of our human rights claims. These national institutions are then followed by our fellow citizens. These institutions and individuals are most in a position to harm us—have the most influence on our vital needs—and thus bear the weightiest duties. But there are cases when foreign or international institutions, associations, corporations and persons find themselves in such a position of influence and impact. The moral logic here demands they be constrained by duties too, even if such duties are of lesser import than those borne by the entities more proximate to the person. The upshot is this: we all have human rights and, in exchange for them, we all have to play our part in realizing, and above all not violating, the human rights of our fellow human beings.

Content of the Duties

We have delved into this issue at multiple points in the text already. Since it is so central and crucial to the debate, this comes as no surprise: we do not know the full scope of our human rights until we know that the duties correlative to them can be performed at a reasonable cost. Generally, a reasonable cost means one proportional to the merits of the thing being paid for, in this case human rights. Even if we concur about the identity of the duty-bearers being both individual and institutions, on this side of the border and beyond, we still have to determine which exact duties these duty-bearers bear. We know that there *are* duties correlative to human rights, we now need to know what the *content* of each duty is.

Up until the late 1970s, the duties correlative to claims of human right were largely seen as being *either* negative *or* positive. For each human right, it was thought there correlated exactly one duty, and it was either negative or positive. The difference between negative and positive was seen solely in terms of whether or not the duty-bearer had to perform an action. A negative duty was one of strict factual inaction. It was a duty of omission, of forbearance, of non-interference, of *refraining from doing something*. A positive duty, by contrast, required factual action. It demanded performance, commission, assistance, *providing something* or otherwise doing something beneficial for the right-holder. Frequently, it was contended that the rights correlative to such duties should, in fact, be named after them: hence, the rights correlative to negative duties were "negative rights," and those correlative to positive ones were "positive rights."

It was often contended, on the basis of these assumptions, that the duties correlative to the so-called civil and political rights—e.g., to security, liberty, property and standard participatory and due process rights—were wholly negative. It was thought, for example, that all that others have to do for one to enjoy one's right to free speech is simply to refrain from interfering with one's speech. Civil and political rights, thus viewed, appear to have only costs of forbearance in this regard and, as a result, seem quite affordable and reasonable. Asking people and institutions to restrain themselves and refrain from interfering in people's lives is not asking too much of them. Negative rights, a.k.a. first-generation human rights, are readily absorbable in terms of cost. It was often thought, by contrast, that the duties correlative to the so-called socio-economic rights were wholly positive. To enjoy a right to material subsistence, for example, would require that other people and social institutions go out of their way to aid, assist, perform and otherwise supply one with the object of one's right, namely, a subsistence income or a bundle of vital goods like food, water, clothing and shelter. By this convenient conceptual linkage, older rights theorists like Maurice Cranston were quick to pronounce on the utter illegitimacy of socio-economic rights. Such rights, they said, really are not worthy of the name, due to the immense costs and onerous burdens that their correlative positive duties mandate. Such rights, they said, simply ask for too much, and so they do not constitute "justified claims," as the definition of rights stipulates they must. So their conclusion was that socio-economic rights are bogus rights; only civil and political rights, correlative to reasonable duties of non-interference, are truly worthy of the distinguished title of "human rights."[13]

Henry Shue, amongst others, formulated a devastating counter-attack on this conception of human rights and their correlative duties. Using the same understanding of the distinction between "negative" and "positive," he pointed out that some very traditional civil and political rights require the performance of duties that are not simply negative ones of forbearance. Consider, for example, the basic set of due process rights, such as the right to a fair trial by one's peers within a reasonable time-period, the right to be informed of what one has been charged with, the right to qualified counsel, the right to question one's accusers, or the right to the presumption of innocence. To enjoy the substance of these rights, is it true that other people and institutions need only to refrain from treating oneself in certain ways? That all they have to do is stay out of one's way? The answer, clearly, is no. The right to be informed of whatever crime one has been charged with obviously requires positive action on the part of whomever is to inform one of the nature of the charge. Furthermore, the right to a trial by peers within a reasonable time-frame requires that a whole slew of positive duties be performed: it requires the presence, selection and participation of jury members and officers of the court, a place to hold the trial, and so on. In fact, the right requires the positive construction and maintenance of an entire well-ordered judicial system charged with expediting one's case. It is clear that these positive actions do, in fact, come at a substantial cost—one that is not merely implicit, in terms of alternatives foregone, but also explicit in terms of the expenditure of time and resources.[14]

It follows from the above considerations, as Shue pointed out, that the enjoyment of some of the most traditional, first-generation human rights requires the performance of duties that are not merely negative but also positive, and ones that can cost a considerable amount indeed. So, one of Shue's most powerful contentions was that, *if* one defines the duties correlative to human rights in terms of a binary distinction between inaction and action, such a binary cannot be sustained. And so the sharp split between so-called civil and political rights, on the one hand, and socio-economic rights, on the other, is fallacious. The critics of socio-economic human rights turned out, on their own terms, to be mistaken. There is no sharp cleavage within the heart of human rights; they seem, rather, to form a unified and coherent whole. One such unified and integrated understanding was developed in the last chapter.

Shue's alternative understanding of the duties correlative to human rights involves not a two-fold but, rather, a three-fold conception. First, Shue still relies on the traditional conception of the difference between a negative and a positive duty: a negative duty is still, for him, one of factual forbearance while a positive duty is one of factual performance. Shue contends, however, that, correlative to any single human right is not one single duty, which must be either negative or positive; rather, there are actually multiple duties, which mix both negative and positive elements. Specifically, he says that correlative to any single assertion of human right are three correlative duties: 1) negatively, not to deprive the right-holder of the object of his right; 2) positively, to protect the right-holder in his possession of the object of his right; and 3) positively, to aid the right-holder, should someone still manage to violate his right.[15]

Why these three kinds of duty, expressed in this manner? The answer, in Shue's mind, is straightforward and compelling: the performance of these three kinds of duty is, in fact, required to supply everyone with the objects of their human rights. Human rights, we have seen, exist to ensure a certain baseline level of decent treatment for all persons, usually by providing for them certain freedoms or benefits and by protecting them from standard, serious threats to the enjoyment of such freedoms and benefits. Shue contends, powerfully, that such protection from standard threats is ensured *only* when the relevant actors and institutions fulfil these duties: 1) all persons refrain from violating the right; 2) effective institutions exist to protect the object of the right; and 3) all those in a position to do so come to one's aid in case such protection fails. This three-fold structure is called for because it holds the greatest promise in terms of actually ensuring that everyone can enjoy reasonably secure access to the objects of their human rights.

Consider an example, involving the human right to personal security. What are the duties correlative to this single human right, as Shue sees them? First, there is the negative duty, on the part of others and institutions, to refrain from inflicting serious injury or death upon a person. Second, there is the positive duty, on the part of others and institutions, to protect a person in the possession of the object of that right, which is life and physical functioning. It seems, for Shue, that this second duty involves especially the construction of those social institutions that would reliably protect one from being seriously injured in unjust fashion: an effective and decent system of law and order. Third, there is the positive duty to aid a person in the event such institutional protection fails and some people violate their foremost negative duty not to inflict serious and unjust injury. Shue calls this three-fold structure of duties the three successive "waves of duty" that ought to be seen as correlative to any single assertion of human right.[16]

Shue's account is compelling, at the least making clear progress on past views. In fact, I believe that Shue's account suffices as a skeletal structure to which flesh and blood can then be added to achieve some satisfaction. There is, in particular, one "big picture" aspect that needs to be added to Shue's understanding.

This big picture aspect deals with Shue's reliance on the old understanding of the distinction between negative and positive. One might feel that Shue's account fails to pay enough respect to the fact that many—perhaps even most—people persist in the belief that negative duties are more important than positive ones. I suggest that we can both keep this belief and yet retain Shue's essential elements, if we make the following adjustment: we redefine the meaning of "negative" *away from* factual inaction and *toward* the norm of not inflicting harm.[17] A negative duty thus becomes a duty not to inflict grievous and unjust harm on another, whereas a positive duty becomes a duty to do someone some good, like being polite to him. Let us call this redefinition the normative, or *prescriptive*, understanding of negative and positive, as opposed to the older *descriptive*, or factual, understanding that has hitherto been in use. On reflection we can see how this redefinition squares with Shue's efforts: for it may well be part of one's duty not to inflict harm that one must *both* refrain from performing some act *and* perform some further action. For example, it may well be part of one's negative duty not to inflict harm on a person that one should *both* refrain from injuring that person *and* vote on election day for sound policies of law and order. To the extent to which one fails to do either, one has harmed that person. If we make use of this normative reconception, we can retain our intuitions about negative duties being more important than positive ones: we agree that it is more important to avoid inflicting harm than it is to do someone some good. Some thinkers, like Marcia Baron, refer to this normative distinction as being equivalent to the one between duties of justice and duties of benevolence.[18]

Duties of justice, or normatively negative duties, are duties that it is imperative to perform. So important are they that one's failure to perform them properly exposes oneself to both resistance and punishment. The duties correlative to human rights, I suggest, are all duties of justice. Duties of benevolence, or normatively positive duties, are of lesser importance. Though one should still perform them—though they still confront one with an "ought," with the force of a moral duty—one's failure to perform them properly exposes oneself to nothing more than blame and criticism. If some insensitive clod violates a duty of benevolence—say, by being supremely rude and insulting—then the rest of us may well criticize him but we may not thereby throw him in jail. The moral violation is simply not serious enough. The man is a jerk, not a criminal: he violates our sensibilities, not our rights. Normatively positive duties are irrelevant to human rights. Human rights serve to secure and protect vital human needs, and the benevolence of others is not one of them. We can live minimally good lives without people being as gracious as we might prefer. Benevolence is, of course, still a wonderful thing and it still makes sense for us to frame moral requirements around it, since most of us enjoy life well above the threshold of minimally decent treatment that human rights specify. But benevolence is simply a topic that is not within the scope of this text: I leave the refined topic of benevolence, and its associated virtues of character, to other moral theorists.

There are two important things to note about the normative conception of a negative duty, defined here as a duty of justice not to inflict grievous and unjust harm. The first, as mentioned, is that it enables us both to keep our intuitions about the relative importance of negative over positive duties, and also to remain faithful to Shue's advances on past accounts of correlative duty. The second thing is that this normative definition fits in beautifully with the main justification of human rights offered at the end of Chapter 3. The main appeal there was to the wrongness of inflicting grievous, unjustified harm on another person. Such harm was then linked to either depriving a person of one of the objects of her vital need, or else failing to do one's fair share in providing all such objects to her. This is to say that what justifies human rights, or at least one compelling justification for them, is precisely an appeal to the moral force of the normatively negative duty not to harm. The justification ultimately rests on an appeal to a negative duty. Violating human rights inflicts on the victim of the violation harm that is grievous, since it attacks the victim's vital human needs in living a minimally good life, and unjust, since the victim is owed the objects of such needs as a matter of minimally decent treatment. Human rights are violated—the negative duty not to harm is violated—whenever anyone, or any institution, violates one of Shue's three duties: 1) do not deprive without just cause; 2) protect and secure; and 3) aid and provide.

Our understanding of these considerations can be aided by drawing on a distinction between first-level and second-level specifications of duties, analogous to the last chapter's helpful distinction in connection with rights specification. Correlative to any human right, there is one universal, general and abstract duty, namely, the normatively negative duty of justice not to inflict grievous and unjust harm. This duty is mandated by the ultimate principles justifying human rights. What this one normatively negative duty specifies at the second, or more concrete and applied, level is Shue's three duties.

First, if the right-holder *already has* the object of the human right in question, then all persons and institutions *must not deprive* the right-holder of that object, be it an aspect of security, subsistence, liberty, equality or recognition. If someone already has the objects of his human rights, no person or institution may take such objects away. The only reason for doing so deals with comparatively rare instances of forfeiture discussed in Chapter 2.

Second, Shue is correct to take things a step further when he points out that full realization of human rights requires not merely that right-holders *possess* the objects of their rights but that, additionally, they need to be *secure in their possession* of those objects. They need to be able *to count on having* such objects at their disposal as they go about living their lives. The importance of what human rights protect—namely, lives of minimal value—tells us this is so. There is little point in having possession if such possession is in constant and serious jeopardy. One wants reliable, socially acknowledged and protected possession, not merely luck-of-the-draw, safe-for-the-moment possession. Non-deprivation is not enough: reliable protection against future non-deprivation is also required. Of course, we cannot ever fully guarantee, one hundred percent and totally in all circumstances, that people are going to have secure possession, or even simple possession, of all the objects of all their human rights. Human fallibility, swiftly changing circumstances, emergencies and crises, all underline this truth: human rights are not absolute, fail-safe entitlements. But they do remain vitally important entitlements that generally trump rival claims and call for the most serious efforts in ordinary circumstances. While we cannot guarantee unfailing possession, we *can* guarantee the establishment of a social context in which one's possession of human rights objects is secure against the most serious and standard threats. Such threats include the force and fraud of people, the malign design of wicked social institutions, and conditions of severe personal deprivation regarding both the material necessities of life and basic health care and education. The duty of establishing such a secure context—of protecting people in their possession of the objects of their human rights—falls, in the first instance, on social institutions. With their power and scope, they are the most capable of achieving the secure society-wide conditions sought after. The very point of social institutions, it might be said, is to fashion such a protective context for all individuals living within their scope. This is clearest with those social institutions devoted to ensuring law and order. Most police forces, in fact, have as their motto some version of "to serve and protect." Even though the duty of protection falls in the first instance on social institutions, this does not utterly unburden individuals, who must take secondary responsibility for doing their part to ensure that the social institutions they share have adequate resources to provide such protection, and indeed are structured with the aim of achieving such protection in the first place. This secondary responsibility requires of all persons some degree of social engagement, political participation and reasonable sharing of the tax burden required to fund such institutions.

So much for those cases when the right-holder already has possession of the objects of his human rights, and subsequently demands both non-deprivation and protection. If the right-holder *lacks* the objects of her human rights, then she *must be aided* in this regard, and indeed provided the objects in question. This third requirement, of aid and provision, assumes, importantly, that the objects can be provided at reasonable cost. If they cannot be so affordably provided, the requirement dissolves. This duty should likewise be seen as falling in the first instance on institutions, and only secondarily upon individuals. Why? The answer is that institutions can more effectively and efficiently provide such objects to people, and can do so at a cost that can be intelligently and fairly spread out amongst all members of society, over generations. Having such cost fall on the shoulders of an individual would run a much greater risk of both failing to ensure that the right-holder gets her object, and imposing potentially ruinous costs on the duty-bearer. Individuals do not make good providers for more than a very small number of people, such as parents for their children. But when individuals pool resources, delegate authority, and establish effective social institutions authorized to facilitate such provisions, then widespread success is much more likely to result. We saw, in Chapter 3, that Judith Thomson's thought experiment regarding the dying violinist establishes the firm outside limits on the costs we can reasonably expect people to bear, even for the sake of something as important as human rights. We can never ask an individual, for example, to shoulder a cost that thwarts his own ability to both have and lead a minimally good life. We cannot require that people sacrifice the objects of their own human rights for the sake of providing such objects to another. That would be paradox and contradiction. If the cost to an individual is that high, the duty dissolves. Institutions, of course, are importantly different: they are not themselves human rights-holders, their actions have much more widespread effect, and they can absorb costs of an entirely different order of magnitude than individuals can. In abstract terms, a cost ruinous to an institution would be a cost so high that, if paid, the institution could no longer perform the very function it was established to secure. This sets the firm outside limits on the costs we can require institutions to bear, on behalf of us all, for the sake of providing the objects of human rights.

A simple chart sketches the overall relationship between rights and duties, and between the levels of specification in this regard:

Fig. 5.1.

Ultimate Principles Justifying Human Rights

First-level Specification of Human Rights Objects	**First-level Specification of Correlative Duty**
(*i.e.*, to security, subsistence, freedom, equality, and recognition)	(*i.e.*, do not inflict grievous and unjustified harm)

Second-level Specification of Human Rights Objects	**Second-level Specification of Correlative Duties**
(*e.g.*, freedom of expression, conscience, religion, movement, association, to emigrate, *etc.*, and so on for each first-level object)	(if *having* possession: do not deprive, and secure and protect) (if *lacking* possession: provide and aid)

What exactly do these illustrations, and reflections on cost, imply in terms of actual social organization and personal behaviour? What confidence can we have that human rights as sketched are, in fact, affordable? Two core premises by way of beginning a response: first, human rights are neither free nor cheap; second, the vital importance of human rights for all demands we pursue their realization unless the costs of doing so are genuinely unaffordable and ruinous. How can human rights be made affordable? The answer probably lies in an analysis of the social structures of those societies where human rights have already been more or less realized on a mass scale. What do they share in common? First, a shared moral culture that enshrines respect for the value and worth of each person. Simply providing a decent moral education that develops some scruples and a sense of basic humanity can go a long way toward developing a rights-respecting culture. Secondly, rights-respecting societies allow people, in the first instance, the freedom and opportunity to secure the objects of their human rights for themselves. It seems plausible to say that most people, given the chance, will be able to find for themselves the means needed to live a minimally good life. The average person has at least that amount of practical intelligence and industriousness. Third, such societies are ruled by law and order, providing a social context secure enough that it makes sense for people to strive after what they want, not having to worry constantly about the security of themselves and their possessions. The threat of legal punishment for human rights violations is also an effective inducement against such acts, serving as the punitive "stick" complementary to the "carrot" of a sound moral education. Fourth, rights-respecting societies make it clear that the provision of human rights objects by public institutions will be available only to those who genuinely cannot provide for themselves. This is a reasonable measure to take to reign in costs, since it sends out appropriate incentives in favour of self-reliance, yet is also humane in guaranteeing to the unfortunate that they will not be left to fall below the minimally decent standard of living denoted by human rights. This implies the presence of some social security assistance, some kind of welfare state protections, in the midst of an otherwise free society that allows and rewards effort and industry. Institutions often reign in their costs further, in this regard, by making the provision for children the main responsibility of their parents, and so recourse to welfare payments is limited, generally, to those adults who genuinely cannot provide for themselves. Such a welfare state need not be big and bloated, and seems readily affordable. We are, after all, talking about providing *only* a finite set of objects of vital human need to those who do *not* already have such objects *and* who genuinely cannot provide such for themselves. The fifth thing that rights-respecting societies share in common is institutional accountability. Since social institutions play such an important role in whether or not people enjoy the objects of their human rights, it follows that there must be some mechanism for holding them accountable for fulfilling that function. Different societies differ here, but prominent options include the following: a division of power between institutions, designed to get them to serve as checks-and-balances on each other; efforts to keep the overall size of the total set of such institutions under control; and a system of democratic entitlements, allowing people to vote for and against those people with ambitions to run social institutions.[19]

Societies that respect human rights, then, most often have a pre-existing moral culture that believes in the worth of the human person; a culture with a presumption in favour of freedom and providing for oneself where one can; the rule of law and order; ways for holding social institutions accountable to the public good; and at least a minimal welfare state, in terms of ensuring basic education and health care, and subsistence income payments for food, water, clothing and shelter. The fact that so many societies have either succeeded, or made large strides toward success, in this regard demonstrates the affordability of the overall costs of human rights. And the moral case has already been made that such costs are well worth absorbing, for the enormous payoff is ensuring that every human being can both have and lead a minimally good life in the modern world. Against the cost of realizing rights, we have to weigh the severe costs of failing to do so: the moral cost of inflicting such harm on people, and the prudential cost of damaging the peace and stability of our societies as a result of such infliction.

What about the poorest of the poor countries, though? Do such statements hold true for them? If our duty is to ensure that literally everyone in the world has the objects of their human rights, can we still confidently predict the overall affordability of a *global* realization of human rights? Here, too, I believe that the most plausible answer is yes.[20] We are not talking about making such countries flush with wealth; rather, we are talking about only doing our fair share, as citizens of comparatively privileged countries, to ensure that poor countries at least have enough to fund a minimally decent life for all their people. We are not talking about impoverishing ourselves so that they too can drive fast cars and drink French wine; we are talking about establishing genuinely global protections for everyone against the infliction of grievous and unjust harm. Such establishment may imply a duty of development assistance, or resource transfer, from the wealthiest nations of the global community to the poorest. This is hardly a radical proposal: most wealthy nations already have programs of development assistance in place, some for generations. The aim of such assistance, obviously, is not to engender perpetual dependence but, rather, to create a stable and sustainable set of human rights-respecting institutions within countries genuinely needing such assistance. Quite often, past programs of "development aid" have been thinly disguised forms of international political patronage, or of cementing military alliances, or of trying to enhance the bottom line of businesses back home.[21] Often, the genuinely humanitarian component of development assistance has been small, or even completely absent. This is to say that institutional checks-and-balances are needed to ensure that international human rights aid effectively advances its aim and end. And not just from the point of view of the wealthy "donor" countries: recent research has shown that often the major factor in mass deprivation, or massive human rights violation, has *less* to do with global disparities in stages of development and *more* to do with decrepit national institutions. Acclaimed economist Amartya Sen, for instance, has determined that the main cause behind modern famines—i.e., emergencies of mass starvation—has been corrupt and wicked local institutions, and not a genuine lack of food.[22] Thus, the givers of human rights aid have a right to insist on needed institutional reforms within recipient countries. Indeed, helping with such reforms is probably better in the long run than simply throwing cash or food at the problem and wishing it would go away.

What might such help consist of? Several examples come to mind: training lawyers and judges in such countries to act out the rule of law, as opposed to enacting the will of some tyrant; helping such countries to write new constitutions to transform the very way law is made there; training police officers how to work with the people to ensure public safety, as opposed to how to lord it over the people, making them cower in fear and resentment; programs of human rights education would also help, exposing children to basic moral virtues as well as needed life skills; perhaps even introducing democratic reforms, like holding elections, to start making social institutions accountable to the public good and not merely serving private interests. In general, the help should be oriented toward developing in that country the five conditions rights-respecting societies share: widespread belief in the value of humanity, a presumption in favour of freedom, a peaceful social context ordered by laws, institutional accountability, and minimal welfare protections. Sometimes, of course, raw resources will be needed, and should be provided if they come at absorbable cost. But most of the time it is institutional transformation that is needed: not so much physical goods but more the services of sound advice and expertise in basic social design.

The main responsibility in connection with the very poorest countries rests first and foremost with the national institutions and citizenry of the disadvantaged society in question. Next in line come those foreign countries that may have contributed to this disadvantage through prior historical entanglements, such as war or colonialism. Finally come all other foreign countries that can afford to contribute something meaningful to this important process, noting the residual yet resilient duty that even individual persons in remote countries have to press their own institutions to play their part where and when they can.

Conclusion

This chapter advanced an understanding of who or what bears duties in connection with human rights satisfaction. This integrative understanding stipulates that both individuals and institutions, whether here at home or abroad in a foreign land, bear duties of a kind. The general principle here is this: the more power and influence one has over the objects of another's vital needs, the greater the degree of responsibility one has in connection with that person's human rights. What are the contents of these correlative duties? There is both a first- and a second-level specification of this content, which corresponds nicely to the split in specification of rights offered in the last chapter. The first-level duty, correlative to any human right, is not to inflict grievous harm unjustly on another human being. The second-level duties implied by this first-level obligation are as follows: first, do not deprive others of human rights objects if they already have them; second, do play one's part securing and protecting everyone's possession of their human rights objects; and finally, where others lack the objects of their human rights, do one's fair share in aiding or providing them with such objects. We saw that, even though social institutions probably bear the heaviest practical responsibility in this regard, this does not unburden us as individuals. For institutions remain the products of individual thought, choice, action and effort, and so it remains true to say that all of us, everywhere, bear duties in connection with the realization of human rights.

Notes

1 See J. Nickel, *Making Sense of Human Rights* (Berkeley: University of California Press, 1987), 41-45; D. Luban, "Human Rights and the General Welfare," *Philosophy and Public Affairs* 2 (1976/77): 113-29; and H. Shue, *Basic Rights: Subsistence, Affluence and U.S. Foreign Policy*, 2nd ed. (Princeton: Princeton University Press, 1996). The "Afterword" in this second edition deals with this debate.

2 T. Pogge, "How Should Human Rights be Conceived?" *Jahrbuch für Recht und Ethik* 3 (1995): 103-20; T. Pogge, "The International Significance of Human Rights," *Journal of Ethics* 1 (2000): 45-69.

3 T. Pogge, *Realizing Rawls* (Ithaca, NY: Cornell University Press, 1989), 15-63.

4 T. Pogge, "Cosmopolitanism and Sovereignty," *Ethics* 44 (1992): 48-75; T. Pogge, "A Global Resources Dividend," in D. Crocker and T. Linden, eds., *Ethics of Consumption* (Boston: Rowman Littlefield, 1998), 501-35.

5 Pogge, "How Should Human Rights be Conceived?", 103-20.

6 Pogge, "How Should Human Rights be Conceived?", 103-20.

7 For more on the French Revolution and rights, see the section on the French Declaration in the last chapter, as well as the forthcoming part on historical context.

8 A more detailed analysis of the ethics of this stance can be found in Chapter 5 of my *War and International Justice: A Kantian Perspective* (Waterloo, ON: Wilfrid Laurier University Press, 2000) as well as in T. Pogge, "The Bounds of Nationalism," in J. Couture *et al.*, eds., *Rethinking Nationalism* (Calgary: University of Calgary Press, 1998), 463-504.

9 M. Walzer, "The Moral Standing of States," *Philosophy and Public Affairs* 4 (1979/80): 209-29. See also Chapter 7 of my *Michael Walzer on War and Justice* (Montreal: McGill-Queen's University Press, 2000).

10 C. Beitz, *Political Theory and International Relations* (Princeton: Princeton University Press, 1979); F. Lechner and J. Boli, eds., *The Globalization Reader* (Oxford: Blackwell, 1999); T. Spybey, *Globalization and World Society* (Cambridge: Polity Press, 1996); Pogge, "Cosmopolitanism," 48-75.

11 For more on humanitarian intervention, see my "Crisis in Kosovo: A Just Use of Force?" *Politics* 19 (Sept. 1999): 125-30.

12 M. Walzer, *Thick and Thin: Moral Argument at Home and Abroad* (Notre Dame, IN: University of Notre Dame Press, 1996).

13 M. Cranston, *What are Human Rights?* (New York: Basic Books, 1973); R. Nozick, *Anarchy, State and Utopia* (New York: Basic Books, 1974); J. Narveson, *The Libertarian Idea* (Philadelphia: Temple University Press, 1989).

14 Shue, *Basic Rights, passim*; Nickel, *Making Sense*, 147-70; R. Peffer, "A Defence of Rights to Well-Being," *Philosophy and Public Affairs* 3 (1978/79): 65-87; J. Donnelly, *International Human Rights* (Boulder, CO: Westview, 1993), 13-39.

15 Shue, *Basic Rights*, 3-65.

16 Shue, *Basic Rights*, "Afterword."

17 I first suggested this reconceptualization in Chapter 4 of my *Kantian Perspective*.

18 M. Baron, *Kantian Ethics Almost Without Apology* (Ithaca, NY: Cornell University Press, 1995); M. Baron, "The Moral Status of Loyalty," in D. Johnson, *Ethical Issues in Engineering* (Englewood Cliffs, NJ: Prentice Hall, 1991), 225-40.

19 G. Sorenson, *Democracy and Democratization* (Boulder, CO: Westview Press, 1998); L. Diamond, *Developing Democracy* (Baltimore: Johns Hopkins University Press, 1999); M. Robinson and G. White, eds., *The Democratic Developmental State: Politics and Institutional Design* (Oxford: Oxford University Press, 1999).

20 The Bi-annual United Nations *Report on Human Development* provides a wealth of information about the material well-being of people world-wide, with often a special focus on the developing nations. See also the World Bank's annual *World Development Indicators*.

21 J. Moore, ed., *Hard Choices* (New York: Rowman Littlefield, 1999); World Bank, *Assessing Aid: What Works, What Doesn't and Why* (Washington, DC: World Bank, 1998); and M. Maren, *The Road to Hell* (New York: Free Press, 1997).

22 A. Sen, *Poverty and Famines* (Oxford: Clarendon Press, 1981); A. Sen and J. Dreze, *Hunger and Public Action* (Oxford: Clarendon, 1989); P. Dasgupta, *An Inquiry into Well-Being and Destitution* (Oxford: Clarendon, 1993); and D. Landes, *The Wealth and Poverty of Nations* (New York: W.W. Norton, 1998).

Chapter 6

Can Human Rights
Withstand Criticism?

The only task remaining in our development of the concept of human rights concerns the capacity of the idea to respond to forceful criticism. I am not talking about criticism *amongst* human rights theorists, as witnessed in Chapter 4's debate between supporters of first-generation and those of second-generation human rights. The topic is not sibling rivalry within the human rights family. It is, rather, those who reject entirely the idea of human rights and its associated trends in social and political life. I am talking about non-believers in human rights of any kind. In my judgment, such skeptics ask five compelling critical questions of the human rights defender:

1. Do human rights *exist?*
2. Are human rights *justified?*
3. Are human rights *affordable?*
4. Are human rights *universal?*
5. Are human rights *beneficial?*

Prior chapters offered satisfying answers to at least the first three questions. Human rights do indeed exist: not as properties of persons but, rather, as reasons for treating persons in a minimally decent way. Rights are reasons, and we have reasons aplenty for treating everyone in such a way that their vital human needs get satisfied. Human rights have also enjoyed some success in getting translated into effective legal rights, a palpable demonstration of their reality. Human rights are also justifiable, and Chapter 3 detailed numerous strategies of justification. A number were found to be sound. Consequentialist appeals to prudence, first-principle appeals to fairness, and appeals to inference from special rights all seemed plausible and persuasive. Found especially strong was a strategy combining a sober and minimal conception of vital human needs with an appeal to the moral duty not to inflict harm on a person's fundamental interests in both having and leading a life. Human rights are also affordable. As Chapters 4 and 5 demonstrated, human rights are by no means free. While coming with a price, human rights remain absorbable at reasonable cost, both in explicit resource expenditure and in implicit cost of alternatives foregone. Human rights are, in fact, worth every single penny spent on them, since they are designed to secure for all their holders the essential ingredients of a minimally decent life in the modern world.

We have, of course, dealt with the final two questions listed above, at least in some fashion, throughout this text. Chapter 2, in particular, devoted itself to the issue of universality. But there remain aspects of these last two questions, on universality and beneficial results, which require a fuller response. Such a response is needed not only to achieve theoretical completeness on the conceptual issue but also because these last two queries contain some of the most resilient, pointed and frequently repeated criticisms of human rights.

Against Chapter 2's conclusion that human rights are universally held, critics contend that human rights are biased in favour of Western civilization, relevant only in developed free market economies, and/or are expressive of a narrowly male perspective on morality and justice. The general idea, shared by all such critics, is that human rights defenders generalize from their own particular view of the world and project it onto those who do not share it. Human rights are seen as an aggressive imposition, of one narrow vision, upon others of different—yet equally legitimate—political orientation.

Western Bias?

The critics allege that human rights, in spite of the rhetoric about universality and equality, are in fact pieces of Western liberal democratic ideology that are not applicable to societies with non-Western and undemocratic political structures. Human rights also enshrine a degree of individualism that simply is not shared by some cultures, where social belongingness and group success rank higher in concern. The fact that ideas about human rights originated in Western Europe, they say, is not merely an accident: it is an important fact about the world-view contained in the human rights idea. This idea bears the indelible stamp of a European, or European-derived, culture and it is naïve at best, and arrogant at worst, to assume that this culture speaks to everyone, or is applicable to every existing social context regardless of local history. If human rights express what Western people believe should be provided to everyone in their culture as a matter of minimally decent treatment, then that is wonderful and so be it. But, the critics ask, who are Westerners to insist that the idea also expresses an equal commitment to such treatment in every other culture? This is just the latest idea, with its accompanying set of institutions, in a long history of the same old thing: arrogant Westerners using their power advantages over other cultures to re-make the world in their own image. Where Westerners see the promotion of universal truth and betterment, non-Westerners perceive the infliction of one narrow, and foreign, set of values over another set that was already there and doing just fine—thank you very much—prior to Western intervention. While Westerners might plausibly point out that many improvements were brought about by such "intervention," we all know the historical record remains spotty and sullied. Some cultures—especially Aboriginal or Native cultures—were essentially destroyed by contact with Western civilization. There is, to say the least, no evidence from history to conclude that all ideas and institutions transposed from Western cultures onto non-Western ones have been beneficial. So if a non-Western culture tells us, sincerely, that human rights are at odds with its own local customs and commitments, then on what grounds can we say that such a culture should nevertheless adopt them, and change its institutions accordingly? Are our imaginations so limited that we can only see the world through our own eyes, refusing to acknowledge any other kind of political legitimacy than that conferred through the realization of human rights? Finally, some critics claim that it is no accident that human rights have risen to such special prominence in the period following World War II. For that period has been dominated, internationally, by the United States, which has had a bedrock commitment to the idea of natural or human rights dating back to the first days of its own revolutionary origins. Whether by design or sheer dint of its power, America has put human rights front and centre. In doing so, it has availed itself of the rhetoric of universal truth and betterment but, in reality, it is simply doing what all dominant powers in history have always done: re-make the world in its own image, and assure the world it looks all the more beautiful as a result. This is, skeptics say, more a matter of extending the security, comfort and power of the dominant civilization than it is of genuinely bettering the welfare of all humanity.[1]

Any effective response to this accusation of Eurocentrism, or more accurately Western bias, must start off by acknowledging the mixed record of the history of Western involvement with non-Western cultures. Some sensitivity must be shown to this fact. It is also probably true to point out that American hegemony has been one of the reasons for the sharp rise in the prominence of human rights in the past fifty or so years. One wonders whether human rights would be so influential had history taken another course and a different power come to enjoy global primacy. All these admissions, however, are not devastating to the human rights defender.

The human rights defender could, at this point, raise caution about the so-called "genetic fallacy." The genetic fallacy refers to a flaw in reasoning. The flaw here is this: rejecting an argument, or theory, not on the basis of its own merits but, rather, on the basis of the irrelevant personal characteristics of the person or group who invented it. Perhaps the most notorious real-world example of the genetic fallacy occurred in Nazi Germany, when it was briefly official policy to reject the theory of relativity because it was devised by a Jew, Albert Einstein. This is, obviously, an instance of poor reasoning, since the personal characteristics of Albert Einstein have no relevant bearing whatsoever on whether the theory of relativity he invented offers a true, or at least compelling, account of time, space and the movement of physical objects in the universe. Similarly, we might say that, from the fact that the idea of human rights was probably first devised in Western European culture, it does not follow that the idea is therefore limited in application only to that part of the world. The criticism of Eurocentrism, as a criticism of human rights, errs because it does not deal with the merits of the human rights idea itself but, rather, with the characteristics of the people and civilization out of which it first came. The Eurocentrism criticism offers no conspicuous criticism of the moral merits of realizing human rights, and as such misses the mark. It throws the baby out with the bathwater. Furthermore, from the fact that the human rights idea originated in Western Europe, it does not follow that Western European culture is thereby revealed to be a blessed, and utterly superior, cultural form. Good ideas come from all over the place, and wisdom consists in knowing when to adopt a good idea and make it one's own, as opposed to refusing to do so out of a misplaced stubborn pride. Just because the good idea of human rights came out of Western European culture does not mean other cultures should resist it, any more than it denotes the sheer supremacy of Western culture. After all, some of the most grievous and appalling human rights violations have occurred right in the very heart of Europe.

The human rights defender can also point out that the criticism of universality is often put forward in bad faith. It is surely no coincidence that this criticism is most prominently made by governments in countries with poor human rights records. Such governments—that of China being one of the most forceful—have every self-interested reason to denounce human rights, since the realization of human rights in their countries would challenge their own power, perhaps resulting in institutional transformation. One of the most effective means of denunciation in such countries is often to link it to anti-Western biases and convictions. The result is a bogus denunciation of human rights, since it is not on their own merits but on the back of official propaganda that manipulates popular prejudices for the gain of a small cadre of politicians thinking only about themselves. When officials in repressive and rights-violating societies criticize human rights as alien to their culture, we can reply by asking what makes such officials the authority on declaring what is, and is not, part of their culture? One presumes, for example, that opponents of such officials—e.g., political dissidents languishing in jail—would not acknowledge the right of such officials to speak for them about the desire for human rights in their culture. Against the cost of being accused of being arrogantly Eurocentric, human rights defenders have to measure the larger cost of abandoning those courageous activists committed to realizing pro-rights changes in the face of repressive regimes. Furthermore, and frankly, it seems no less arrogant to suggest, as the skeptics seem to, that whole chunks of humanity fail to discern the basic sense and moral power of the reasons supportive of the existence of human rights and the need to realize them. It does not seem arrogant at all, on our part, to suggest that everyone wants their own vital needs met, and that reasonable people agree that it is only fair that everyone else also get the objects of their vital needs, assuming absorbable costs. It is not arrogant to presuppose that everybody wants to have and lead their own life; it is arrogant to suggest that some do not have such wants, and thus are not entitled to live in a minimally just social and political context.

The skeptic's claim, that significant chunks of humanity do not endorse human rights, runs afoul of the evidence in favour of cross-cultural consensus on the propriety of human rights and the desirability of what they are designed to protect. How are the skeptics to explain the fact that nearly every country in the world has joined the United Nations, and that the Charter of that organization commits all its members, among other things, to respect human rights? How to explain the fact that the overwhelming majority of countries have ratified various international human rights treaties, the most important of which being the International Bill of Rights, composed of the Universal Declaration and the two subsequent International Covenants? How to account for the fact that, within their own national constitutions, a great number of non-Western countries confer to individual citizens civil rights that are consonant with the human rights we are concerned with? It may interest readers to know that many non-Western countries, in addition to the above activities, have devised their own articulation of what human rights mean within their own cultural traditions. There is, for example, the African/Banjul Charter on Human and People's Rights (1981) and the Cairo Declaration on Human Rights in Islam (1990). These international treaties contain substantially the same core ideas about the need for minimally decent treatment of human beings as the supposedly "Western" understanding. Of course, such treaties include references and emphases not found in other documents—e.g., to Allah in the Cairo document—but they are not inconsistent with the elemental moral vision contained within the very idea of human rights and within other documents. Indeed, there are various treaties amongst Western countries themselves which do the same, adding nuances to the core idea for application to their own neck of the woods. Examples include the European Convention on Human Rights (1953), the Inter-American Convention on Human Rights (1969) and the Charter of Paris for a New Europe (1990).[2]

This cross-cultural consensus comes as no surprise, since the human rights idea is so thin and minimal, so elemental and fundamental to people's understanding of how a person ought minimally to be treated. Most of the world's moral traditions contain the idea that the human person has worth, and there is recognizable overlap among traditions regarding basic ethical propositions, such as the wrongness of murder and the desirability of forwarding human happiness. Furthermore, basic rational prudence is distributed pretty much regardless of ethical tradition, and we saw in Chapter 3 that self-regarding prudence can go a surprisingly long way toward persuading people about human rights. The minimal and baseline nature of human rights protection blunts much of the sharpness in the skeptic's accusations regarding Western arrogance, and the associated intolerance of difference. Human rights are not the be-all and end-all of moral and political debate: there is much to ethical life that is not captured in them. We glimpsed this in the last chapter, in the distinction between duties of justice and duties of benevolence. Thus, respecting human rights does not demand the utter sacrifice of one's own unique cultural traditions and peculiarities. There is much room *above the minimal threshold* for cultural difference, ethical pluralism, and the maintenance and enhancement of unique customs and traditions. So promoting human rights is not the same thing as promoting the Western, or American, way of life. Promoting human rights is about establishing everywhere the moral, legal and political protections designed to allow everyone the opportunity not just to live but to lead a minimally decent life—a life worthy of a human being. It is true that the logic of human rights demands the sacrifice of those practices that attack that value: it does set a limit on the degree of pluralism that reasonable people should tolerate.[3] Like any other moral value with real substance, the human rights idea does draw a line, and specifies that crossing it subjects one to legitimate resistance and perhaps punishment. Human rights, after all, would be completely empty and devoid of function if they ruled nothing out. Like anything else that is real and valuable in this life, human rights come with a price. But this price is not excessive and is well worth paying, since it amounts to nothing more than refraining from the infliction of grievous harm, and to nothing less than securing everyone's shot at enjoying a minimally decent life.

The final argument for the human rights defender to appeal to, in this regard, refers to globalization. Like it or not, we now live in a world where there are clear and powerful connections among all peoples. These connections include international trade, diplomacy, military alliances, travel and tourism, educational exchanges, development aid, the transmission of culture both high and low, and so on. Indeed, there is even a robust set of international institutions, ranging from regional associations—such as the European Union and the North American Free Trade Agreement—to genuinely global organizations, like the United Nations, the World Trade Organization, the International Court of Justice and the International Monetary Fund. This globalizing trend appears to be both widening and deepening: the world is drawing ever closer together. Now that our interconnections are genuinely international, we need core ground-rules to govern our interactions and our shared institutions. These ground-rules, at the very least, must make sense: they cannot permit the performance of contradictory practices. A relevant example of a pair of contradictory practices would be one that respects human rights and one that violates them. The global community must decide on a consistent set of ground-rules for everyone: we can no longer indulge contradictions like permitting rights violations abroad but insisting on rights realization at home. The *one* set of international institutions demands *one* set of coherent, plausible and defensible ground-rules. I suggest that such ground-rules importantly involve human rights. Human rights not only have their own moral force but also attract cross-cultural consensus. They are thin and minimal yet still vital and substantive. They establish core values yet still allow for some cultural pluralism and the expression of diversity. They fit the bill perfectly for inclusion in that set of ground-rules needed to forge further a developing international society.[4]

Needed Only in Free Market Societies?

The problem with human rights, according to Karl Marx, is that in spite of their supposed universality, they are useful only in the context of a mature, developed free-market society. Human rights, like all other kinds of rights, are part-and-parcel of capitalism. Capitalism is that mode of social organization which combines three elements: private property ownership of the means of production, free markets as the means of distribution, and money as the means of exchange. People and companies are allowed to own things like money, natural resources, land and technology. They use these things to produce articles for sale. The selling price is determined not by government fiat but by the interaction between supply and demand, and the deal is sealed with money. The motive driving a capitalist economy is personal profit, i.e., the desire to increase the amount of what one owns, the level of resources one has to realize one's dreams. Versions of capitalism have been the dominant forms of social organization in Western civilization, starting around the Industrial Revolution in the 1700s. Use of the term "capitalism" has waned in recent years, replaced by the softer-sounding "free market society." But the two terms are, by and large, interchangeable. They describe very important facets of the societies in which we live.

Marx, the philosophical fountainhead of modern communism, makes two important points in this regard. The first is that rights, human or otherwise, have a function only in a free-market society and thus are not universal. The second is that capitalism, in his eyes, is deserving of serious criticism, and ultimately of resistance and transformation. This is to say that human rights are, despite appearances, actually complicit in a deficient and decrepit mode of social organization. Rights are the children of capitalism, and the sins of the father are visited upon the son.[5]

Dealing with the first of Marx's claims, we must note his keen insight into the origin of rights thinking. It is no accident, he says, that the rights idea originated in Europe, for that is where the first free-market societies developed historically. It is also no coincidence that the consensus of human rights historians regarding the date of the advent of the natural or human rights idea is around the time of the transition between medieval feudalism and the early modern era, somewhere between 1300 and 1600. That was the time when the seeds of the modern economy were sown: the discovery of the New World; the development of freer trading relations between people; the decline of the Church and the rise of the secular nation-state; the decline of bartering and the rise of money-based transactions, which spurred the growth of banks; and the rise of an educated and entrepreneurial merchant class, who were members neither of the land-owning aristocratic "nobility" nor of the peasants labouring on the land as tenant farmers or outright serfs. The idea of natural, and eventually human, rights was not the product of people coming at last to discover the universal truths of morality and justice. The idea was invented because it suited the social situation then developing into the dominant mode of economic organization. The rhetoric of natural rights was first employed, historically, by the rising urban middle classes—such as merchants and professionals—to claim new powers and opportunities for themselves: opportunities they lacked in the pre-industrial *ancien régime*. Essentially, Marx suggests that the educated and ambitious middle classes, from the time in question, did to the land-owning aristocracy what the aristocracy had previously done to the monarchy, as we saw in connection with the Magna Carta of 1215. In the Magna Carta—as we saw in Chapter 4—the aristocracy offered the King tax contributions, but only in exchange for the Crown's recognition of their rights to due process, political participation, and land-ownership. Several centuries later, the middle classes did much the same thing: used their rising influence to demand recognition, this time from the aristocracy, of their own rights to property and participation. The middle classes were able to turn the aristocratic rhetoric of rights and entitlements against the aristocrats themselves, forcing their way onto the political stage and into higher levels of wealth and status.

Marx invites us to pay special attention to the centrality of private property in capitalism. The motor behind a free-market economy is the profit motive: capitalism elicits so much entrepreneurial energy and market competition because, in it, people are allowed to keep the fruits of their labour as their own private property. The lure of more profit and wealth, more resources and luxuries, is a powerful incentive in favour of productive activity for which there is market demand. The market rewards such activity with more money, which can in turn be used to generate even more, and so on. That is how people become enormously wealthy. But, generally, people would not be so productive if they were not guaranteed that they themselves will personally benefit from their own production. Would you work hard if you knew that the rewards of your work would go to someone else? Would you work at all if you knew that the fruits of your labour would become the property of another, or even public property for the state to distribute as it sees fit? It is essential to the capitalist way of life that people be given incentive to produce:

the best such incentive is to institute a system of private property rights whereby people are guaranteed ownership of the fruits of their labour. People will work because they know they will benefit from it: they get to keep the money they make and spend it however they like. The lure of even more money will drive them to keep it up, and before long we will have a thriving market economy. This is to say that, in Marx's view, the core right, historically, is the right to own and dispose of one's property as one sees fit. All other rights, human or otherwise, have been modelled after the primordial right to own property. Property is the prime mover; all else follows in its train. Indeed, the central image of rights thinking is modelled after that of the property-owner: there is the holder of rights, enjoying his space and using it however he wants. There he is, telling his neighbours what he is entitled to with regard to his property, and demanding from them that they respect his claims. The line between property-owner and right-holder is very fine indeed, and is no coincidence. Marx would say that, historically, they go together hand-in-hand. Human rights are essentially designed to make us all feel like property-owners, whether we really are or not. All of us, at the least, have "property" in ourselves, if not in other things. The very idea of human rights, Marx says, is shot through with a capitalist world-view.

Marx asserts that we do not have human rights to security, subsistence, liberty, and so on, because of genuine moral conviction. We have such rights, rather, because they are needed to grease the wheels of a free-market economy. People need food to be productive workers, so ensure they get it. They need freedom to engage in market bargaining, so give it to them. People need possession of their own property secured from force, theft and fraud—otherwise they will have no incentive to work—so set up an effective system of law and order, and so on. Morality and justice, in Marx's eyes, have nothing to do with it. Human rights were created, and enjoy such prominence today, because a free-market economy needs them to operate as best it can. Human rights are part-and-parcel of capitalism, and thus are not applicable to those parts of the world that sport different modes of social organization.

Large chunks of the planet do not have genuinely free markets. Examples include China, other parts of Southeast Asia, parts of the Middle East and Africa. Attempts to persuade such societies to adopt human rights, Marx would say, should be seen for what they really are: not attempts at genuine moral improvement but, rather, attempts at converting such countries to a capitalist organization. Trying to transform non-capitalist societies into ones that respect human rights is not so much an act of moral rescue as it is an attempt to crack open those markets and make more money. The rhetoric of universal morality, Marx believes, is employed as a kind of cosmetic cover-up for what is really going on, namely, the drive to convert the world into one big free market, open for business. The current trend toward globalization, the widespread adoption of capitalism and democracy, the dominance of the United States, and the spread of human rights are not isolated events all coming together by sheer happenstance. They are interwoven together into a nexus which, by intention or default, is structured to transform the world into one which is more productive and profitable. It is not about justice; it is about greed. It is all about bucks; the rest is merely diverting conversation.

Human rights defenders are seen by Marx, and his fans, as gullible suckers: sincerely believing in something which is not at all what it appears to be. Human rights seem to be genuinely moral, but are actually just one more tool in capitalist social engineering. The tool is all the more ingenious and effective because it is conceptual and not concrete, and so people do not often associate it with its real function. The real function is this: people should be educated about human rights, and human rights should be codified effectively into law because that will institutionalize some of the pillars needed for a free-market society.

Marx's second claim is that being complicit in the construction of such a society is not a praiseworthy enterprise. Marx, of course, is one of history's most ferocious and influential critics of capitalism. He levels three specific charges against it: exploitation, alienation, and instability.[6] Capitalist societies are composed of two social classes: those who own such major means of production as money, land, natural resources and technology, and those who own little more than their own labour power. Those who own the means of production are the capitalists, or "bourgeoisie," and they enjoy dominance in free-market societies. They form the wealthy and powerful elite, they do not have to work to survive, and they live a life of affluence and influence. Those who own only their own labour power are the workers, or "proletariat," and they do indeed have to work to survive. The workers are the underclass, and Marx believes that capitalists exploit workers by taking advantage of their neediness, paying them less than what they are really worth, i.e., less than what they produce for the capitalists. Workers have very little bargaining power with those who employ them. They need their jobs to survive; they cannot fall back on vast stocks of wealth. Capitalists realize this, and as a result they refuse to pay workers more than that amount needed to keep them coming back to work. Marx believes that, to the extent to which workers produce economic value for capitalists in excess of the amount capitalists pay them to keep them coming to work, they are exploited. The capitalist creams off all the "surplus value" of what his worker employees produce for him, refusing to spread the wealth around and exploiting the relative poverty, vulnerability and neediness of his fellow human beings.

Workers, when they realize their status as people whose vulnerability is being taken advantage of for another's gain, become alienated. This is to say that they become unfriendly and hostile; they experience separation from society and come to view it bitterly and with resentment. Capitalism also alienates people because it is, in Marx's eyes, a form of social organization at odds with human nature. Our nature as human beings is to become fully developed, well-rounded and self-actualized. We all want to flourish in this fashion. But capitalism prevents this. Since production is more efficient through the division of labour, capitalism forces most people to focus on developing but one small set of skills, and then to trade on it for the rest of their working lives. This one-dimensional existence—where one's life becomes dominated by the role one plays in the production process—is at odds with full human development, and so over time generates alienation.

Alienation, by causing resentment, produces instability. Bitterness and hostility will call forth resistance and agitation on the part of the workers for change in favour of a more equitable share of wealth and those resources needed to live a more diverse and well-rounded life. Capitalists will themselves resist such resistance, and eventually we will have a full-scale social conflict, a violent class struggle over social control. Marx hoped, and predicted, that the workers would win such a conflict and institute communism, a more equal form of social organization. Until that point, we should not be surprised to note that developed capitalist societies are plagued by serious, destabilizing problems that have their roots in the experience of exploitation and alienation: things like drug addiction, alcoholism, property theft, violence, labour strikes, and so on.

Marx denounced the "myths" of capitalism and argued that the idea of natural, or human, rights is one such fiction. Which myths? They are best captured in the very slogan of the pro-rights advocates behind the French Revolution: liberty, equality and fraternity. There is no denying that such concepts play a big role in human rights thinking today. In spite of this, Marx contends that none of these values can be realized in a free-market society. Are people truly free? His answer is no, since most people in a capitalist society have no choice but to go to work in order to survive. The mythology of free choice, autonomy and self-direction is flatly at odds with the fact that the vast majority have their socio-economic destiny—their very quality of life—in the hands of another. The extent of freedom in capitalism, according to Marx, is the freedom to choose which capitalist to be exploited by. Capitalists themselves, of course, enjoy much wider freedom of action, but even they are not the utterly free and self-directing beings presumed by the ideals of human rights slogans. Capitalists are like spiders caught in their own webs: they fret about their own profitability, they still have to compete against each other for market share, and so on. For Marx, the commitment to freedom is a fiction and illusion that ignores the dominant role that the economy plays in our lives: what use is telling people who are economically unfree that they nevertheless have the human right to be free, in some unspecified further sense? Marx's cynical reply: the use is precisely to take people's minds off their own economic entrapment and exploitation. Making them think they are free in one sense will undermine their anger and resistance about being unfree in the more important sense of their role in the economy.

What about fraternity and recognition? Is there, or can there be, a meaningful sense of fraternity in a free-market society? Marx again is skeptical: the capitalists themselves compete against each other over market share, social status, wealth and power. At best, they will feel among themselves a shared sense of superiority, but not a genuine spirit of brother- or sisterhood. The workers also have to compete against each other over jobs and promotions. In fact, capitalists do everything they can to encourage such competition, because they are the major beneficiaries of it in terms of quality of labour and quantity of output. Marx thus viewed attempts to get people to think in terms of fraternity, in the midst of a free-market economy, to be a sham. Whether it be nationalism, or ethnic, racial or religious commonality, or even an appeal to human solidarity, all such phenomena wither in the face of the most powerful social force under capitalism: economic competition. It is a dog-eat-dog world, and attempts to gloss it over by appealing to a human right of social recognition are doomed to fail.

Marx reserves his greatest rhetorical venom for the supposed right to equality in a free-market society. Capitalism is a necessarily unequal form of social organization, split sharply between the two great classes of capitalist and worker. This class divide generates enormous disparities between people regarding both standard of living and quality of life. Does an equality of legal rights, as citizens of a given country, change this? Marx's answer is no, because capitalists are clearly in a much better position than workers actually to enjoy their legal rights. Does a homeless person care that his right to freedom of movement is the exact same legal entitlement as that enjoyed by a wealthy factory owner? Do the rich and the poor really enjoy equal rights in a court of law, when the former can afford the very best lawyers and the latter get saddled with over-burdened public defenders? Can a poor woman just as readily take advantage of her right to run for public office as a wealthy woman can? Does a hard-working middle-class kid really enjoy an equality of opportunity with another child who stands to inherit millions upon reaching the age of majority? For Marx, these are all rhetorical questions, and they reveal that genuine equality—socio-economic equality—is simply not found in a free-market society. Indeed, equality is one of the values farthest away from the core commitments of a capitalist country. To what extent, then, can a human rights defender hope for success in persuading such a society to enact anything more than empty proclamations about an equality of dignity, respect, welfare, opportunity, and so on? Marx claims that only revolutionary transformation—wholesale institutional change—can bring about real equality, wherein everyone enjoys equal access to those productive resources which shape the structure of all our lives.

Marx offers cogent criticisms, but the human rights defender has the resources to reply. The first must, of course, refer to the abject failure of real-world communist regimes. Admittedly, such regimes—the former Soviet Union and Warsaw Pact countries, China, North Korea, Cuba, etc.—were not exactly what Marx had in mind when he defended communism, but the complete collapse of his project in real-world terms is relevant evidence of a kind. We simply have no other choice, at this historical moment, but to deal with human rights within non-communist contexts. Besides, real-world communist regimes were revealed to be horrible human rights violators. Soviet dictator Joseph Stalin was responsible for the deaths of millions; ditto for Cambodia's Pol Pot; the Cultural Revolution in China slaughtered tens of thousands; North Korea still cannot feed its own people, and negligently refuses outside food aid; and the natural environment in all such countries is appallingly dilapidated. All this is leaving unsaid the gross restrictions on personal freedom that are part-and-parcel of the communist perspective. This is not to deny that free-market societies have serious problems. It is, rather, to deny that communist regimes treat their people better than do free-market ones.

Indeed, it is a fact of some irony to note that, when communist regimes did flourish—i.e., during the Cold War, from the late 1940s to the early 1990s—they actually supported the human rights idea in spite of its capitalist origins. Cold War communist regimes were very vocal supporters of socio-economic, or "second-generation," human rights. They fancied themselves more progressive in this regard than free-market societies. Most of the communist countries even ratified the International Covenant on Economic, Social and Cultural Rights in the mid-1960s, while rejecting the International Covenant on Civil and Political Rights.[7] Did such societies fail to grasp the core anti-rights commitments of their own social doctrine? Marx would probably, in his imperious way, say so. But the rest of us might observe that such societies knew a good idea when they saw one, and tried as best they could to fit it into their own interpretation of social justice. This raises a powerful rejoinder to Marx: if human rights are applicable only to capitalist contexts, how is it that there is such a large cross-cultural consensus in favour of the notion that human rights specify genuinely universal minimum standards of decent treatment? Do people in non-capitalist countries who support human rights somehow err with regard to their own fundamental interests? Are they all just gullible dupes—the term used to be "running dogs"—of Western business interests? Which is the more plausible claim here: Marx's, or the idea that these people do indeed recognize that their own fundamental interests would be protected by human rights but the leaders of such societies do not want to extend such protection, and show such respect, because it would diminish their own power? Such leaders therefore brand the human rights idea as foreign: not only to their native culture but also to the path of economic development they have chosen. Against the self-serving claims of capitalist profiteers we have to weigh the self-serving claims of ruthless communist overlords.

It is important to note the degree of difference between the free-market societies of Marx's day and those of today. The industrial capitalist societies of Marx's time—the mid-1800s—were much more brutal than those we live in today. Conditions for factory workers right after the Industrial Revolution were truly degrading and disgusting. Workers had to put in impossibly long shifts, under dangerous conditions, in exchange for a pittance of a wage. Widespread access to health care and education was non-existent, and no one but the wealthy could participate in politics. There was not even an effective system of law and order of the same calibre we have today. Marx's call for the workers of *his* world to unite, to improve their lot in life, probably meets with a surprisingly large degree of historical consensus regarding its justice. But the magnitude of the transformations within free-market societies— over 150 years later—mitigates his criticism of capitalism. Nowhere today does there exist the kind of unconstrained, winner-take-all free market that Marx blasted. We have enacted a number of sensible laws to regulate the market and improve everyone's lot: laws against pollution, child labour and sexual harassment; laws against fraud and anti-competitive collusion; and regulations protecting the health and safety of both workers in their workplaces and consumers in their homes. In most developed free-market societies, we have made basic health care and education not just accessible to all, but actually enjoyed by the vast majority. Furthermore, everyone of age can vote, and most capitalist countries have functional systems of law and order. The most important changes between then and now, in this regard, have to do with the spread of democracy and the invention of minimal welfare state benefits to protect those not faring well in market competition. These twin forces of democracy and welfare have humanized the fierce capitalism of Marx's day and made it more responsive to everyone's well-being. This is not to say that each, or even any, of today's free market societies fully satisfies everybody's human rights. But it is to say that clear progress has been made on that front, and moreover to assert that the power of the very idea of human rights played a role in bringing about such progress.

Such changes were brought about in free-market societies because, among other things, people thought that human rights demanded them. So citizens agitated for the right to vote and to run for public office. This was granted on a mass scale in the industrialized West by the early 1920s. Following World War II, citizens demanded the provision of welfare benefits and investments in health care, education and unemployment insurance as a matter of elemental human dignity, as payback from the state for all their wartime sacrifices, and also to ensure that the desperate poverty of the Great Depression of the 1930s would not be repeated. Success was generally achieved. Defenders of human rights contend that it was no coincidence that these concrete improvements were made during a time featuring the increased prominence of the idea of human rights. We might say this: we can judge an idea's merit by looking at the real-world consequences of its implementation. By these lights, the idea of human rights seems, if not perfect, then at least far better than communism regarding the morally necessary aspects of individual behaviour and social ordering. Communism in practice has been a disaster, whereas human rights remain a real force for practical, progressive change.

Communism, moreover, can itself be subjected to moral criticism, on the grounds that it fails to pay sufficient respect to the worth of each and every individual person. Individuals are seen by communists—from Marx's day forward—as mere means to bringing about the end of a classless society. Persons are but props, mere pawns in the grand chess game of crushing capitalism. It was no accident that many communist societies experienced a number of slaughters and massacres—of thousands of people, sometimes more—in the name of achieving the collective good of socio-economic equality. The rights of workers, as a massive group or collective entity, were cited as "justifications" for gross violations of individual human rights. This was not some kind of deep paradox whose truth could be grasped only by Marxist gurus: it was a flat-out contradiction. We know now that a human rights-respecting society cannot be built using tools that themselves violate human rights. If it is garbage in, then it is garbage out: communism shows this. There must be a comprehensive consistency between means and ends in shaping a society that can fulfil the requirements of minimal justice.

Marx's conviction that the human rights idea serves only as a conceptual cover-up for the sins of capitalism stands in need of refutation. Marx displays real historical insight when he writes about the link between the rise of rights and the rise of free-market economies. There are indeed clear similarities between the idea of a right-holder and that of a property owner, and the right of property probably was among the very first ever to win acceptance and codification into law. But from these truths the rest of Marx's criticisms do not follow. For they are predicated on the idea that human rights are always, so to speak, in a passive position: always explaining things away after the fact; always distracting people from gritty reality with pretty pictures of morality. But this is not always true: human rights sometimes occupy an active position, insisting that changes be made in a long-held practice, or transformations begun of a powerful institution. Examples abound, including those of democracy and welfare mentioned already. Sometimes an appeal to human rights *is* an appeal to the stark reality of how a person or group has been brutally treated, and why such treatment must be stopped and punished. This is to say that human rights, in addition to justifying a certain way of life, also *provide a critical standard for judging ways of life*. Human rights can be used to criticize shortcomings in capitalist countries as readily as they can be used to justify or even praise those other things such countries get right. This is what Marx got wrong: he failed to appreciate the critical function of human rights, because he focussed exclusively on the flip-side function of justification. If human rights provide a justification for something, then they also provide a criticism when that something fails to happen. I know of no human rights defender who believes that the developed free-market democracies have nothing to improve on in connection with human rights. All countries can—and morally must—make progress in this regard. Some countries have further to go than others, but pointing that out is neither Eurocentric nor pro-capitalist: it is the simple truth. Human rights thus serve as genuinely universal, and minimal, standards of decent treatment, according to which we can both justify some, and criticize other, social conditions.

Male Bias?

There is a handful of feminist thinkers[8] who object to rights, whether human or more specialized, on the grounds that they are expressive of a man's point of view. Such feminists are apt to point to the fact that, not only were human rights first devised in Western European capitalist countries, they were moreover devised by prominent *men* in such countries. So, like previous criticisms, the feminist one suggests that the source of the human rights idea reveals something important, and importantly limited, about the idea itself. Given the historical suppression of women by men, we are well advised to beware of ideas with such a pedigree. The dissemination of the human rights idea has been just that: the transmission of specifically male values from one culture to another, from one generation to the next.

The contemporary origins of this line of rights criticism stems from Carol Gilligan's landmark 1982 study, *In a Different Voice*.[9] Gilligan, a psychologist, did some empirical studies on the ethical attitudes of a group of 29 female research subjects. She concluded from them that women generally are disposed to think about normative issues in a way unique from men. Whereas men are much more likely to view moral issues in terms of universal rules and rights, or of promoting everyone's fundamental interests, women view ethics more through the prism of a particular relationship. Whereas men demand that their rights be realized, or insist that utilities be maximized, women prefer that people develop the character traits displayed by those engaged in a rewarding personal relationship. So men praise traits like impartiality, objectivity, autonomy, reasonableness and the performance of duties whereas women look more for empathy, sympathy, loyalty, community and a sense of responsibility for nurturing others. In short, Gilligan carved a sharp distinction between "an ethic of rights" and an "ethics of care." Her main aim in doing so was to call attention to the purported facts of how women perceive morality differently: how they speak about ethics "in a different voice." She was less concerned about comparing the strengths and weaknesses of each such ethic. But others such as Annette

Baier, Nel Noddings and Virginia Held have been glad to do so. In their works, they suggest that the male ethic of rights, with its insistence on abstract universality, ignores the degree to which human beings are concrete creatures with deep ties to other people and to particular historical communities. The male ethic, with its insistence on claims and rights, alongside correlative duties and obligations, expresses a kind of aggressive selfishness: this is what *I* am entitled to, and this is what *you* must do to ensure I enjoy it. The male ethic presupposes a separation between people that not only assumes a background potential for conflict, it actually makes such conflict more likely by modelling personal relationships in this way. The male ethic, in short, is artificial and assertive, calculating and competitive, disconnected and disadvantageous. It is, more than anything, about keeping score: who is entitled to what, and who owes whom. The world would be a better place if we could manage to move beyond this traditional, male-dominated understanding and toward an ethics of care. What would that involve, exactly? Instead of competition, cooperation; instead of disconnection, community; instead of artificiality, reality; instead of asserting oneself, nurturing and enabling others, and being cared for in turn. Care for others mean sympathizing with them and supporting them, helping them develop their skills, being committed to a personal connection with them based on trust and mutual respect, taking on responsibility to do what one can to ensure their well-being. It is far better to raise children, and to encourage each other as adults, to be people who care for others in this way than to portray the social world as a mere collection of separate and selfish individuals, each shouting about their rights and what the world owes them.

The defence of human rights from such accusations would first involve a skepticism regarding whether men and women genuinely have such different views on morality and justice. Of course, there are real and substantial differences between the sexes, but does it follow that, "generally," there is such a sharp, gender-specific split in world views? Is it really true that, morally speaking, men are from Mars and women from Venus? There are serious questions to raise about Gilligan's method of generalizing from 29 research subjects in a controlled experimental environment to women in general living their lives in the world at large. In fairness, Gilligan herself admits that there *can* be men who have more the ethics of care approach, just as there can be women who live and breathe the ethics of rights approach. We have all met nurturing men as well as competitive and assertive women. The main problem this feminist criticism runs up against is the degree to which women have shown themselves to be not simply committed to the human rights idea but sometimes among its most energetic advocates and activists.

From the very start of human rights movements, women have employed the language and moral substance of the idea to combat male suppression and unjustified social superiority. For instance, barely a year had passed following the 1789 proclamation of the French Declaration of the Rights of Man and Citizen than Olympe de Gouge published her own *Declaration of the Rights of Woman*. In it de Gouge criticized the male revolutionaries for leaving out of their work a concern for equality between the sexes. She then proceeded to offer an article-by-article re-wording of the original Declaration as it might appear if it also took the fundamental interests of women to heart. Two years later, and on the other side of the English Channel, Mary Wollstonecraft published her *Vindication of the Rights of Women*, making a special plea for the provision of decent education to girls and young women.[10] Over the next few generations, socialist groups took up issues of women's rights—particularly regarding access to education and to decent working conditions—and of course by the mid-1800s there began a sustained campaign to secure for adult women the right to vote and participate in public elections. The movement for female suffrage ended up being successful, at least in Western countries, by the 1920s. During this time and beyond, women secured effective rights to own their own property, to enter the work force *en masse*, to get a divorce if desired, to control their reproductive choices more soundly, and ultimately to compete for, and win, some of the very top positions in business, the professions and government.

All of the above considerations underline the notion that women have been able to make very effective use of the human rights idea to secure greater equality, alongside other fundamental interests in liberty, security, subsistence and recognition. Most national constitutions enshrine norms prohibiting discrimination on the basis of gender, and in 1979 there was an international treaty signed called the Convention of the Elimination of Discrimination Against Women. This Convention was followed, in 1993, by powerful passages on gender equality in the Vienna Declaration, and more recently in the 1995 Beijing Declaration. Such is the appeal and meaningfulness of the human rights idea that women have been able to make use of it to forward their interests and even to resist precisely the very kind of male oppression feminists criticize. This is not to say that everything is fine, and that all women have all of their human rights satisfied, anymore than it is to say that all men have all of theirs satisfied. The point, rather, is that there seems to be very little to the feminist suggestion that the human rights idea has itself been part of the traditional male suppression of women. Indeed, the opposite seems more historically accurate: the idea has proved to be a powerful tool in woman's struggle for secure access to her vital needs, including the need to be free from suppression and discrimination based on an arbitrary characteristic like gender.[11]

The further observation might be made that the ethics of care can seem itself to be based on a kind of gender stereotyping that feminists criticize chauvinists for. The sharp split that some of the feminists make seems itself based on the idea that men are assertive, independent, competitive and reasonable whereas women are supportive, dependent, cooperative and emotional. I have not done formal, empirical studies to prove this in a scholarly way, but my own experience in life suggests to me that these claims are, at best, exaggerated and, at worst, inaccurate and stereotypical. The split is simply not as sharp as the feminist criticism makes it out to be. This is true regarding not only people's behaviours but also moral theory itself. Theories of ethics and justice, some already discussed in detail in this text, have always included references to both reason and passion, both obligation and emotion, both justice and benevolence. There is no reason why we cannot have both as parts of our shared social existence. It is undeniable that to live in a caring community would be a desirable thing and a real pleasure to experience. But from this fact it does not follow that we can dispense with all talk of universal rules and human rights. We can actually see the two supposedly separate projects inhabiting one coherent world-view. This world-view would insist on relying, first, on ideas of justice and human rights to secure a social minimum guaranteeing to all secure access to the objects of vital human need. This still leaves open the subsequent pursuit of a social maximum, an ideal of aspiration that the ethics of care may well furnish. In other words, the ethics of rights is designed to secure the floor and foundations, whereas the ethics of care is better thought of as constructing the ceiling, for the structures of our shared social life. Human rights do *not* provide us with everything we want out of moral life: the ethics of care do reveal our aspirations for more than a minimum. But human rights were never, or at least should never be, thought of in that way. Winston Churchill once made a witty remark when he first heard of America's decision, in 1941, to get involved in World War II. He cautioned: "This is not the end, nor even the beginning of the end. But it is, perhaps, the end of the beginning." An analogous point holds true of human rights, when properly perceived. They do not answer all our concerns and hopes, and so they do not exhaust moral and political life. What human rights are designed to do is ensure the security of a social minimum of decent treatment for all. The rest— the pursuit of the maximum, of an even more just and pleasant society— is still up for argument and effort, still up for grabs among ourselves and future generations.

Selfish and Antisocial?

We turn now from criticisms surrounding the universality of human rights to those surrounding their consequences. The first major criticism under this heading is the accusation that human rights disrupt social cohesion, since they express and reward selfish and antisocial attitudes. We have already glimpsed shades of this accusation from both Marx and the feminists. Marx once remarked that "none of the rights of man go beyond egoistic man." Feminists sometimes argue that rights express male self-assertion and competitive individualism. The image of the rights-holder they share is very much like the picture of the character Shylock in Shakespeare's play, *The Merchant of Venice*: greedy, narrow-minded, self-centred, insensitive to others, insisting on getting his own pound of flesh even though he does not need it and regardless of the damage done to other people. More recently, Mary Ann Glendon has written that our contemporary obsession with "rights talk" in all its forms has had the effect of diminishing both the width and depth of the common life we share.[12] With each right we enumerate—each second-level object specification we come up with—we take something out of the realm of public policy and put it into the realm of private entitle-ment. Not surprisingly, this leads ordinary people to put most of their time and energy into forwarding and asserting their own rights claims, as opposed to working, in a publicly spirited way, toward the common good. Since rights-claiming necessarily involves individual assertion, this trend can only undermine people's skills at, and willingness to engage in, the development of such vital virtues as taking on responsibility, negoti-ating, and being willing to make reasonable compromises so that progress can be made on public policy issues. Rights talk, critics fear, has this disturbing tendency to crowd other issues out of the limelight, forc-ing them backstage. Rights are not just major political stars: they are out-rageous prima donnas, demanding everyone's undivided attention and respect. But since rights do not capture everything important in moral and political life—something we just admitted at the end of the last sec-tion—it follows that political discourse and social action are impover-ished by rights, whether human or more specialized.

Communitarians, like Michael Sandel and Amitai Etzioni,[13] have written eloquent testimonials about a collapse in public-spiritedness since rights talk came to dominate political life. Their complaints are not simply nostalgic laments for a lost way of life; they are rooted as well in a fear that this phenomenon can only lead to more antisocial behaviour, brazen selfishness, and ultimately fragmentation and conflict. Over time, rights rupture: they tear apart a shared sense of public life and the common good, finally leaving every man and woman to fend for themselves. What the idea of the rights-holder does, above all, is shove to the side the idea of the good citizen. Instead of the ethics of rights, the politics of atomistic individualism and stubborn insistence on selfish entitlements, we need the ethics of the good citizen, the politics of the common good and a willingness to compromise one's claims out of public spirit and with an eye toward preserving a life rich with community feeling and interconnecting support structure.

This is an interesting criticism but it, too, fails to persuade. For example, it is deeply unclear whether the rise in rights talk has *actually caused* a collapse in public-spiritedness, or rather whether such a collapse was brought about by something else, and that an ethic of rights simply speaks more accurately and honestly to the aspirations of the new age. It seems to me, to the extent to which the common ground has shrunk, that it has been because of major shifts in social structures and not because of the supposedly corrosive individualism of the rights idea. Some closely-knit communities have indeed been ruptured and transformed by emigration and immigration, by technological innovations (especially in communications) and by changes in the economy that stress the value of mobility and the development of a skill set that is saleable worldwide. These social shifts have mixed people of different backgrounds like never before. The differences in their beliefs and values have put pressure on political structures to pay less attention to preserving a traditional way of life and more attention to ensuring basic fairness for all. Rights, far from rupturing, actually fill in a moral gap left behind by the collapse of traditional "community values." Rights are actually a more appropriate and plausible candidate to dominate moral and political life in our time, because they reflect, better than any of their competitors, the salient aspects of life in the modern world. As the world becomes more globally interconnected, we can actually predict with some confidence a further rise in rights talk. This trend is for the better, because it shifts public discourse away from controversies regarding whose traditions should prevail toward a more neutral set of concerns regarding equal entitlements for all regardless of background.

This is to say that an emphasis on rights may actually help to smooth over political ruptures, as opposed to provoking or even creating them. The idea that rights, including human rights, are essentially selfish and antisocial fails to carry with it the stamp of necessity. Sure, there are selfish bastards out there who only care about their own private concerns, and the rest of the world be damned. Some people really do seem to use their rights in a Shylockean, belligerently self-assertive way. They treat their rights like sticks to beat back the rest of the world, preventing it from horning in on their own personal universe. But that is more a matter of such people's own psychological shortcomings than it is a legitimate criticism of the very idea of rights. Consider the fact that rights necessarily presuppose a social context. Rights were not invented so that modern man could fancy himself a rock, or an island. They were invented to try and ensure elemental fairness between people living together in society. Remember, there are no rights-holders without correlative duty-bearers. An emphasis on rights necessarily comes hand-in-hand with an emphasis on responsibilities. Rights can be made real only when relevant others and institutions behave appropriately. So there is not the one-sidedness alleged by rights critics. Furthermore, the idea of human rights especially seems as much a wonderful affirmation of social solidarity as it does a glorification of the individual person. It *is* true that human rights are rights that individuals have, but *all* individuals get to have them: membership in the human rights club is much more socially inclusive than membership in any other kind of moral or political community. How can that be consistent with selfishness? The institutions demanded by human rights thus actually seem to be an expression of values shared between people, as opposed to those that tear them apart. We ought never to overlook the minimalism of human rights in this regard, realizing that such a focus on ensuring a baseline of decent treatment for all still leaves communities with plenty of room to preserve local customs, traditions, and ways of life.

Finally, if respect for rights supposedly generates fragmentation and conflict, try on the other hand the violation of rights. I suppose it *is* true to say that any moral idea of genuine substance and worth is going to generate some controversy. Fine, but what is the alternative? Against the risk that some people will use their rights as an excuse to opt out of social togetherness, we have to weigh the much more serious risk of not enshrining respect for human rights at all. That risk, we know from history, would involve not only actual rights violations but also—through them—the production of division and conflict, resistance and violence.

The violation of human rights is much more damaging and divisive than the respect for them ever could be.

At Odds with Good Governance?

Some critics allege that in making respect for rights—especially human rights—the foundation for social policy is at odds with sound public administration and good governance. These critics base their allegation on the notions that rights are too rigid and inflexible, that rights are neither particular nor practical, and that rights elevate private advantage over general public welfare—something that they insist must be the overriding aim of any praiseworthy politician.

A fellow named Edmund Burke made memorable remarks on how the idea of rights can be based on assumptions that are too general and impractical. Burke was a prominent parliamentarian in Britain during the era of the first rights revolutions in America and France. In 1790, Burke published his *Reflections on the Revolution in France,* a polemic critical not only of that particular revolution but also of the general idea of universal rights.[14] A skilled statesman, in Burke's eyes, is one who is an experienced legislator and a polished politician. A good political leader is a person firmly rooted and experienced in the community he hopes to lead. Such a leader should have paid his dues over time, gaining insight and exposure into all different matters of statecraft. So he should know about national defence and municipal road repair, about promoting trade abroad and levying appropriate taxes back home, and be as comfortable talking about public health and safety as he is about proposed reforms to the criminal law. A good governor is, above all, a man of his time and place: someone who knows his own people, who has gained their trust, and who has demonstrated real skill in handling their affairs for the better. These traits can only be developed over time, through trials of experience, with hard work and real attention paid to particular details of the community in question. No good political leader operates as an island, in abstraction from his own time and place, and lording it over his "subjects." He must, rather, get along well with other political leaders and, frequently, make sound compromises between competing interests amongst his people. Rights, Burke says, are at odds with good governance—as thus defined—because they insist, in extreme fashion, on their own satisfaction, come hell or high water. Rights advocates are extremists unskilled and untested in the pragmatic arts of political compromise. "What is the use," Burke asks, "of discussing a man's abstract right to food or medicine? The [real] question is upon the method of procuring or administering them. In that deliberation I shall always advise to call in the aid of the farmer and the physician, rather than the professor of metaphysics." "The pretended rights" of universal rights advocates, in Burke's terms, "are all extremes: and in proportion as they are metaphysically true, they are ... politically false."[15]

Burke views the concern with universal rights as an artificial and rigid construction of theory, as opposed to a more natural and flexible application of practice. Universal rights form a simplistic, cookie-cutter approach to politics, when most often it is complex negotiations and well-crafted compromises that are in order. The world of politics, in Burke's eyes, does not usually admit of the clear-cut, black-and-white distinctions favoured by rights advocates, such as those drawn between right-holder and duty-bearer, entitlements and objects, individuals and institutions, and so on. He asserts that "the rights of man are in a sort of middle, incapable of definition, but not impossible to be discerned. The rights of men in government are their advantages; and these are often in balances between differences of good; in compromises sometime between good and evil, and sometimes between evil and evil." We note, in this quotation, that Burke does not utterly reject rights: what he rejects are rights that are universal and abstract, i.e., human rights. He takes particular aim at rights to equality and to political participation: he once labelled democracy "the most shameful thing in the world." Of equality, he assures us that "those who attempt to level, never equalise. In all societies ... some description must be uppermost. The levellers, therefore, only change and pervert the natural order of things; they load the edifice of society, by setting up in the air what the solidity of the structure requires to be on the ground."[16] One cannot square the circle: all people are not equal, and pretending so as a matter of human right is dangerous nonsense, since it will create false hopes in those of lesser talents and real resentment in those of greater. Burke's vision of political entitlements is elitist, hierarchical and conservative: he believes in a privileged class of well-trained and wise legislators coming together to rule a community in accord with its best traditions and interests.

The only rights that Burke respects are those specific to a certain country, entitlements that flow naturally out of the shared way of life a particular community has built for itself over generations. Such rights are to be trusted over time. The very fact that they have prevailed, and are preserved, shows for Burke that such rights serve a function that that community values. "You will observe," Burke intones, that from Magna Charta to the Declaration of Right, it has been the uniform policy of our [i.e., British] constitution to claim and assert our liberties, as an entailed inheritance derived to us from our forefathers, and to be transmitted to our posterity; as an estate specially belonging to the people of this kingdom, without any reference whatever to any other more general or prior right. By this means our constitution preserves unity in so great diversity of its parts.[17]

New-fangled rights that defy historical reality and political recognition—rights that have merely been claimed but not yet acknowledged—actually destabilize a political community, threatening to usurp rightful authority from experienced statesmen to the unwashed mob.

Jeremy Bentham, writing around the same time, shared Burke's fear of destabilization. He wrote that defenders of the universal rights of humanity speak "a terrorist language," one that enshrines the idea that "the madman has as good a right to govern everybody, as anyone to govern him." Human rights, for Bentham, express "anarchical fallacies." Bentham preferred a system of political leadership wherein wise legislators, versed in utilitarianism, would rule for the betterment of the entire public. He admitted, though, that democracy was probably the only way to ensure that public policies would tend to public welfare over time.[18]

Utilitarianism, of course, is a view of morality, politics and law that places prime emphasis on achieving "the greatest happiness for the greatest number." The most desirable form of social organization is the form that provides us with the most desirable things and experiences. Pleasure and happiness are the utilitarian's focus, and Bentham suggests that the best political leaders are not those guided by grand visions or sublime horizons but, rather, those mindful to make concrete and measurable improvements in people's lives. The best politicians have public spirit and make those decisions that increase the amount of pleasure and happiness in their communities. A successful statesman is one who leaves his people subjectively happier, and objectively better off, than they were before he came to power through their vote. It should be noted that Bentham practised what he preached. He was not just a theorist: he involved himself in policy reforms designed to enhance public welfare in Great Britain in the late eighteenth and early nineteenth centuries. These reforms focussed on promoting public health and safety, literacy, higher education, the right to vote, and on humanizing the kinds of sentences and punishments routinely meted out by the criminal justice system. Utilitarianism used to be the dominant doctrine on these, and related, issues until human rights rose to prominence in the mid-1900s, but it probably still today captures a very widespread belief regarding the purpose of politics. Many people seem to agree with Bentham's idea that political leadership is about tending to the public good: making smart policies that increase the common person's health, wealth and happiness. Rights critics like Bentham argue that rights get in the way of this process. Rights often serve as roadblocks on the journey toward maximizing public welfare and happiness. Rights, among other things, carve out a protected space wherein people are free to do what they wish, regardless of whether the public finds it pleasing, tasteful, productive or sensible. Think of homeowners who keep their property poorly, or who stubbornly refuse to sell their land to make way for a much needed highway. Or think of those inventors who refuse to share beneficial information or innovations—like a promising new medicine—without first being assured of making their own fortune. Think of those people who refuse to donate their bodies for medical purposes after they die, in spite of the great good that could be done and the total lack of harm and cost to themselves. Or think of those charged with serious criminal offences doing everything they can to exercise every last one of their rights without regard to the public interest or to those they have victimized. Indeed, rights are designed, as Dworkin has said, to serve as trumps, outranking the pursuit of the greatest happiness for the greatest number. But Bentham suggests that it is precisely this function that makes rights unsuitable as a sound basis for social policy. For such policy must, almost by definition, serve the common or public good, else the fabric of society dissolves. Smart policy serves the majority, and will succeed over its rivals in generating the greatest happiness for the greatest number. Individual claims of human rights, as trumps over the public welfare, not only reduce overall social happiness, they also threaten the balance of good political judgment and ultimately the stability of our shared social existence. The real danger of rights, in Bentham's mind, is that they put private advantage and personal entitlement over public gain and the common good. In doing so, rights shrink the solidarity needed in society, reduce fellow-feeling, make sound compromise very difficult and ultimately make the world worse off by erecting barriers and roadblocks to the maximization of people's pleasure.[19]

The resources to reply to both Burke and Bentham on this topic of rights and governance are deep. A human rights defender should, first, stress the minimalism of human rights. This, for example, blunts much of Burke's critique: there is plenty of political space left, after human rights have been realized, for the kind of historically sensitive and culturally relative political compromising that Burke so admires. As to rigidity, it has been noted repeatedly that gone are the days when human rights were thought to be absolute. Human rights are high-priority reasons that *generally* trump rival claims but they can themselves be overturned, by utilitarian appeals, in the face of a genuine social emergency. Human rights remain firm, but not rigid; they are high-priority, but not invincible, reasons for personal and political action. As to their simplicity, this should be seen as a clear virtue. No one can deny the complexities of political leadership in a modern society. But the basic requirements of morality and justice are not complex. To say that everyone is owed a minimally decent standard of treatment is not to indulge childish naïveté: it is clearly compelling to even the most worldly sophisticate. The minimalism of the human rights idea again saves it from Burke's criticism here: surely we want the basic elements of morality and justice to be clear and simple, as opposed to controversial and complex. There indeed comes a point in personal and political life where one simply sees the better reason over the worse, and the use of firm, black-and-white distinctions—e.g., between right and duty, right and object, or respect and violation—flows from this fact. The foundations of political life *should* be simple and reasonable, clear and morally compelling.

Burke and Bentham both allege that respect for human rights jeopardizes social stability. We know now that their comments were exaggerated by their own fears of how the French Revolution was then unfolding. Sure, *that* Revolution generated violence and terror, and then paved the way for Napoleon's military dictatorship, but over the long term it heightened European consciousness regarding the treatment of people and the need for more inclusive and progressive forms of governance. Other pro-rights revolutions, notably the American, turned out more successfully—even in the short term. Realizing rights may, admittedly, destabilize those regimes that violate rights, but it is by no means obvious that tranquility and stability ought to be the overriding values in such countries. It remains plausible to suggest that it is far more divisive, over time, to violate or ignore human rights than it is to pursue their realization.

The issue of democracy divides Burke and Bentham. Burke the conservative criticizes it and, since he associates human rights with it, blasts them both. Bentham, a more liberal social reformer, supported a widening of the vote, but suggested that human rights are, in fact, antidemocratic. Rights get in the way of the public good with their assertions of private entitlement. They try to take things away from the claims of the commonwealth for the sake of purely personal possession and enjoyment. I will not spend more time refuting Burke's criticism, since the sun has so clearly set on his brand of hierarchical conservatism and anti-democratic elitism. The man was a fervent monarchist, and perhaps that says enough. Bentham's suggestion, however, is more serious. Most human rights advocates support democracy and so it would be a major setback if it turned out that human rights are essentially anti-democratic.

In a way, Bentham's claim contains real truth: human rights have anti-democratic aspects to them. They are designed to ensure, for everyone, secure access to the objects of vital human need *regardless of what the majority prefers*. Human rights were established not only to challenge conservative elitism and to crack open hitherto closed institutions but also to resist what Alexis de Tocqueville first diagnosed as "the tyranny of the majority." Many of the major human rights disasters of the twentieth century involved the persecution, and worse, of disfavoured minority groups. Individuals need protection not only from criminals and dictators but also from a malign majority abusing its democratic control over core social institutions. Respect for rights may thus call for the implementation of some so-called "counter-majoritarian" measures. Important examples of these include a codified bill or charter of rights, a judiciary and police system that operate independently from those legislative bodies that enact the democratic will of the majority, and the empowering of the judiciary with the authority to review and perhaps reject legislative measures that violate human rights. Most of these measures are features of the societies in which we live, and they help to ensure that a robust respect for democracy does not degenerate into a nasty mob rule that takes unjustified aim at disfavoured individuals or unpopular groups. Judicial review, in particular, continues to serve as a major tool for human rights protection in even the most developed democracies.[20]

Bentham is correct to say that, sometimes, human rights get in the way of legislative schemes to maximize overall public pleasure and social happiness. What he is wrong to say is that this is something human rights defenders should apologize, and be criticized, for. That is precisely what human rights are designed to do: provide everyone, and not just "the greatest number," with secure access to the objects that they vitally need to live a minimally decent life in the modern world. Human rights defenders insist that it is far more important to secure for everyone the social minimum of decent treatment for all than it is to secure the maximization of the majority's happiness. The idea that society should try to maximize the majority's happiness, when there are still people who are not being treated in even a minimally decent way, is for human rights defenders what stands in need of criticism and apology. Bentham's "greatest happiness for the greatest number" is not only consistent with, but may actually call for, outrageous individual sacrifice in the name of the common good. Bentham says "so be it" if that is needed to generate more social utility, whereas a human rights advocate says "resist it" and insists on the principle that individuals have rights not to be treated as mere tools or toys to further the pleasure of others. Human beings, as those who both have and lead their own lives, do *not* have to apologize for refusing to sacrifice their own vital needs and fundamental interests in favour of further social advancements. If a conflict between the two threatens, a just society does not have the authority to sacrifice the individual; he or she has the right to be left alone. A society that does not respect human rights is not a society sporting sound and balanced social policy. Such a society is one that has failed to give every one of its members reason to sign on to its social contract.

These reflections and admissions do not add up to Bentham's belief that rights are necessarily anti-democratic. The relationship is more complex. Surely the raw historical fact that concern for human rights first fully flourished in democratic societies shows some positive correlation between the two. Furthermore, most human rights advocates argue that the first-level human rights objects of liberty and security imply second-level specifications to political participation. It is clear that the spirit of democracy and the spirit of human rights still share much in common. Democracy is inspired by the vision of "one person, one vote": this vision contains norms of universality and equality, which we have already shown are central to human rights ideals. Democracy arose, historically, out of anger at severe social exclusion and official oppression: human rights defenders also struggle against such things. Democracy is, above all, about everyone's right to participate in those institutions that have a major impact on one's life—that indeed shape the structure of our shared social existence. Democracy is ultimately about self-governance. It is about letting people live their own lives. Human rights are likewise expressive of autonomy and personal freedom for self-direction. In both cases we note that people should be free to govern themselves, so long as they do not abuse such freedom by unjustly harming others. If they do so, they forfeit their rights. We have discovered that, historically, some counter-majoritarian measures are necessary to prevent whole societies from abusing their right of self-governance to harm others in their midst. Thus, we at last understand how such apparently anti-democratic measures actually remain faithful to democracy's deepest purpose.[21]

Conclusion

Since human rights are so prominent and powerful, they attract much criticism. It is important to note that such criticism comes from all sides of the political spectrum and focuses on whether human rights are really universal and truly beneficial. It is even more important to note that the defender of human rights has the resources to reply to all such criticisms in a satisfying way. Human rights are neither perfect nor invincible but they remain both vital and reasonable. Those who deny the idea of human rights, and the moral minimum it stands for, occupy a poor position, and they have their work cut out for them.

Notes

1 A. Pollis and P. Schwab, eds., *Human Rights: Cultural and Ideological Perspectives* (New York: Praeger, 1979); A. Milne, *Human Rights and Human Diversity* (London: Macmillan, 1986); T. Dunne, ed., *Human Rights in Global Politics* (Cambridge: Cambridge University Press, 1999); and T. Evans, *U.S. Hegemony and The Project of Universal Human Rights* (New York: St. Martin's, 1996).

2 For a sampling of national constitutions that attempt to enshrine global human rights norms, see pp. 348-50 of H. Steiner and P. Alston, *International Human Rights in Context: Law, Politics, Morals*, 2nd ed. (Oxford: Oxford University Press, 2000). For more on various international law documents, consult not only Steiner/Alston but also *Twenty-Five Human Rights Documents* (New York: Columbia University Center for the Study of Human Rights, 1995). See also Appendix B's human rights research tool.

3 J. Rawls, *The Law of Peoples* (Cambridge, MA: Harvard University Press, 1999), 78-82.

4 I owe this point to Thomas Pogge. See his "The International Significance of Human Rights," *Journal of Ethics* 1 (2000): 45-69.

5 The material in this section draws upon Marx's entire body of work, for instance as collected and edited in E. Kamenka, ed., *The Portable Karl Marx* (New York: Penguin, 1983). See especially "On The Jewish Question," pp. 95-115. See also: T. Campbell, *The Left and Rights* (London: Routledge Kegan Paul, 1983); S. Lukes, *Marxism and Morality* (Oxford:

Oxford University Press, 1985); and P. Kain, *Marx and Ethics* (Oxford: Clarendon, 1988).

6 For these criticisms, see especially Marx's *Communist Manifesto* (203-42) and *The German Ideology* (162-97) in Kamenka, ed., *Portable Marx*.

7 We saw in Chapter 1 that these two covenants, alongside the Universal Declaration, form the so-called International Bill of Human Rights.

8 A. Baier, *A Progress of Sentiments*, 2nd ed. (Cambridge, MA: Harvard University Press, 1994); N. Noddings, *Caring: A Feminine Approach to Ethics and Moral Education* (Berkeley: University of California Press, 1984); V. Held, *Feminist Morality* (Chicago: University of Chicago Press, 1993); and R. Tong, *Feminine and Feminist Ethics* (Belmont, CA: Wadsworth, 1993).

9 C. Gilligan, *In a Different Voice*, 2nd ed. (Cambridge, MA: Harvard University Press, 1993).

10 For the most relevant excerpts from both de Gouge and Wollstonecraft, see M. Ishay, ed., *The Human Rights Reader* (New York: Routledge, 1997), 140-58.

11 See Ishay, *Reader*, 461-68, 479-91 for texts of the Convention and Declarations. For more, see A. Wolper and J. Peters, eds., *Women's Rights, Human Rights: International Feminist Perspectives* (New York: Routledge, 1995); and M. Agosin, ed., *A Map of Hope: Women's Writings on Human Rights* (New Brunswick, NJ: Rutgers University Press, 1999).

12 Marx, "Jewish Question," 96-97; and M.A. Glendon, *Rights Talk: The Impoverishment of Political Discourse* (New York: Free Press, 1991).

13 M. Sandel, *Liberalism and The Limits of Justice* (Cambridge: Cambridge University Press, 1982); and A. Etzioni, *The Spirit of Community* (New York: Touchstone, 1994).

14 E. Burke, *Reflections on the Revolution in France* (London: Macmillan, 1988). See also the superb study and collection of J. Waldron, *Nonsense Upon Stilts: Bentham, Burke and Marx on The Rights of Man* (London: Methuen, 1987).

15 Burke, *Reflections*, 10-12.

16 Burke, *Reflections*, 16-19.

17 Burke, *Reflections*, 23-24.

18 J. Bentham, *Introduction to the Principles of Morals and Legislation* (Oxford: Oxford University Press, 1981), 47-52.

19 R.G. Frey, *Utility and Rights* (Oxford: Blackwell, 1985); R.M. Hare, *Moral Thinking* (Oxford: Clarendon, 1981); A. Sen and B. Williams, eds., *Utilitarianism and Beyond* (Cambridge: Cambridge University Press, 1982); and J. Glover, ed., *Utilitarianism and Its Critics* (London: Macmillan, 1990).

20 A. de Tocqueville, *Democracy in America* (New York: New American Library, 1991); J.S. Mill, *On Liberty* (New York: Penguin, 1987); J. Waldron, *Law and Disagreement* (Oxford: Oxford University Press, 2001); and J. Waldron, *Liberal Rights* (Cambridge: Cambridge University Press, 1993).

21 H. Koh and R. Slye, eds. *Deliberative Democracy and Human Rights* (New Haven, CT: Yale University Press, 1999); D. Beetham, *Democracy and Human Rights* (Oxford: Blackwell, 1999).

Part Two: Context

Chapter 7

History I:
Origins to the Nineteenth Century

We have, of course, already referred to the history of human rights at many points throughout this text. Try as we might, it is impossible to separate totally the concept from the context. Whether examining rights justification or object specification, whether identifying duty-holders or responding to rights criticism, we have seen the history illuminate and make vital the very idea. At the same time, there is much to the historical context that has yet to be mentioned. It is thus worth our while, as we pursue the goal of having an adequate grasp of *both* theory and practice, to turn our attention to the history of human rights. Which bodies of thought have contributed to the idea? Which events have shaped its realization? Who has challenged, and who has supported, human rights? In other words, how exactly have we come to be where we are today? Can we project from this history into the future, and see where further work and action are needed?

Traditional Religions

Most of the world's major religions—Judaism, Christianity, Islam, Hinduism, Buddhism, etc.—support in some form the idea that each human person, as the creation of some Divinity, has worth and value, and accordingly should be treated with a measure of dignity and respect. Of course, sometimes believers have failed to act in accord with this tenet of their faith, but that kind of hypocrisy is not our main concern here: the *idea* that everyone deserves some decent treatment and respectful regard clearly plays a major role in human rights thinking, and it probably first came to such thinking through the influence of the major religions.

Most of the major religions also subscribe to the notion that there are enduring standards of morality and justice against which people's actions, and the community's laws, must be evaluated. Indeed, the core ethical imperative of most religions is to meet and implement such standards through one's actions: to do one's part in ensuring the realization of such values concretely in the world and not merely abstractly in the after-life or in one's dreams. Human rights supporters also subscribe to this important idea that laws and actions ought to conform to compelling moral principles. Very few modern rights defenders cite God's will as the source of such principles, but the commitment to an authoritative set of values against which actions and institutions ought to be judged endures.

It needs to be conceded that the enduring standards of morality and justice subscribed to by the major religions started out first as articulations *not of rights* but, rather, *of duties*. Intellectual history shows that the concept of a duty predates that of a right—indeed, by a considerable stretch of time. It was to take centuries for people to hit upon the notion that often there is a right at the other end of a duty, thereby establishing the correlativity thesis between rights and duties first discussed in Part One.[1] For now, though, we must note that rights came later, and duties were first. It was thought that the Divinity's will placed upon all of us a set of requirements that had to be followed to ensure blessedness and divine favour. We are all God's children, so to speak, and like a loving parent God has laid out for us certain standards and expectations we must meet. We are all duty-bound to conform to God's commands; failure to do so leads to perdition and damnation in God's eyes, and to shame, suffering and humiliation in our own.

A number of ancient religions—perhaps Judaism most prominently—sought to render concrete which exact duties were expected of adherents to the faith. They did this by cataloguing such duties in written, law-like form. The Ten Commandments of the Old Testament, or the Torah, are only the most famous examples.[2] The rest of the Old Testament enumerates rules for living, the Levitican code, that are astonishing in scope and detail. This desire to see general moral principles codified into law-like clarity and with associated widespread publicity lives on in the human rights movement. We saw, in Part One, how the drive to codify human rights norms into both national constitutions and international treaties serves as one of the primary energizers of contemporary human rights activism.

It does not seem an exaggeration to suggest that, of the major religions, Christianity has probably had the biggest influence on the development of human rights. Christianity was the first religion clearly committed—at least in principle—to the twin values of universality and equality, which pulse at the heart of the human rights idea. Some of the other religions were first rooted in ethnic ties, class membership or particular political identities; many rejected vehemently the notion that all were or could be chosen, or divinely favoured. Religion, in ancient times, was often a way of cementing communities together *in opposition to* others. This is not to say, of course, that the Christian commitment to universality and equality was problem-free, or that it has always been adhered to flawlessly. But it was the first major religion open to all, sporting as one of its ideals that all could be saved if they convert-ed of their own will, and that each and every one of us has the spark of the Divine in us, as children of God. The New Testament's Golden Rule clearly enjoins upon adherents a norm of universality: treat all others as you yourself would like to be treated by them. The spirit of the New Testament is also clearly egalitarian, and not just in the sim-ple sense that we all have a soul that needs salvation. Jesus clearly asso-ciates himself with the downtrodden, most famously in The Beati-tudes. He castigates those with authority and power, and counsels adherents to remove the sticks in their own eyes before commenting on the specks in those of others. He stuns the frenzied mob by telling them that only those who have not sinned may cast the first stone, and so on. Moreover, the core norm of love expressed in the New Testa-ment contains within it such warm humanitarianism that it clearly inspires current commitments to ensuring a level of minimally decent treatment for all.[3] Of course, love is far too ambitious to serve as the goal of the human rights movement. Treating each other with love is indeed a matter best left to religious inspiration and devoted personal relationships. Decent treatment may be a thin substitute for love, but it may be the most we can ask from social institutions in particular. In any event, there is real work to do just to ensure minimally decent treatment, and if such work can find inspiration in, and common cause with, religious humanitarianism, then so be it. The key idea both norms share is that it is horribly wrong to treat other people with cru-elty and brutality, and that such treatments must be resisted and pun-ished, and ultimately converted in the direction of decency and respect.[4]

Classical Civilizations: Greece and Rome

Ancient Greece is the cradle of Western civilization, and since Western civilization served as the cradle for human rights, we must turn to exploring Greece's contribution. This offering was probably not so large, since ancient Greece was highly class-structured internally and sported fierce external rivalries with outsiders of different ethnicity and religious belief. Most of the Greek city-states were slave societies, and all were quite chauvinist. Ancient Greece was dominated by wealthy and well-educated male aristocrats. In spite of this, however, ancient Athens was the world's first democracy. For a period of time, all citizens could vote, run for office, and sit on juries. It did not last and, while it did, citizenship was severely limited to adult men who were both free and wealthy. Still, it was the first attempt at broad-based self-governance, a form of social organization consonant with human rights, as we saw at the end of the last chapter. Democracies were not to reappear until the medieval Swiss canton, revolutionary America and France, and even then not on a widespread and deep scale until well into the twentieth century.

The main Greek contribution to the human rights idea resides in the conception of natural law. This can be thought of as an extension, or even better a reinterpretation, of the commitment to divine law inaugurated by the traditional religions. The idea behind natural law is that the source of authoritative moral principles, by which we judge people's actions and society's laws, is not God but, rather, nature. The source to look to for moral and political guidance was for the Greeks not the supernatural but the natural. The Greeks, of course, placed great emphasis on our faculty of reason and accordingly founded most of our disciplines of intellectual inquiry, ranging from philosophy to the hard sciences. This is not to deny that the Greeks also had faith in their own set of gods; it is rather to point out the *distinctive* contribution they made to modern human rights thinking.

For ancient Greek thinkers like Aristotle, it is the combination of reason and observation on which we are to rely for guidance in life. When considering how something should act, or how something should be used or treated, we should investigate its nature or essence. The nature of a thing tells us what that thing is for, and how it should be treated. Reflection upon such observation informs us, Aristotle says, that human beings are both rational and political animals. They should thus pursue the life of reason, either in its theoretical sense of philosophical meditation and scientific inquiry, or else in its practical sense of political deliberation. The Greeks thus secularized an appeal to pre-existing moral and political standards, taking them out of the fickle hands of the gods and into the more regular and clearly discernible realities of the natural world. The famous Greek legend of Antigone makes for perhaps the clearest example of Greek views regarding natural law. She was ordered by the King not to bury her brother but went ahead and did it anyway, claiming that nature itself demanded that her brother be laid to rest in his homeland.

The Greek city-states never forged an over-arching alliance among themselves and as a result were vulnerable to attack and conquest by larger outside powers, first the Macedonians and then the Romans. Rome, of course, forged one of the largest and most enduring empires in world history. Its imperial reign over the Mediterranean world lasted from at least 250 BC until AD 476, and for much longer than that in various European and Near Eastern regions. The Romans had powerful armies, slaves to fuel their economy and engineers of unrivalled genius. These engineers not only designed such enduring symbols as the Coliseum, they also built vitally needed infrastructure projects—roads and aqueducts especially—by means of which Rome cemented its control of far-flung areas. Above all, the Romans mastered the art and science of government: over centuries of time, over millions of people and over thousands of miles. The Romans were a very practical people, as opposed to the more theoretical and artistic Greeks. It is often said that, while the Romans conquered the Greeks militarily and politically, the Greeks conquered the Romans culturally. For example, the gods of ancient Rome were exactly the same gods as those of ancient Greece: the Romans merely adopted them and changed their names. Athens remained the seat of higher learning, even during the pinnacle of Rome's power. The Greeks developed an idea that the Romans took to especially: this was the doctrine of Stoicism.

The Stoics believed that the universe was one organic whole, organized by the laws of a rational God. There are physical laws that govern the movement of objects, and there are moral laws that govern the free choices of human beings. It is our duty as human beings to obey these moral laws. These laws express rules of "right conduct" and are discernible through the faculty of "right reason." The content of these laws and rules inspires our modern notion of what a Stoic is like: someone who eschews worldly goods and pleasure; someone strong, disciplined and self-supportive. The core appeal of Stoic ethics is the duty to conform one's private will to the unfolding universe. Like the Christians who were to follow shortly thereafter, the Stoics believed their ethical code to be universal, capturing the objective truths of morality applicable to all persons and peoples. In a radical departure from earlier Greek isolationism and narrow ethnic nationalism, the Stoics were truly cosmopolitan in their outlook.

It is easy to see why Stoicism was adopted by the Romans, especially the most powerful classes—among them such legends as the senator Cicero and the emperor Marcus Aurelius. For the Stoic doctrine fitted in perfectly with Rome's grand imperial project: the appeal to duty over private gain; the militaristic glorification of strength and discipline; the implicit appeal to weaker societies to succumb to the "fate" of Roman control; and the explicit cosmopolitan conviction that ethnic, religious and national differences cannot preclude the need for one overarching rule of law and order. Roman lawmakers and leaders enacted Stoic principles into the canons of their positive law: They thereby provided an additional source for the universality of the human rights idea, with a concrete political cosmopolitanism not obviously present in Christianity.

Speaking of Christianity, it must be noted that, several hundred years after Stoicism first came to enjoy influence in Rome, the emperor Constantine made Christianity the official religion of the Roman Empire. This point—about AD 330—marks the beginnings of the development of the Roman Catholic Church as an important institution in Western, indeed world, civilization. It should be noted that the switch from Stoicism to Christianity was not that radical, since both were universal moral codes that taught self-discipline and an emphasis not on worldly happiness so much as on personal obedience to the objectively true laws of the Divine. The nexus between Greek Stoicism, Roman law and Christianity proved to be one of the history's most influential forces, especially in terms of persuading people about the universal requirements of morality and justice.[5]

Dark and Middle Ages

The Roman Empire collapsed in Western Europe in the fifth century AD, fragmenting in the face of repeated barbarian invasions from the north. It had grown too large to govern efficiently and too often its governors were corrupt and incompetent, so the Empire fell. It managed to endure in the Near East for over a thousand years more, but in the West the only institution to survive the collapse of Roman civilization was the Catholic Church. The western empire otherwise dissolved into a series of small ethnic groups and tribe-like families, and many wars between them ensued. Not much information survives from this period and so we call it the Dark Ages. What little does survive tells us, sporadically, of an anarchical and bloody existence, a dirty and decrepit life. Europe took major steps backwards during the Dark Ages, which lasted anywhere from AD 500-1000. At the same time, Islamic civilization in Persia and Africa and Far Eastern civilizations in China and India flourished.

During the Dark Ages's latter years, starting around AD 800, attempts were made by ambitious local warlords to consolidate their control over larger pieces of territory. Alfred did this in Britain and Charlemagne on the Continent. While not immediately successful, these efforts pointed the way toward the future: local tribal heads gradually winning control over larger and larger pieces of territory, declaring themselves champions of the people in the process. They re-established law and order, by force of arms, farm by farm and forest by forest. A handful of such warlords eventually became self-styled kings, monarchs of their realms. All the while, such warlords had to deal with the Church: its longevity, its land holdings, its moral authority over its flock. Most warlords were eager to win the Church's approval, for it was a powerful ally and could provide to their rule a strong stamp of legitimacy. As a result, many European warlords heeded the call when the Church demanded a series of military crusades, between AD 1000-1200, against the encroachment of Islam into Europe. These Crusades were massive armed invasions of Muslim strongholds in Eastern Europe, the Middle East and North Africa.

The local warlords also had to deal with fierce rivalries amongst themselves, especially over who got to call himself the one and only king of the entire nation. Such rivalries sparked murders and wars, as well as marriages and alliances, and also one of the very first codifications of rights. We saw previously, in Chapter 4, that in 1215 King John of England signed a "great charter," or Magna Carta, recognizing the titles, lands and privileges of some successful local warlords, who now preferred to call themselves "nobles" and "aristocrats." In return, these nobles gave King John enough money to stay afloat as king.

Where exactly came the transition from duties to rights, no one knows: such is probably lost in the sands of time. But by the medieval period we see, clearly, claims of rights and entitlements on the other side of certain duties. The king has duties not just to God and to his subjects, the nobles said, but to us as well: duties to stay off our lands, to allow us to travel, to tax us only in reasonable amounts, to have us thrown in jail only after a fair trial, and so on. And if the king has duties to do such things for us, they concluded, then we must have rights that he do such things. We have justified claims—authoritative entitlements—to the performance of such duties. In short, they said, we have rights. Marx was thus on to something real when he speculated that the origins of rights thinking was in the hands of those property-owning aristocrats who either had ambitions for the throne themselves or at least wanted to protect themselves from whoever was able to win the throne. Entitlement equals empowerment, and historically the influential and the affluent are in the best position to win such acknowledgment, with its corresponding aggrandizement. Those who have the most are in the best position to ask for even more, and moreover actually to get it. The concept of rights then widened as each inferior class rose, acquired more influence, and could use the language of rights against the one who used it last, as part of their own designs to pole-vault into better social standing and a higher standard of living. So we probably have the nobles of yesteryear to thank for getting the ball rolling on rights, and thus ultimately on human rights. Even back then, medieval philosophers like Thomas Aquinas, himself a Church theologian, were hinting at the idea that, if we all have duties to God and to society, then we might have rights to claim at least those objects we need to be able to perform such duties. Reflection on the duty brings forth the demand for the right as a natural matter of moral logic: one cannot perform the duty without the object required to fulfil that task, and thus one must have a right to the object. This idea was to inspire John Locke in the period leading up to the Revolutionary Era.[6]

Early Modern Era

Medieval society was transformed by a series of shocks. Most important among these shocks, for our purposes, were the discovery of the New World in 1492 and the Protestant Reformation in 1517. Of course, the "New" World in the Americas had been there for a long time and was populated by thousands of Natives, or Aboriginals, prior to European contact. But it was new to the Europeans, who proceeded to do everything in their power to exploit the new-found riches of this new-found land. The discovery of the New World was partially a product of the development of nation-states, then well underway, and it also accelerated the process in turn. In most cases, the expeditions to discover parts of the New World were financed by national monarchs—especially in Portugal, Spain, England, France and the Netherlands—desperate to forward their own wealth and power. Once found, the New World lured even more expeditions, fuelled by nationalist competition and the desire for supremacy. The New World also attracted colonists from the Old World, who set up new settlements modelled closely after those left behind. This process is relevant to human rights for at least two reasons. The first is that European contact with Natives at times produced major humanitarian catastrophes—e.g., mass slaughters—which called into question the European commitment to moral universalism and also foreshadowed similar acts in the future. The question of the treatment of Native peoples in the New World produced serious and heated debates in the Old. These debates, and the human rights implications of European colonialism, would be felt well into our own time. The colonial period—wherein European powers set about conquering other continents and forging new settlements modelled after themselves—technically lasted from about 1500 until our own day in the 1990s. Colonialism has had a major impact on contemporary living.[7] The second reason for the relevance of this process to human rights is the fact that colonialism spurred the formation of European nation-states, a mode of social organization destined to dominate modern life and, as such, any contemporary concern with human rights. "Nation-state" refers to a form of governance that is territorially concentrated in a compact, contiguous area, and that represents a people sharing a common language and history, and perhaps ethnicity and religion as well. The state, or government, exists to protect and represent the nation, a people of shared heritage living in the same area. Nation-state governance differs clearly from, say, Roman cosmopolitan governance, wherein one city governed a far-flung, non-contiguous area and represented diverse and multiple groups of people.

The relationship between the structure of the nation-state and the state of human rights satisfaction is one of the most complex and important in the field of human rights. On the one hand, some of the world's most appalling human rights violations were committed by European, or European-derived, nation-state mechanisms. On the other, some nation-states have more or less succeeded in providing human rights satisfaction for their citizens. The fact that the state has been the foremost protector, as well as violator, of human rights in the modern world only underlines its status as the dominant social institution in the modern era.

Colonialism also had a massive impact on economic and technological development. As we glimpsed when discussing Marx in Chapter 6, colonialism brought vast new resources into European cities, generating wealth greater than any seen until that point. Huge banks grew to handle such wealth, displacing the outdoor market in the town square as the scene of economic action. Huge colonial plantations created new economies of scale and called forth new management techniques. International "trade" created room for middle class merchants and professionals who were neither land-owners nor tenant farmers. These people were to become the main agitators, and beneficiaries, of the first rights revolutions.

Nationalism was also spurred on by the Protestant Reformation, begun by Martin Luther in German lands in 1517. Luther, a priest and thinker, rejected aspects of Catholic teachings, was ex-communicated by the Pope and started his own break-away church, later named after him. The main reason the Reformation became a major upheaval in Western civilization had less to do, however, with the power of ideas and theology, and more to do with the ambitions of local aristocrats and national kings who saw, in the Reformation, their chance to free themselves forever from the age-old need to court the Roman Catholic Church and keep its favour. Such figures were now—thanks to their armies, their lands, and resources from the colonies—strong enough to do away with the connection to Rome. A number of such kings and princes sided with the religious reformers and formed new national churches. The case of England's King Henry VIII and his establishment of the Church of England, with himself as its head, provides the clearest example. The Reformation deeply divided Europeans, and a severe split developed between the Protestant north and the Catholic south. Religious antagonisms grew positively poisonous, and some horrendous violence ensued. Arguably the worst carnage occurred in German areas, when the Thirty Years War (1618-48) ended up killing fully one-third of the region's population. The peace treaty that ended this war, known as the Treaty of Westphalia, is very significant. First, it is cited as the first ever document of modern international law, a topic human rights defenders are indeed keen on. Nation-states came together to sign a treaty committing each of them to respect certain standards of conduct in their dealings with each other. Second, the Treaty of Westphalia enshrined an early form of a very modern principle, namely, that of tolerance for different beliefs and alternative, reasonable ways of life. The carnage of the wars over religion in the West showed that the only way out of constant, horrifying war was to acknowledge the enemy's right to entertain whatever (reasonable) religious beliefs and practices he wanted. This was perhaps the earliest glimpse of our own value of religious liberty and freedom of conscience, belief and association. We began to agree to disagree and yet still to tolerate and recognize each other.[8]

Protestantism sports other aspects of interest. The individualist flavour of Protestant theology, for instance, has obvious affinities with human rights thinking. Just as an individual must come to his own personal relationship with the Divine, so too persons need to be free to live their own lives as they best see fit, subject of course to reciprocity on their part. Rights were designed, partially, to form a protective perimeter around people, creating a space for them to both have and lead a life of minimal value. And the sociologist Max Weber became famous by asserting a link between the rise of Protestantism and the rise of capitalism. The link, he supposed, was ideological: Protestant beliefs resulted in actions conducive to free-market exchange. Which beliefs? Those in favour of hard work and saving for the future over sloth and praying for last-minute divine intervention. Above all, the Protestant belief that success in this life was a sign of divine favour and selection for the next called forth the kind of entrepreneurial energies out of which contemporary capitalism grew. It was no accident, Weber wrote, that the very first free-market societies developed in such early Protestant strongholds as the Netherlands, England and America.[9]

The Revolutionary Era

The Revolutionary Era probably began a hundred years before what most people would guess: 1689, as opposed to 1789. The late 1680s saw strong conflict in England between Catholics and Protestants over who should sit on the throne, and how he or she should deal with residual religious antagonism once there. The reason why the throne was disputed refers back to the English Civil War of 1640-60. This civil war was between defenders of the monarchy and supporters of a commonwealth or republic, i.e., a political community with a non-hereditary head of state. The republicans, under Oliver Cromwell, briefly succeeded in establishing a commonwealth: King Charles I was executed in 1649 and Cromwell declared himself Lord Protector of the Realm in 1653. The tide turned, however, and by 1660 a new king, Charles II, re-established the monarchy. In 1685, James II came to the throne as a Catholic. Protestants took umbrage at how he governed at odds with their interests, and successfully conspired to overthrow him in a "Glorious Revolution." Then, in 1688-89, they invited the Protestant monarchs William and Charles's daughter Mary, originally from Orange in Holland, to occupy the British throne. The two did so, and in return signed the English Bill of Rights. As we saw in Chapter 4, this Bill established a constitutional monarchy in Great Britain: future kings and queens now had to exercise authority within the confines of legal limits defined for them by Parliament. Additionally, both Crown and Parliament acknowledged various rights of British citizens, notably to run for Parliament, to bear arms in self-defence, and to be free from cruel and unusual punishment.

In the following year, 1690, John Locke published his *Second Treatise of Civil Government*, which remains the classical expression of the doctrine of natural rights. Locke himself was a strong supporter of the Glorious Revolution, so it is important to note that the book was not just abstract philosophy but also very much a product of its time, almost like a sophisticated political pamphlet justifying the change in government. In the *Second Treatise*, Locke argued that natural rights flow from natural law. Natural law has both a religious and a secular side. On the religious side, and accessed through faith alone, Locke asserted that God the Creator establishes for us the laws by which we ought to live. These laws are contained in the Bible, for instance in the Ten Commandments and the Golden Rule. On the secular side, and knowable through reason alone, there are principles of action that every normal human being agrees should be followed. These include rules regarding self-preservation. The commands of natural law, however, cannot be followed without first having secure access to a small number of abstractly-defined yet essential items. For one to follow the Ten Commandments, for example, one first needs to be alive. For one to secure oneself, one needs to be free from the domination of others. Since both life and the exercise of liberty consume resources, one also needs some property. Thus, commands of natural law lead to the entitlements of natural right: if we need an object to obey the natural law, it follows that we must have the natural right to claim, and indeed possess, that object. Locke argued that we all have natural rights to life, liberty and property. Governments are formed by people to realize these natural rights and to ensure protection of them against criminals. This is the sole justification for government, and so any state that fails in this task—or, moreover, violates natural rights—is illegitimate and may be overthrown, with force if needed.[10]

When American colonists began to resent British rule, especially regarding taxation and the desire to have their own views represented in the laws that governed them, they cited Locke as one reason to revolt. Indeed, the first few lines of the Declaration of Independence sound, almost word-for-word, as if they had been written by Locke himself. There can be little doubt that Thomas Jefferson, the Declaration's principal author, absorbed Locke's writings and was influenced by them. The War for Independence began in 1775-76, and lasted until 1783. In 1789, local representatives of the various American states ratified the U.S. Constitution, including the first ten amendments to it, which form the American Bill of Rights. These rights were discussed in Chapter 4. As important as the Bill of Rights for our purposes is the division of governing authority elaborated in the Constitution itself. The American founding fathers took very seriously Locke's idea that one of the best ways to ensure that a state respects rights is to carve out checks and balances within the state itself. Government, if it is to be prevented from becoming tyrannical and rights-violating, needs to be broken up into units that can limit each other's power. The Glorious Revolution set some parliamentary limits on the Crown's authority, and the Americans went even further in elaborating detailed divisions between the executive, legislative and judicial branches of government. The very point of the American system, in many ways, is precisely to make governance quite difficult: rival institutions check each other's designs and ambitions, thereby limiting what any one of them can do. The result, the "founding fathers" reasoned, should be a minimal government and maximal freedom for the people, while not hindering effective state action on issues which enjoy broad-based popular consensus. These innovations were clear contributions to the important idea, discussed in Chapter 5, that institutional accountability is a necessary condition for a rights-respecting society.[11]

Just as Locke, and Britain's Glorious Revolution, inspired the American colonists, so too did the American experience inspire the French. At the start of the American Revolution, France was governed by a monarch who essentially enjoyed unlimited power. French kings were absolute monarchs, ruling with the advice of ultra-privileged aristocratic members of their royal court. King Louis XIV once said, "The state, that's me," and he and his descendants ruled accordingly. So French dissidents and malcontents drew inspiration from this new idea of the natural rights of man, which they set in direct opposition to the traditional idea of the divine right of kings. They too yearned and planned at least for a British-style constitutional monarchy and at most for an American-style republic. They were to experience both these options, and much more, once the French Revolution got underway.

One of the major causes of the French Revolution was severe miscalculation on the part of the French aristocrats and monarch. For they, too, supported the American Revolution. But they did so not out of genuine sympathy with revolutionary ideals but, rather, out of bitter hatred for their ancient rivals, the British. The French reasoned that an American win in the War of Independence would be a devastating loss to England. The loss would not only take a huge chunk out of Britain's resources, it would also be utterly humiliating. The French at this time were especially eager to humiliate the English, since just over ten years earlier, in 1763, the French had signed the Treaty of Paris. This Treaty ended the Seven Years War, which Americans call the French-and-Indian War. That war saw Britain achieve a crushing victory over France, winning from it control over vast colonial holdings in North America and the Caribbean. France saw the American Revolution as paying the British back. Accordingly, they funnelled huge amounts of cash, weapons and military expertise to the Americans, and probably played a major role in sustaining the American colonists during the long, hard years of the Revolutionary Wars.

The problem with this vengeful policy was that it bankrupted the resources of the French government. By the time the American war ended in 1783, the French till was all but empty. Accordingly, King Louis XVI was forced to re-establish the Estates General, the French Parliament, which had been defunct for nearly two centuries. His goal in doing so was to get the parliament to levy new taxes on the French people, restoring the solvency of his government. The situation paralleled that surrounding the Magna Carta: a broke king needed cash, but those from whom he sought the cash were not about to simply fork it over. They demanded more power and participation. They wanted more respect and recognition. They demanded access to privileges until then reserved for the aristocrats. They wanted greater freedom to trade and own property. They had the money, and if the king wanted it, he had to do something for them, by doing what the British kings had done, namely, sign a Bill of Rights and agree to constitutional limits on his royal power. The king, seeing how his plans had backfired, tried to backtrack, dissolving the Estates General and wishing them all away. But the members of that parliament refused to be intimidated. They re-named themselves the National Assembly and in 1789 passed the Declaration of the Rights of Man and Citizen, discussed in Chapter 4. Some of the more energetic supporters of the Assembly raided the Bastille, a royal prison, with force of arms. They freed the Bastille's prisoners both political and otherwise, and the fight was on between supporters of the monarchy and those of the revolution.

The French Revolution got everyone's immediate attention in Europe, ranging from the support of the street people of Paris, to feminists like de Gouge who wanted it to go further, to the hostility expressed by Burke and Bentham, to the shock and fear felt by the other monarchs of Europe. A revolution in America was one thing; but one in France—one of Europe's leading nations, and so close—was quite another. Everyone waited anxiously to see what would happen. At first, the Revolution proceeded much like its English and American counterparts, with the monarch accepting constitutional limits and supporting the Declaration of Rights. The National Assembly became an active legislative body, with teeming factions and political intrigue. Well-placed middle-class merchants and professionals won more rights, prestige and wealth. But what makes the French Revolution so unique was that it did not stop there. The urban street poor of Paris saw what the middle class

got, and they demanded more for themselves. When refused, they riot-
ed, spurred on by hunger and the high price of bread. Class divisions
and hatreds rose to new heights during the French Revolution. Revolutionary radicals like Maximillien Robespierre supported the demands
for greater equality by the poor. The radicals also saw that mob support
might catapult them into greater positions of power, over the heads of
the moderate middle-class activists who had hitherto been at the helm.
The Revolution became increasingly more violent and extreme: civil
order began to dissolve as these groups struggled over control of the
state. Robespierre and his crowd soon seized power, and then had King
Louis XVI and his Queen Marie Antoinette executed in public by guil-
lotine. They began to radically restructure governing institutions from
the top down as they sought to create a "Republic of Virtue." The monarchs of Europe, for their part, prepared to invade France and to crush
the regicidal radicals by force. The radicals, in turn, saw war with foreign powers as the perfect way to unify the French people behind them.
They also wanted to export the Revolution's ideals throughout Europe.
What resulted was years of armed conflict in Europe, appropriately
known as the Revolutionary Wars.

Back in Paris, the radicals were desperate to restore law and order and
to refashion society in their own image. A Committee of Public Safety
was formed, led by Robespierre, and it instituted a Reign of Terror,
unleashing state-sanctioned violence against all supposed enemies of the
Revolution. Blood flowed in a crimson tide from the guillotines. When
executions were limited to the despised aristocrats, they enjoyed some
support: but as more and more people from the middle and lower classes also fell victim to the blade, support shrivelled. The people, horrified
at the carnage, came to view Robespierre as a dangerous fanatic, well on
his way to becoming a brutal tyrant. For his trouble, he suffered the
same "close shave" he had administered to others. After his death,
France collapsed into chaos, for years lurching from government to government, besieged from the outside by war with European powers and
hampered on the inside by conditions verging on anarchy.

Order returned to France in the very late 1790s riding the coattails of
a crafty, Corsican-born soldier named Napoleon Bonaparte. Napoleon
served in the French army during the Revolution and effectively
deployed force against both foreign armies and domestic street mobs.
He was a military genius of first rank, sporting as well the physical energy and courage of perhaps ten men and the ego and ambition of at least
a thousand. Through competence, cunning and chutzpah, Napoleon
worked his way from being a mere private to becoming the general in

command of all France's armies. When one of the weak, post-Robespierre governments, seeking stability, invited him to join them, he agreed. He then rapidly outmanoeuvred everyone in that government and became France's first military dictator. In short order he won absolute power, in fact crowning himself Emperor. He set about to achieve what the revolutionaries merely wished: to modernize and transform French society, and to export the ideals of the Revolution throughout Europe. He did the latter following an incredibly successful series of military campaigns during which the Emperor personally won himself an Empire. By 1810 Napoleon was, in one way or another, the master of all Europe, excluding England, Russia and parts of Spain. Napoleon's relevance to human rights rests first, and on the good side, on his exporting the ideas of modern rights throughout Europe. He believed in order, in property, in public education and in promoting people on the basis of merit rather than heredity. On the other side of the ledger, Napoleon had a dark record on rights realization. Historians agree that Napoleon established a degree of control over state and society that no older monarch had ever dreamed of. He controlled the army and the legislature, he ran the press and established the curricula for public education. He employed an extensive network of spies and essentially practiced martial law. He ran French society as if it were one of his own army regiments, and had his cronies—many of them his own family members—do the same for his colonies. Essentially Napoleon ran the world's very first modern police state, and in so doing provided a model for some of the twentieth century's most fearsome dictatorships.[12]

The Nineteenth Century After Napoleon

Napoleon's reign came to an abrupt and spectacular end. He had long abandoned plans to invade arch-enemy England, but by 1812 felt it was a different story with Russia. He gambled and lost: the Russians, instead of fighting, withdrew, drawing Napoleon's army deep into the countryside, farther from its supply source at home in France. Winter came and killed his soldiers and horses by tens of thousands. It also froze the food. Napoleon ordered a retreat; and that is when the shrewd Russians launched their attack, picking apart his starving, diseased and decimated army chunk-by-chunk. As the Russians drove Napoleon back, other conquered European peoples—especially the Germans—rose and picked up where they left off. The French army was smashed, Napoleon lost power, and he was exiled. He tried to come back in 1815, but was famously bested by the British at the Battle of Waterloo. He was then exiled to the island of St. Helena, one of the remotest places on earth at that time, where he died.

At the Congress of Vienna of 1815, the peace treaty after Napoleon's defeat was signed by European powers. It re-established quite conservative monarchies throughout Europe. There was revolution, and then reaction. This had the virtue of restoring some stability and achieving peace, but the vice of ignoring and shutting out many dispossessed peoples who had not forgotten revolutionary ideals. It became very fashionable in nineteenth-century establishment circles to denounce the idea of natural rights. This elite criticism of the rights idea by the politically conservative and the intellectually skeptical continued in the corridors of power and in the halls of academe at least until the turn of the twentieth century. We surveyed, and responded to, such criticism in Chapter 6. In the twentieth century, as we will see, the horrors of war, and the conceptual switch from natural to human rights, brought about the end to this hostility.

Back on the ground in the wake of the Congress of Vienna, those dispossessed by the aristocratic diplomats refused to be ignored. Pro-democracy movements spread, seeking to expand the number of those who could vote. These movements won victories of a kind with the election of US President Andrew Jackson in 1828 and with the 1832 passage of Britain's Great Reform Bill. There was a promising moment of continental European democratization in 1848 but it was not as successful.[13]

One of the least known things about the Congress of Vienna was that it featured quite extensive, but unproductive, talks on the future of the international slave trade. Slavery, of course, was still being practised at this time in the southern US states and throughout the Caribbean. There was a brutal yet lucrative trade to be had in shipping slaves from Africa to slave-holders, usually plantation owners in need of cheap and plentiful manpower to mass-produce labour-intensive agricultural products like cotton, tobacco and sugar. Slavery has always been a divisive issue in American politics, and by the mid-1800s international politics came to be quite concerned over the slave trade. The move to abolish the international slave trade was led by the British government for two reasons: its own people expressed moral outrage at the institution, which it had previously abolished domestically; and it was thought that ruining the slave trade would hurt American interests. Official Britain had a long and hard time getting over its loss of the US colonies. From the 1830s to the 1860s, many international treaties banning the slave trade were signed and, moreover, implemented with effectiveness. Of course, during this time inside America, the issue of slavery came to dominate the political agenda, eventually sparking a bitter and bloody civil war from 1861 to 1865. The war was won by the North, and its leader Abraham Lincoln paid the price with his life. Still, his Emancipation Proclamation of 1863, which freed the slaves and declared slavery forever illegal, must count as one of the most important human rights documents of the nineteenth century.[14]

The Napoleonic Wars and the US Civil War were ferocious conflicts. Bitter hatreds combined with industrial-era productivity and management efficiency to produce disciplined mass armies capable of new heights of death and destruction. The fierce commitment to ideology— whether pro- or anti-Revolution, whether pro- or anti-Napoleon, whether pro- or anti-slave—only increased the bloodshed. So appalling was nineteenth-century warfare that it led to the formation of the world's first humanitarian non-governmental organization (or NGO): the International Red Cross, formed in 1863 as a neutral body to care for those injured by war. There was a movement starting in the mid-1860s to devise international laws to regulate and restrain warfare, in the hopes of reducing such fearful rates of casualty, both military and civilian. The US Army issued guidelines to its own soldiers during the Civil War, and in ·1868 representatives of various nations signed the Declaration of St. Petersburg. There followed a period of intense research, debate and reflection which generated, between 1899 and 1907, four extensive international treaties on the laws of war, known collectively as the Hague Conventions. They established rules to regulate and minimize the reasons for launching a war and to render less destructive the means used to prosecute a war. They are still referred to today when soldiers are put on trial for alleged war crimes.[15]

We only now mentioned the Industrial Revolution, even though it began as early as the mid-1700s in such spots as Manchester, England. The Industrial Revolution refers to a transformation in Western economies, away from agriculturally-dominated production to industrially-dominated production. It refers to the invention of the steam engine and steel, the discovery of oil and electricity, the growth of factories and cities at the expense of farms in the country, the development of mass-production manufacturing and the modern corporation at the expense of craftsmen and small shop-keepers. By the mid-1800s, industrialization had done much more than revolutionize warfare, making mass killing easier than ever before. Industrialization had also created disparities of wealth on an enormous scale, and left-leaning critics like Marx responded by calling for more socio-economic equality—perhaps even violent revolution. Socialist parties and movements spread like wildfire, and had as their focus the formation of unions to advance worker interest in shorter working hours, better health and safety conditions in the factories, and of course higher wages. The mid- to late 1800s saw the birth of the modern labour movement. This period offered the first suggestion that, in addition to "first-generation" human rights to security, liberty, property and various civil and due process rights, there may also be "second-generation" claims to vitally needed socio-economic objects, like a subsistence income, basic social services like education, and such public health and safety measures as water treatment and vaccinations.

The labour movement allied itself with those "suffragettes" who, starting in the mid-1800s, took up where early feminists like de Gouge and Wollstonecraft left off and campaigned for the right of women to vote. The role of women in the professions and politics was a hot topic by the late 1800s, but the right to vote was not actually granted on a widespread basis until after World War I. In the meantime women did win rights to enter hitherto male professions, such as medicine, and to the schools which provided advanced training for them. One of the most important effects of the Industrial Revolution was that it called forth major new investments in education, both public and private. A more complicated economy demanded more knowledgeable workers, and this educational investment spurred the development of a genuinely broad-based middle class in the West. This class came to comprise the majority of decently-educated, literate, hard-working, reasonably healthy and moderately wealthy people. As more people learned more and earned more, they came to think of themselves as being just as entitled to fundamental freedoms and core social protections as the well-off and the well-born. The rise of the Western middle class no doubt contributed mightily to the eventual rise in human rights consciousness that was to burst forth in the twentieth century.[16]

Notes

1 A. Monahan, *From Personal Duties Towards Personal Rights* (Montreal & Kingston: McGill-Queen's University Press, 1992); R. Tuck, *Natural Rights Theories: Their Origins and Development* (Cambridge: Cambridge University Press, 1979).

2 W. Harrelson, *The Ten Commandments and Human Rights* (New York: Mercer, 1997).

3 See especially the Sermon on the Mount, in the Book of Matthew, Chapters 5-7.

4 See also M. Perry, *The Idea of Human Rights* (Oxford: Oxford University Press, 2000).

5 S. Hornblower, *et al.*, eds., *The Oxford Companion to Classical Civilization* (Oxford: Oxford University Press, 1998).

6 N. Cantor, *The Civilization of the Middle Ages* (New York: Harper, 1994).

7 D. Abernathy, *The Dynamics of Global Dominance: European Overseas Empires, 1415-1980* (New Haven, CT: Yale University Press, 2001).

8 H. Lauterpacht, *International Law* (Cambridge: Cambridge University Press, 1978).

9 S. Ozment, *The Age of Reform, 1250-1550* (New Haven, CT: Yale University Press, 1986); W. and A. Durant, *The Reformation* (New York: Simon and Schuster, 1983); and M. Weber, *The Protestant Ethic and The Spirit of Capitalism* (London: Unwin, 1992).

10 J. Locke, *Two Treatises of Civil Government* (Cambridge: Cambridge University Press, 1988).

11 B. Bailyn, *The Ideological Origins of the American Revolution* (Cambridge, MA: Harvard University Press, 1992); J. Alder, *A History of the American Revolution* (New York: De Capo Press, 1989).

12 S. Schama, *Citizens: A Chronicle of the French Revolution* (New York: Vintage, 1989); W. Doyle, *The Oxford History of the French Revolution* (Oxford: Oxford University Press, 1990); and L. Hunt, ed., *The French Revolution and Human Rights* (London: Bedford Books, 1996).

13 E. Hobsbawm, *The Age of Revolution, 1789-1848* (New York: Vintage, 1996).

14 W. Klingamen, *Abe Lincoln and the Road to Emancipation, 1861-65* (New York: Viking, 2001).

15 W. Reisman and C. Antoniou, eds., *The Laws of War* (New York: Vintage, 1993). See also my *War and International Justice: A Kantian Perspective*

(Waterloo: Wilfrid Laurier University Press, 2000); and *Michael Walzer on War and Justice* (Cardiff: University of Wales Press, 2000).

16 T. Ashton, *The Industrial Revolution, 1760-1830* (Oxford: Oxford University Press, 1998); T. Blanning, ed., *The 19th Century: Europe, 1789-1914* (Oxford: Oxford University Press, 2000).

Chapter 8

History II:
Twentieth Century and Beyond

The twentieth century really began with the outbreak of World War I in 1914. The period prior to that is largely seen by historians as having more in common with the nineteenth century than with what was to follow. Indeed, World War I broke out owing to the interconnection between two very nineteenth-century phenomena: nationalism and colonialism. The international system in the 1800s was dominated by the imperial powers of Europe: Britain, France, Austria-Hungary, Turkey and Russia. Britain, in particular, enjoyed dominance in the system, seeing its world-wide empire flourish to its fullest extent under Queen Victoria. International trade, secured by the Royal Navy, ensured that it was "Rule Britannia" over much of the global system.

The European powers still competed for new territories but had switched their focus from the Americas and Caribbean islands to Africa and southeast Asia. New nations were developing; and they sought not merely their own states but even empires. The German and Italian nations managed to unify themselves, in modern form, by the mid-1860s, and thereafter got in on the colonial game in parts of Africa. Germany in particular made rapid progress in terms of developing a modern industrial economy as well as large and effective armed forces and in throwing its foreign policy weight around within the political map of Europe. A quick win in a war against France in 1871 fired German pride and ambitions for aggrandizement. Some scholars even date the founding of the modern welfare state to German Chancellor Otto von Bismarck's provision of extensive and generous social services and state-secured benefits to the German veterans of that conflict, called the Franco-Prussian War. The German people had long chafed under the influence of the Austro-Hungarians and then of Napoleon's cronies and were keen to make up for lost time. They quickly emerged as a major force on the international scene, rivalling the industrial and population growth rates of America and challenging the military and political primacy of Britain itself.

Imperial rivalries between these ambitious European empires finally boiled over in 1914. What was expected to be a lovely little war on behalf of national pride and honour degenerated into a long and tragically pointless slaughterhouse of destruction. The bleak and barren killing fields between the muddy trenches heralded the dawn of the twentieth century and the major challenge it would pose to human rights, in both theory and practice.

The big break in World War I came in 1917, when one major power, Russia, left the war and another, America, entered it. Russia left because that year it experienced a *coup d'état*: communists, inspired by Marx's philosophy, succeeded in their violent overthrow of the czar and his government. They then withdrew Russia from the battlefields of Europe so that they could consolidate their rule at home and concentrate their energies on converting Russia into a communist society they soon dubbed the Union of Soviet Socialist Republics (USSR). It was the world's first communist revolution but was not to be its last: more on that when we come to the Cold War. America's entry into World War I following a period of neutrality tipped the war in favour of Britain and France over Germany. Peace came on November 11, 1918, now commemorated widely as Remembrance, or Veterans', Day. The peace treaty that ended the war is one of history's most influential, and infamous.[1]

The Treaty of Versailles

The Treaty of Versailles was not signed until 1919 and did not come into force until the following year. It was a wide-ranging agreement destined to have major impact on the unfolding of the twentieth century. The most significant aspects of the treaty can be roughly divided between those that Britain and France insisted on and those that America demanded. Britain and France, especially, insisted that Germany be made to accept very tough terms. Germany, which was not at all consulted on the negotiations, was presented with a number of stiff conditions. It had to accept responsibility for the war's outbreak and accordingly to accept the burden of reparations payments to the Allied side. It had to return the borderlands of Alsace-Lorraine to France, which it had acquired in the Franco-Prussian War. France also got to occupy parts of Germany, and other parts were ceded to Poland, Belgium and Denmark. Firm limits were also placed on Germany's ability to rebuild its armed forces. German diplomats protested vigorously when presented with these terms but in the end had little choice as the defeated nation but to accept them. These terms sparked simmering rage amongst much of the German people, and the burden of the reparations payments caused severe economic dislocation, which in turn fed social and political instability. An ambitious group of thugs, organized into a political party called the National Socialists, was to take advantage of these pressures and feelings and ultimately seize power in the 1930s.

American President Woodrow Wilson, at the time of Versailles, hesitated about the terms being imposed on Germany. But he decided to go along with them so that, in return, Britain and France would support his own terms. Wilson was a rather remarkable figure for his time, committed to restructuring international society in a different and quite idealistic way. He thought intrigue amongst old-style European empires had really caused the war, so he had included in the Treaty principles designed to hold empires in check. These principles would, over time, come to figure prominently in the international human rights movement. Such principles included a commitment to the self-determination of nations, protections for minority groups within existing empires, and an impetus toward decolonization. This last was to be first experienced by Germany, which was stripped of all its colonial holdings. The same was true for Turkey. These holdings were to be administered by a brand new international organization, the League of Nations.

The League was Wilson's baby. He thought of it as a much-needed international level of governance to which nation-states could turn in seeking help with their disputes. Far better, Wilson reasoned, for there to be a new, global institution to which nations could turn in order to resolve their disputes peacefully than to continue on with the status quo, where the lack of an international arbitrator meant that nations had nowhere else to go but to war over serious disputes. The League had legislative, executive and judicial branches. Its main goal was the preservation of peace, but it included secondary interests in such apparently unrelated areas as working conditions. Indeed, the League sponsored and forwarded the formation of the International Labour Organization. The League was, ironically, to be far more successful in pushing its member countries to enact humane labour laws and factory health and safety regulations than it ever was in preventing war. The League was severely hampered right from the outset, owing to America's refusal to join. This, of course, was the most bitter disappointment to Wilson, who died while campaigning strenuously among the American people in hopes they would pressure the US Senate to ratify America's membership in the League. The Senators refused. Only 28 countries ever joined the League, nearly all of them from Western Europe and North America. Germany and Japan withdrew from the League in 1933 after fascist regimes came to power there. The USSR ended its long isolation from the international scene by joining the League in 1934 but then was kicked out in 1939 after it signed a co-operation pact with Nazi

Germany. When World War II broke out in 1939, the League was a laughingstock—a powerless failure—and accordingly dissolved.[2]

Roaring Twenties, Dirty Thirties

The period between the wars was one of remarkable transformation, and one of relevance for human rights. Women won the right to vote and run for public office, and in most Western countries all people of the age of majority were permitted to vote as well. The spread of real representative democracy was underway in earnest. In the early 1920s there was widespread labour unrest throughout the Western world. Unions and workers wanting to form unions organized general strikes and political parties, and struggled to get respected and realized some of the second-generation, socio-economic human rights that had appeared on the agenda following the Industrial Revolution. They met with stiff resistance from management and capitalist owners, but also enjoyed some real success. Capitalists feared that the workers might actually rise up in a communist revolution, as they recently had in Russia. Their response was to offer real concessions and improvements in working conditions, expecting that such benefits would dampen any revolutionary impulse. In this they were correct: Western workers, exhausted from World War I, had no desire for more violent struggle: they just wanted higher wages and better work, and eventually won them both. The rest of the 1920s was, for most Western nations, an economic boom time, a period of "roaring" affluence, invention, and cultural growth.

Bust followed boom, and the stock market crash of 1929 eventually developed into a full-blown depression by 1930-31. Economies, far from growing or even slowing, actually contracted. The pie shrank, and so did the pieces, which increasingly looked like little more than crusts and crumbs. Unemployment skyrocketed, and rates of grinding poverty followed it. The desperation and misery, the anxiety and insecurity lasted for years and years. It was one of the most severe economic catastrophes in history and it called forth a major change in the way in which governments dealt with economic growth. Franklin Roosevelt won election as American president in 1932 on a campaign to use the tax-and-spend power of government to stimulate the economy to grow again. This was a radical departure. Most Western governments, at that point, believed that government's role in the economy was, essentially, to get out of the way of free-market enterprise. Government should ensure civil and due process rights—especially to own property and to form contracts with others in free association—and then tend to other functions of state, like foreign affairs. Government should establish law and order, respect first-generation human rights, and then let capitalism, through its profit incentive, work its economic magic on rates of growth and employment. It was a policy that worked in the 1920s but not in the depths of the Great Depression. So fearful was the economic climate that wealthy corporations themselves felt it too risky to spend. Indeed, they were chopping jobs by the thousands to cut expenses, just to remain solvent. Which other agency, then, could stimulate the economy except government? When Herbert Hoover refused to do so after years of despair he was dumped by the American people in favour of Roosevelt's "New Deal." Massive government spending followed, including both unemployment insurance payments to those without jobs and large-scale public works projects to generate new jobs. When these government programs started to work, they were copied by other governments around the world. The result was large-scale state intervention in the economy: the development of the modern, activist social welfare state.

The 1930s brought about an era of big government world-wide. In the USSR the state in the name of communism dominated most aspects of life. In the West the social welfare state was born as governments tried to developed "mixed economies" featuring both private and public presence in economic activity. The goal was to ensure a social subsistence minimum during the gritty grip of the Great Depression. In the colonies of European powers, the state determined the conditions of life faced by the indigenous and conquered peoples. In Germany, Spain, Italy and Japan, there developed fascist and authoritarian dictatorships where government rather fearsomely controlled nearly all aspects of social existence. These fascist dictatorships—which combined fierce nationalism and racism with police-state authoritarianism—soon plunged the world into the most devastating armed conflict ever experienced.[3]

World War II

Adolf Hitler rose to power in Germany by exploiting the recent experiences of the German people and by combining that with ruthless thuggery against all who stood in the way of the Nazi party. He stirred up hatred against the victors of World War I by complaining about the strict peace terms of the Treaty of Versailles. He urged Germany to re-arm and take back the lands it had lost in that settlement. He felt the humiliation imposed by Versailles should be replaced by an arrogant pride. He in fact preached a doctrine of racial and ethnic superiority that suggested that white Germans were destined to rule Europe, if not the entire world. He saved special scorn for the Jewish and Slavic peoples, tapping into ancient anti-Semitic prejudices and more recent wartime feelings about Russians and communism. Finally, he pledged massive state intervention in the economy to put Germans back to work. Since they had suffered real deprivations in the 1920s while the rest of the world roared, his policy found an audience. The Nazis barely squeaked into power through a combination of electoral success and strategic partnerships with other, gullible politicians. Once there, the Nazis promptly swept aside all rivals and in 1933 established the Third Reich, a fascist tyranny with Hitler as dictator. He promptly withdrew Germany from the League of Nations and began to build up the national armed forces in violation of the Treaty . of Versailles. He also began a systematic program to strip Jews in Germany of their wealth and property, their civil and legal rights, and ultimately their very lives. By the late 1930s Hitler started to take, by force, the lands Germany had lost at Versailles. Western leaders alternatively warned him and appeased him, but his decision to invade Poland in 1939 was too much. Britain and France declared war, and the world was at it again, only 20 years after peace had been achieved.

The Nazis enjoyed stunning success at the war's outset. All the build-up and scheming paid off, for within 18 months Germany had either conquered, or at least controlled, all of Europe save Britain and the USSR. The Soviets had signed a non-aggression pact with Hitler in 1939, letting him focus his attention on crushing Poland, Belgium, Holland and France, on cowing the Swiss and Scandinavians into harmless "neutrality," and on consolidating the control he already enjoyed over most of the former parts of the Austro-Hungarian empire. His "blitzkrieg" had left him master of Europe. He forced all those countries under his control to implement the same kind of anti-Semitic policies as existed in Germany. For example, some of the very worst discrimination and violence against the Jews happened in Poland.

On the other side of the world, Japan had throughout the 1930s used armed force to assert control throughout Asia, especially against such ancient rivals as China and Korea. The Japanese signed an agreement with Hitler and the Italians, committing each to respect the others' conquests, and moreover to come to their aid in case of difficulty. This agreement actually played a significant role in the development of the war. For after 1939 the United States remained officially neutral, even though it obviously had pro-British and anti-German sentiments. There is, after all, not much for a pro-rights democracy to admire in a fascist dictatorship. Even after Hitler's blitzkrieg America stayed out, much to the consternation of a desperate Britain, which was able to stave off

Hitler's attempts at conquest only through a combination of geography, courage, and massive assistance from such colonies and ex-colonies as Australia, Canada and India. In late 1941 the government of Japan somehow decided that it should bomb American military assets at Pearl Harbor in Hawaii. America, accordingly, declared war on Japan; and Hitler, citing his agreement with Japan, in turn declared war on America. This was not the only dumb decision Hitler made in 1941. While keeping his deal with Japan, he decided to break his other one with the USSR. He had come to the belief that no self-respecting racist fascist could deal with a communist, much less a Slavic one. So he tore up the agreement with the USSR and invaded that country too.

By bringing both the US and the USSR into the war, Hitler sealed his fate. Germany was now smack-dab in the middle between the world's two largest fighting forces. Bit by bit, the Nazi war machine was torn apart, conquered lands were liberated, and the Nazis rolled back to within their own borders. Hitler, perhaps seeing the writing on the wall, set in frantic motion the madness of the Holocaust, his "Final Solution" to the presence of Jewish people in Europe. The Holocaust involved, within all Nazi-controlled areas, the systematic identification and separation of Jews, their arrest and forcible confinement, and then their subjection to forced labour and mass murder. The forced labour and execution facilities came to be known as "concentration camps," and in them were murdered some six million Jews. While Jews were the main targets, gypsies, other visible minorities, communists, homosexuals and the physically handicapped were also included in the slaughter. It is probably fair to say that the contemporary human rights movement was born in appalled reaction to the Holocaust's horrors. The drive to ensure that "never again" would such brutality be inflicted upon others motivated the drive to secure respect for the bare minimum of decent treatment that the idea of human rights enshrines and seeks to protect.[4]

War's End

The end came relatively fast and furiously for Hitler. By 1945 fully 50 countries from around the world had joined the Allied cause against him, and Germany was pounded on the west by a coalition led by the Americans, and on the east by the Soviets. Hitler committed suicide in his bunker beneath Berlin at the very moment Soviet troops entered his capital. Germany, then in utter ruin, surrendered unconditionally. Attention turned to the Pacific War, where the Americans led a different coalition still squaring off against Japan. The US was tired of fighting and had no appetite to invade the island nation. In a bid to put the war to bed quickly, American President Harry Truman ordered the dropping of two atom bombs on Japan. Faced with the prospect of continuing to fight a country now possessed of such ferociously destructive weaponry, Japan surrendered.

The settlement of World War II altered the course of history. The USSR was allowed to control the countries of Eastern Europe, as a "security buffer" against the threat of any future German invasion. The US was authorized to occupy and reconstruct Japan, and consolidated its control of Hawaii and other Pacific islands. Britain and France were allowed to keep their colonial holdings but their postwar exhaustion quickly inclined them to begin a process of decolonization. Simply put, the cost of the war was so severe on them both that they could barely afford to keep control of their former empires. Many of their colonies rapidly realized this and began to mobilize campaigns for national self-determination and an end to European control. As for Germany it was carved in two, with the Soviets controlling the East and the Americans, British, and French the West. Instead of inflicting reparations on Germany, the Allies this time decided to invest in and re-build the country and to create new, more peaceable, and humane institutions to govern German society. What remained of the Nazi leadership was put on trial for war crimes.

These Nuremberg trials also served as a human rights landmark, establishing the world's first international criminal trials for those accused of committing massive human rights violations. Lesser-known war crimes trials were also held in Tokyo for Japanese officers and soldiers, for such barbarities as torturing Allied prisoners of war. To add further clarification and strength to the existing laws of war, the international community got together and in 1949 signed the Geneva Conventions. These Conventions continued the work of the older Hague Conventions—mentioned in the last chapter—by dealing with acceptable conduct during wartime. But they did so in response to radically different weaponry and in light of the terrible experience of World War II. The Hague and Geneva Conventions remain to this day the definitive pieces of international law regarding our on-going struggle to constrain both the incidence and destructiveness of war, and to hold those who unjustly unleash it accountable for their actions.[5]

The victorious powers at war's end referred back to Wilson's old idea of a League of Nations and decided that it had been strong in principle but weak in practice. They sought to keep the idea but make it more effective, notably by cementing American commitment to a new institution. In fact, American wartime president Franklin Roosevelt played a seminal role in the new global authority's birth. The United Nations, accordingly, was founded in San Francisco in 1945 and New York named its headquarters. It endures to this day.

The UN has a three-fold structure, with legislative, executive and judicial branches. It also has a three-fold mandate: to preserve international peace and security, to promote human rights, and generally to promote peaceful co-operation between states in the face of common difficulties. The judicial body is the International Court of Justice (ICJ), located at The Hague in Holland. It hears and decides cases involving disputes between countries, but only those countries that voluntarily submit their issues to judicial resolution. The legislative functions are split between the General Assembly and the Security Council. Every member country of the UN—and there are now almost 200 of them— has a vote in the General Assembly, which debates topical international issues and legislates with regard to new members, the UN's budget, and the UN's own internal bureaucratic structure. Voting in the General Assembly is based on "one country, one vote," with the majority deciding, though overwhelming consensus is usually sought prior to voting. The Security Council is the UN's most powerful organ. It legislates with regard to international peace and security, and thus has the power to authorize member countries to resort to armed force in a manner consistent with the UN's core principles. The Security Council now has 15 members, but only 5 of them are permanent. The five permanent members have a veto over any Security Council resolution, whereas the temporary members have a vote but no veto and serve only two-year terms on a rotating basis. Which countries are the permanent members? Precisely the five major powers on the winning side of World War II: Britain, China, France, the US, and the USSR (now Russia). The winning powers were keen, indeed, on being able to impose their will on a fractious and fractured postwar world. As for the executive functions, the Security Council itself retains the main ones in connection with the authorization and deployment of armed force, but there is also a UN bureaucracy, called the Secretariat, which is in charge of implementing General Assembly legislation and taking whatever actions the Security Council demands. The Secretariat is headed by the Secretary-General, the UN's highest profile position. Far from being the head of state presiding over an international government, the Secretary-General is more like the top diplomat who works day-in, day-out trying to get member countries, in what remains a voluntary association of nations, to negotiate and solve disputes peacefully and progressively. The United Nations is not, and was never designed to be, a world government. It is a voluntary alliance between sovereign states committed to realizing the UN's core commitments to peace, human rights protection and co-operation in the solution of common problems.

On the human rights front, the member countries of the UN quickly negotiated, and passed as a resolution of the General Assembly, the Universal Declaration of Human Rights. This Declaration, passed in 1948, has been referred to throughout this text, and remains the most influential postwar human rights document. Just as quickly, however, one group of member countries lined up behind the Declaration's civil and political rights and denounced its socio-economic rights, whereas another group did the reverse. This reflected a split in international society and resulted in the ratification of two separate international covenants on human rights: the International Covenant on Civil and Political Rights, ratified as a binding international treaty in 1966 by free-market democracies; and the International Covenant on Economic, Social and Cultural Rights, also ratified that same year by centrally-planned communist countries. The split referred to, of course, was the one brought about by the Cold War.[6]

The Cold War and The Three Worlds

The Cold War, which lasted from 1945 until roughly 1990, refers to the struggle between the two superpowers left at the end of World War II: the US and the USSR. It was a war in the sense that two hostile nations faced off against each other in a struggle for both survival and supremacy. But it was cold in the sense that it never erupted into direct armed conflict between them. There *were* wars fought during the Cold War, and they did feature some superpower involvement, but never did America and the Soviet Union directly exchange firepower in a Third World War. The main reason why, it seems, was the fact of nuclear deterrence: both nations developed massive stockpiles of atomic weapons, and each dreaded the prospect of armed confrontation with the other, as it might have escalated into an exchange of unprecedented, and universally ruinous, destructive forces. The doctrine of Mutually Assured Destruction might well have been "mad" but it probably, in paradoxical fashion, staved off an exchange of those fearsome weapons born over the ashes of Hiroshima and Nagasaki. The very severity of the threat that the one posed to the other imposed an odd kind of stability and predictability in the relations between the two superpowers.[7]

How did this Cold War start, develop, and end—and what impact did it have on human rights? Perhaps the best way to examine these issues is on a world-by-world basis. By this I mean the following: the Cold War dominated the postwar era and it both clarified and complicated relations between peoples. The major clarity it brought was by dividing the globe into three distinct spheres. Scholars came to refer to these separate spheres as different "worlds": the First World, of advanced free market democracies; the Second World, of centrally-planned communist countries; and the Third World, of poor and underdeveloped countries with various allegiances to either the First or Second World. The history of the Cold War is the story of how each world developed.

The Third World faced many struggles during the 1945-90 period. The first involved decolonization. Germany, Japan and Italy were all stripped of their colonies by the settlement of World War II. We have also already mentioned that the war had left Britain and France exhausted and all but broke. They could no longer afford their vast colonial holdings, and they began to divest themselves of them with different degrees of reluctance, depending on the territory in question. Britain lost India quickly, in the late 1940s. Mahatma Gandhi's pacific campaign to end British rule, begun in the 1930s, finally bore fruit, and his commitment to non-violent political agitation and demonstration certainly separated him and his movement from others of the era—and indeed since. But India soon found out that national self-determination—the positive flip-side to decolonization—was to prove, if anything, more difficult than throwing off the yoke of Europe. Disagreements over the structure of an independent India led to its split into rival nations, India and Pakistan.

There were several waves of decolonization, and the United Nations set up a Trusteeship Council to help guide the process. The Council disbanded in 1994 after Namibia finally became independent and the Council itself was satisfied that European colonialism—so powerful a force for so long a time—was now finished. But it was a long time getting there: the 1950s and 1960s saw the largest wave of decolonization as it swept over Africa, the Caribbean and southeast Asia. Britain's decolonization marked the largest wave, as it had the largest empire. It sought, in the 1950s and 1960s, to replace the structure of formal empire with a voluntary and informal alliance between independent members of the British Commonwealth. The Commonwealth had residual resonance for a while but today retains little content and glue.

Often, during decolonization, serious rifts and even regional wars erupted as newly liberated peoples proceeded to struggle among themselves over the shape of their new state. Other times the colonial power itself had a hard time letting go, like France in Algeria, and so the people rose up in violence to force it out. A select few times, the process of decolonization and national self-determination attracted the interests of the superpowers, and deadly, protracted wars erupted. Cases of this include Vietnam and Afghanistan. These are now called "proxy wars" because they were fought between the superpowers, to a certain degree, but in Third-World countries and employing local "substitutes" in their place. It is important to note that, when the Cold War did heat up it was in a Third-World location, and that fact probably reveals something about the endurance of Western attitudes of cultural superiority even after colonization ended; conflicts were permitted to break out far away, but never too close to home)

The most salient fact about the Third World during the Cold War was the grinding poverty and deprivation its citizens had to endure. Industrialization had barely touched the Third World; the colonial powers had been exploiting its people and resources for centuries, and massive over-population put severe strains on the amount of resources left over. The poverty had wide-ranging effects well beyond the rates of starvation and misery, disease and deprivation. It led, first, to political corruption: when leaders came to power in a Third-World country, they often used their power to line their own pockets. They employed their power not to ben-efit their people but, rather, to bolster their Swiss bank accounts. Africa, in particular, suffered from this phenomenon. The poverty also led Third World countries to seek assistance from either the First or Second World, in exchange for loyalty and military alliance in the Cold War chess game. The newly liberated countries looked for either a First- or a Second-World "patron"—some even had the gumption to play both sides, turn-ing to both Washington and Moscow for assistance. The human rights implications of the patronage phenomenon were substantial. Often, the human rights record of regimes were overlooked in the interests of the larger Cold War struggle when it came to patronage decisions. Thus America and other First-World countries found themselves in friendly relations with some very unsavoury governments, especially military dic-tatorships in Central and South America, in southeast Asia, and in the Middle East. The Cold War human rights records of countries such as Argentina and Chile, for example, were a disgrace. They included "dis-appearances," jailings, tortures, and murders of political dissidents. Non-governmental human rights groups, such as Amnesty International, were formed to protest these and related actions. The patronage phenomenon, and the use of the Third World as a chess board for Cold War scheming, had the further effect of arming the Third World to an unprecedented scale. This not only fuelled the "proxy wars" of the 1945-90 period; it also facilitated the killing and instability that followed from some of the post-1990 struggles inspired by ethnic hatred and tribal rivalry. At other times something of the opposite phenomenon occurred. Instead of befriending rights-violative regimes there was a deliberate decision not to interfere with such regimes for fear of provoking the other superpower. Thus the world sat by while Pol Pot's Khmer Rouge fanatics committed genocide in Cambodia, and while a racist white minority implemented and enforced apartheid rule over the black majority in South Africa.

Third World leaders tried, throughout the Cold War, to improve their lots either through patronage relationships or the development programs on offer through the United Nations. Aid programs designed to transfer resources and know-how blossomed—to varying and disputed results. Most of the earliest aid was military and did little to improve Third-World economies. Later, most of the aid was "tied," i.e., designed so that it brought greater long-term benefits to the First-World donor country than it did to the Third-World recipient. There is little doubt that today's aid programs have learned much from past failures, but their effects remain difficult to gauge and are of continuing controversy. It remains especially, and perhaps surprisingly, hard to ensure that development aid actually gets to those who need it most. There was, in the 1970s, a call for the establishment of a New International Economic Order (NIEO) to mitigate some of the severe socio-economic inequalities between the First and Third World. People talked about new terms of trade, a transfer of technology from rich to poor nations, debt forgiveness, and even reparations from colonial powers for past exploitation. The NEIO came to nothing. Parts of the Third World did, however, succeed in co-operating on one issue that enabled them to capture added resources from the First World and to make real gains in wealth and development. These parts formed the Organization of Petroleum Exporting Countries (OPEC) in the early 1970s, and since that time have enjoyed success in influencing the world price of oil and gas to their own benefit. The richest OPEC members are the Arab-dominated states in the Middle East. Other parts of the Third World, especially in southeast Asia, were able to carve out specialized niches in free-market trade with the First World. As a result, they were able to make real development gains by the 1980s. Countries such as Taiwan, South Korea, Singapore and Malaysia come to mind.

Reference to OPEC and the Middle East introduces one final consideration regarding the Third World during the Cold War. This deals with the founding of Israel. After the Holocaust, Jewish leaders around the world rallied to the cause of founding a Jewish-based nation-state, to be called Israel, in the Middle Eastern lands biblically associated with the Jewish people. Their compelling argument was that they could no longer count on the protection of a government that was not their own. The Western powers—especially Britain and America—concurred and helped secure land in Palestine, affecting Arab-Palestinian settlements in the area. The founding of Israel in 1948 was, for this and other reasons, rejected by the state's Arab and Islamic neighbours, and conflict between Israelis and Arabs has blown hot and cold for more than 50 years. Israelis have argued an elemental entitlement to their ancient homeland, and cited the Holocaust as proof they need their own state as a matter of human right. Arabs, in turn, have found the way in which Israelis have pursued security and land to be at times rough, and they continue to express concern over the fate of the Palestinians.

The Second World of centrally-planned communist societies was formed in the immediate post-1945 period. We saw previously that Russia experienced the world's first communist revolution in 1917 when the Bolsheviks—inspired by the work of Karl Marx—seized power, executed the czar and withdrew Russia from World War I. They consolidated their control and in short order were able to convert tiny neighbouring countries to communist regimes. In the early 1920s they renamed the whole collection of republics the USSR, or Soviet Union. We saw in Chapter 6 that communism is an ideology hostile to human rights, as such individual protections get in the way of the construction of a mass society designed to radically equalize and to benefit especially the body of workers. Civil and political rights, particularly to personal freedoms, are drastically devalued. Most communist regimes have been brutal, authoritarian dictatorships, but in the name of the welfare of the workers as opposed to, as with the Nazis, the dominance of the Aryan race. The true, rights-violative nature of real-world communist societies was perhaps masked until Joseph Stalin came to power in the Soviet Union. Stalin was a cold and ruthless man who craved power above all and employed the most violent and vulgar methods to seize control in the USSR after the founding revolutionary, Vladimir Lenin, died. Stalin's allegiance to communist ideals is almost beside the point: he professed loyalty to the doctrine but ruled above all in the interests of his own absolute grip on power, which stretched from the 1930s to the 1950s. In his early reign, Stalin launched a series of "purges" to rid the Soviet Union of all who threatened his rule. Figures are difficult to verify, but experts agree that probably millions were jailed, tortured, exiled or killed during this period. By the time World War II broke out, Stalin had perfected the art of running a ruthless police state.[8]

The war had devastating effects on the USSR. Casualties on the Eastern Front, between Germany and Russia, were the war's largest. The fighting was especially ferocious and venomous, involving horrible violations of the laws of war. The Soviets were surprised by Hitler's betrayal of their non-aggression pact and were initially overwhelmed by the scope and strength of the forces the Nazis threw at them. Eventually, though, sheer force of numbers prevailed, and the Soviets—entirely on their own—were able to turn the tide in the East against Hitler. The Soviets did enter into an alliance with the Western powers as the war drew to a close, but it was always uneasy and precarious, with precious little sharing of vital information. The Western Allies were suspicious of communism, and the Soviets returned the feeling. At war's end, when they were all negotiating a peace, the uneasy feelings degenerated into hostility. The Soviets demanded control over Central and Eastern Europe. Their reasons were two-fold: they already controlled the area with armed force anyway, as a consequence of driving Hitler back into Germany; and they wanted a buffer zone between themselves and Germany to better block any future invasion. The Western powers saw little choice but to go along, especially since the USSR already enjoyed *de facto* control. They put up some nominal resistance and verbal objections, but little more. Thus, in Winston Churchill's famous phrase, did an "iron curtain" come to fall across the middle of Europe, separating East from West. The Soviets dominated the East, and the Americans—with the British and French as sidekicks—did so for the West. Suspicions and positions between the two camps hardened. Part of this was predictable rivalry between the powerful. Part was genuine ideological confrontation: they despised each other's political philosophy. The Soviets especially feared American possession of the atomic bomb and raced to develop their own. They also feared the productive capacities and technological sophistication of the American economy and quickly developed "five-year plans" to force-feed advanced industrialization to their own people. The Americans, in turn, feared that the shattered economies of Europe would drive desperate former Allies into the arms of communism. They cited the rise of communist parties in Italy, France and Greece, and Britain's own surprising ouster of Churchill's Conservatives in favour of Labour in the 1945 elections. Quickly, both sides moved to cement their own spheres of influence. The Americans launched the Marshall Plan in 1947 to rebuild Europe's economies, and then followed up with the formation of a military alliance in 1949: the North Atlantic Treaty Organization (NATO). NATO was formed specifically to resist any Soviet invasion of Western Europe. The Soviets, for their part, moved to install puppet regimes in those countries they controlled, and founded their own rival military alliance, the Warsaw Pact. The Soviets even tried to seize sole control of Berlin, Hitler's former capital, in clear violation of the postwar peace agreement. In 1947, the Soviets blocked Western access to the city. The

Americans responded with a year-long airlift of supplies into the Western-controlled sector of the city. The Soviets dropped the blockade, but otherwise refused to budge: the fault lines of the Cold War were now firm.

Then the Second World suddenly grew, and the stakes went up. In 1949, there was a communist revolution in China, which bordered the Soviet Union in the far east. Furthermore, many of the national independence movements on the rise in the Third World following the start of European decolonization started to ally themselves with communist ideology. This was especially true in pockets of Africa and southeast Asia. Americans feared a "domino effect," namely, that one by one vulnerable neighbouring countries would fall to Soviet domination. When communist forces from North Korea moved into the South, the Americans led a "police action" to repulse the invasion. This "police action," which had the UN's authorization, was better known as the Korean War of 1950-53. It was a proxy war between America and communist China (which at that time enjoyed Soviet support, too). It was fought to a standstill, and Korea, much like Germany, continued as two separate states for the rest of the Cold War and beyond.

Shortly thereafter, the Soviets developed the hydrogen bomb, crushed a rebellion in Hungary and launched the world's first space satellite, Sputnik. The five-year plans seemed to be succeeding: the Soviet economy was robust. The Americans reacted vigorously and poured money into their own military, including a new space program. They stockpiled existing weapons, developed new ones, competed over comparative missile counts, and raced to put the first man in space and then on the Moon. An arms race was on in earnest. Things worsened when Cuba fell to a communist revolution in 1959, and the Soviets put up the Berlin Wall in 1961 to prevent refugees fleeing the East for the West. The moment of maximum intensity during the Cold War was the Cuban Missile Crisis of 1962. After Fidel Castro's communist takeover of Cuba, the Americans invaded the island at the Bay of Pigs to try to reverse the revolution. The ill-organized invasion failed. Castro feared a repeat performance and requested that his Soviet allies place nuclear weapons on his Caribbean island to deter the Americans from trying again. When the US discovered the plan, it reacted in outrage. The very idea of nuclear weapons raining down on American cities was too much, and the Americans demanded that existing missiles on Cuba be withdrawn, or else. They further established a naval blockade around the island to prevent more missiles from being installed. The world waited for a very tense time before the Soviets reluctantly agreed to American terms, handing US President John F. Kennedy a shining moment of triumph in his foreign policy. The US had forced the Soviets to back down in the world's first, and so far only, direct nuclear confrontation.

In the meantime, on the other side of the world, the Americans were being dragged into Vietnam. The former French colony was torn between communist and non-communist forces, and the Americans, motivated by the "domino effect" theory, got involved. They had some fresh evidence for the theory, too: the Vietnamese communists were being aided and supplied by both China and the Soviet Union; and the Soviets themselves, in 1968, crushed a rebellion in Czechoslovakia. That year saw the most intense fighting in Vietnam, a war that was eventually fought to an unclear resolution. The Americans, spurred on by public opinion, finally got out in 1974 and within a year the Vietnamese communists took over the entire country. Communist expansionists then set their sights on African countries such as Angola, on Caribbean islands such as Grenada and, in 1979, Afghanistan.

By the time Ronald Reagan became the US President in 1981 the stage was set for the final showdown between the two superpowers. The Soviet Union was no longer what it seemed to be in the 1950s. Its economy was stagnating, its political leadership was elderly and uninspired, the old cooperation with China was over, and the war in Afghanistan became the USSR's own version of Vietnam, wherein the smaller and weaker country was, with the clandestine help of one superpower, able to bog down the other in a conflict without end. There had been a marked thaw in the Cold War in the 1970s, known as détente, when the superpowers agreed to arms control and even signed a shared document affirming human rights, the Helsinki Act of 1975.[9] But the pendulum swung back and the freeze was on again before Reagan's inauguration, mostly owing to the Soviet invasion of Afghanistan.

The key to the final showdown was the USSR's collapse in economic growth. The Soviet economy simply could not sustain the level of military expenditure that the American could. A centrally-planned economy, devoid of profit incentive and free-market interaction between supply and demand, evidently cannot out-produce a capitalist one. In the words of Cold War scholar Martin Walker, the American economy could provide *both* guns and butter whereas the Soviets, eventually, had to choose.[10] At first, the military won out, resulting in real deprivations for the Soviet people. Long lines of prospective customers appeared outside retail establishments, even for basic goods, and severe shortages were rampant. But even an authoritarian communist regime can only disappoint its people for so long. Over the long term, any government must choose—*if* the choice is forced on it—in favour of butter over guns. The people simply will not stand there and starve. The Reagan administration saw this and in the 1980s launched one final, massive burst of military spending, with the aim of forcing the Soviets to choose more quickly than they wanted. Reagan even threatened the development of a new, ultra-expensive laser-guided missile defence system—"Star Wars"—that would render existing Soviet arms beside the point. The Soviets initially attempted to respond, but their economy buckled under the pressure, and a change of leadership was forced upon them. Mikhail Gorbachev came to power and quickly sought to negotiate more arms control agreements with the Americans and to open the Soviet economy to much needed Western investment. The Soviets not only blinked, they folded. When they retreated from Central and Eastern Europe in 1989, the Berlin Wall came crashing down and a wave of national liberation movements swept the region. In 1990 Germany was reunited and the newly liberated nations sat down with the states of Western Europe to sign the Charter of Paris for a New Europe, which commits all signatories to develop democratic and human rights-respecting institutions.[11] The Soviet Union itself ceased to exist in 1991: it was briefly replaced by the Commonwealth of Independent States, which itself soon dissolved into a collection of separate sovereign nations. Russia returned to the map for the first time since 1917. As went the Soviet Union, so went Central and Eastern Europe and many client communist regimes around the world. The "domino effect" went the other way, to the point where today only a handful of countries—Cuba, China, North Korea and Vietnam—still call themselves communist.

So the First World won the Cold War, and we have just seen how, but what else of relevance to human rights happened in the West during the Cold War period? The first thing to note is how the Americans, in particular, learned the lessons of the Treaty of Versailles. Instead of impoverishing, exhausting and humiliating the defeated enemy, the Americans poured massive amounts of expertise and investment into postwar Japan and (West) Germany. The reconstruction and rehabilitation of these two societies, largely by the United States, counts as one of the twentieth century's major success stories. The Germans and Japanese have enjoyed the fruits of a peaceful and prosperous free-market society for generations now, and indeed have the largest national economies in the world after the US. Of course, America's involvement with these countries was motivated not by love or altruism but rather by a healthy prudential regard for its own future security and for strategic advantage against the USSR and China during the Cold War. Still, the transformation of aggressive fascist dictatorships into peaceful, rights-respecting democracies was remarkable, and provides a valuable guide for those interested in understanding what basic structures a society needs to become rights-respecting.[12]

The Cold War also consolidated the post-Depression, and wartime, trend towards a large governmental presence in the economy. After World War II, there were fears that if the state disengaged from economic life there might be a return to the unpredictable boom-and-bust cycle of the 1920s and 1930s. Moreover, many veterans returning from harrowing experiences on the battlefield demanded, as their reward, extensive state-funded favours and benefits, notably subsidized housing and education. Thus the scope of the welfare state originally begun in the 1930s was deepened and widened. Western governments poured money into subsidized housing and education, into building new colleges and universities for retraining, into the roads needed to link them all, into food and health care subsidies, into more generous unemployment insurance systems, and so forth. The goal was the creation of cradle-to-grave benefits designed to ensure that all citizens could count on access to important public goods—like education, health care, housing and subsistence income—regardless of the ups and downs of the free-market business cycle. The state was seen as needed to smooth out the business cycle, to guide overall economic development and, above all, to prevent citizens from falling beneath the floor of a generously-defined social minimum.

It must be noted that the increased state presence in First-World economies was not limited to economic regulation and the provision of public benefits to all citizens. In America especially, the demands of the Cold War also spurred the development of a vast, and enormously expensive, national security establishment. Staggering sums were spent on weapons programs, maintaining the armed forces and funding espionage activities, not to mention the various proxy wars that erupted during this era. For this reason, Americans probably got to enjoy fewer welfare state benefits than did, say, their European, Japanese and Canadian counterparts. Cold War primacy and leadership came at the cost of some real trade-offs in American social policy.

The peak of the Western welfare state was probably during the late 1960s and into the 1970s, when many countries implemented state-run health care systems and ran massive schooling programs to educate the Baby Boom generation. For example, American President Lyndon Johnson in the mid-1960s called his welfare program "The Great Society," and a few years later Canadian Prime Minister Pierre Trudeau followed with his own vision for "A Just Society." By the late 1970s and early 1980s conservative governments around the First World—starting with Margaret Thatcher in Britain and Reagan in America—began to roll back the welfare state in the interests of reducing the taxes needed to fund it, of freeing business from extensive regulation, and of generally shrinking the size of the state for ideological reasons related to personal liberty and some evidence of state inefficiency. The precise role of state intervention in our lives and in the provision of social benefits remains to this day one of the most relevant and controversial human rights topics.

The late 1960s witnessed the birth of some new rights concerns and the vigorous re-birth of older ones. Feminism was front-and-centre, as women capitalized on wartime work experiences to demand greater inclusion, and wage fairness, in the working world. The invention of the birth control pill only accelerated this, and had the added benefit of giving women greater control over their reproductive capacities. There arose a robust women's rights movement that continues to this day. Concerns over industrial pollution and some alarming images of environmental decay and disaster called forth the modern environmental movement. This movement succeeded, in the early 1970s, in pressuring First-World governments to implement the first real environmental protections and regulations. The movement also forwarded the claim that, in addition to first-generation claims to security and liberty, and to second-generation claims to subsistence, there are third-generation human rights to clean air and water, and to access to land which is not so polluted as to be uninhabitable. Difficulties in delivering the objects of established human rights to everyone—especially to visible minorities—generated during this time a robust civil rights movement, especially in America. This movement produced real, rights-related gains for some minority groups and attacked enduring problems of prejudice and discrimination in otherwise advanced societies. Civil rights advocates, student agitators, environmentalists and feminist activists all tended to coalesce with Vietnam War protestors, and by the late 1960s raucous political demonstrations were almost a daily event. The year 1968 was especially active in this regard throughout the entire First World. Some institutional reforms, America's eventual exit from Vietnam, and the maturing of the protestors themselves took much of the wind out of the sails of this interesting coalition. The liberal, left-leaning flavour of the 1960s and 1970s were supplanted by a more conservative, right-leaning sensibility in the 1980s and 1990s.

Partially in response to the American public's hostile reception to the Vietnam War, the role that respect for human rights should play in a country's foreign policy was highlighted in the late 1970s. American President Jimmy Carter prided himself on making respect for human rights a foundation for US foreign policy. He wanted to distance himself from the cold and calculating, power-focussed foreign policy that had character-ized the thinking that went into the Vietnam War and into US support for questionable client states in Latin America. Carter was strongly criticized for this apparent "softening" in the midst of the Cold War. Reagan replaced him and got rid of all talk of a more sensitive foreign policy. Reagan favoured a return to the nuts-and-bolts issue of Cold War strug-gle. But for all his realist rhetoric, Reagan was also animated by a con-cern for human rights, especially for freedom, in his foreign policy. He just thought that the main moral and prudential imperative was to defeat the Soviet Union, and only then to deal with Latin American dictators. Concern for the advancement of certain rights ideals has always been a facet of American foreign policy since at least the days of Wilson: Carter simply made it more explicit. It remains to this day a vital and contested issue to what extent a country should use its foreign policy to influence human rights elsewhere, especially when such advancement may hinder such other goals as military security or the promotion of trade.[13]

After the Cold War and Into the Future

The immediate post-Cold war period, from 1989-91, was one of eupho-ria. Nobody predicted that the Soviet Union would simply back out of the arms race and then withdraw its armed forces and support from Warsaw Pact allies. It all happened so quickly. For all the American pres-sure and strategy, these decisions of the new Soviet leadership—espe-cially Gorbachev—must also be credited with contributing to the Cold War's end. A wave of democratization swept over Central and Eastern Europe, as Soviet client states discovered they could not hold on to power without Moscow's help. Communists were swept out of office, some peacefully and politically, others with violence. The Berlin Wall was torn down, Germany reunified and the USSR itself dissolved into Russia and various other republics. New regimes were eager to prove their human rights credentials, and as first steps held elections and signed The Charter of Paris, as mentioned. Over time, they took steps to modernize and free their economies and to pass constitutional pro-tections of basic rights and freedoms. Above all, the new nations of Cen-tral and Eastern Europe lined up, mainly for economic reasons, to join the European Union (EU). The EU is the successor to the European Economic Community, first formed in the early 1950s to coordinate economic policies and enhance political cooperation between the states of Western Europe and Scandinavia. It has since evolved into a supra-national form of governance, setting fiscal and monetary policies and much else throughout the entire region. Europe now sports a common currency and a central bank, and increasing cooperation is being developed in areas such as criminal justice, military security and foreign affairs. There is an elected European parliament, a European bureaucracy, and even a European court. This last is especially relevant for human rights. If citizens alleging human rights violations have exhausted the court processes in their own countries without favourable resolution, they can be entitled in some instances to take the case to the pan-European court. The idea is to set up supra-national institutions with the power to enforce human rights norms throughout the Union, even in spite of a national government's reluctance. Furthermore, membership in the Union itself has requirements of good governance and respect for human rights. The European regional human rights courts have been copied in the Americas and Africa, and even in the United Nations itself. Citizens of member countries can be entitled to take human rights complaints to the Inter-American court, the African court, or to one of several United Nations human rights committees and commissions, provided they have received no satisfaction within their own national court system. The UN also requires regular reports on human rights implementation from all its member states. Generally speaking, though, all these latter arrangements are not nearly as developed as the European system. They currently result in little more than publicity and political pressure, whereas the European court often has the actual power to enforce its decisions. Still, the trend towards the further development and greater authority of genuinely *international* enforcement of human rights is clearly established.[14]

The year 1989 also witnessed a democratic up-swell within communist China. After several days of hope for a swift, Eastern European-style transition, the Chinese leadership crushed the movement with military force in a massacre at Tienanmin Square in Beijing. To this day, the government of China remains one of the last and most stubborn opponents of human rights reforms. The reform of China, accordingly, is near the top of the agenda for many of the countless human rights organizations which have sprouted up around the world.[15]

The human rights movement now counts amongst its members not just like-minded individuals but also governments with pro-human rights foreign policies, lawyers' and judges' associations, international human rights institutions, student groups, non-governmental organizations, development agencies, think-tanks and academic institutes. There is also a clear trend in favour of human rights education; indeed, this book seeks to contribute to that trend. The human rights movement itself has a history and has, moreover, recently developed a critical mass not only to sustain itself over time but also to effect real change.[16]

It is hard to recapture the incredible optimism that came with the Cold War's end. Serious people sincerely believed that the collapse of the Soviet Union not only ended the world's last European empire; it also marked victory for pro-rights democratic capitalism as the most just and proper mode of social organization yet on offer.[17] There was a sense of triumphalism at the time, which was only underlined by America's quick and complete victory in the Persian Gulf War against Iraq. It was expected that the Cold War's end would also produce a "peace dividend," in that military expenditures could now be cut and the resources transferred to more humanitarian causes like social services. Furthermore, one of the great scourges of the human rights movement—the apartheid government of South Africa—also collapsed, paving the way there for progress toward democracy and human rights. Everything seemed to be coming up roses for those who cared about peace and justice.

What undermined the wave of optimism was the eruption of armed conflict in Central Europe and Central Africa. Various national groups who had had their distinctive identities and cultures suppressed by communism took advantage of the Soviet withdrawal by pressing forward their own claims, often to full-blown national independence. The conflict of these claims boiled over in the former Yugoslavia, and Serb, Croat and Muslim nationalities came to armed conflict. What followed was a long and brutal civil war in Bosnia, from 1992-95. Civil war also broke out in 1994 in the African country of Rwanda between the rival Hutu and Tutsi people. Brutalities and barbarities committed during these two wars, which were fuelled by ethnic nationalism and vicious group hatreds, shocked the world's moral conscience. In Bosnia, civilian populations were deliberately targeted with lethal force, mass rape campaigns occurred, and concentration camps reappeared for the first time since the Nazis scarred Europe's face. In Rwanda, venomous communal hatreds produced mass murder on a near-genocidal scale. The international community failed to intervene effectively in these killings, but still saw fit to establish the first international war crimes trials since the Nuremberg and Tokyo trials in 1945-46. As of the time of writing, people are still being charged and tried at The Hague in Holland for their actions during these wars. Furthermore, the international community in 1998 passed a treaty to create a *permanent* and independent international court for the prosecution of war crimes and other crimes against humanity. Not enough countries have ratified this treaty as of writing, but they are expected to, and it should be up and running soon.

This permanent court will further the previously mentioned development of international human rights courts and institutions.

The controversial question of when to intervene militarily in a country where massive human rights violations are occurring was highlighted in Bosnia and Rwanda. It remains a difficult issue for human rights advocates. Partly out of guilt for failing to intervene in Bosnia, Western nations did so in Serbia in 1999. The Serbian government, which had been very much involved in the Bosnian civil war, was applying its authoritarian nationalism against the Albanian minority within its borders. The Serb army tried to force the Albanians out of the province of Kosovo. The West, making use of the old NATO infrastructure, deployed armed force and made the Serbs back down. Within a year of its defeat, the Serbian government fell and its former strongman, Slobodan Milosevic, found himself under arrest and facing trial—not just in Serbia but also at The Hague.

The post-Cold War period has witnessed the growth of international co-operation not only in war crimes prosecution but also in the promotion of trade. We are now, it is often said, operating in a fully global free-market system. Communism's defeat has left capitalism as the only plausible method for organizing an economy, and so all but a few holdouts—like North Korea—have adopted it in some form. Borders no longer have the relevance they once did: businesses, people and money now flow around the world in search for the best rewards they can get. Goods and services now get produced for world-wide, and not merely national, consumption. Computers and communications connect the world: there is even something of a global pop culture developing. Globalization is here; McLuhan's "global village" is all but built. Advocates of globalization say that this is good, not only because it raises living standards but also because history shows that free-market capitalism, and the other salient trend toward more democracy, go hand-in-hand with human rights. We should thus expect not only economic but also moral and political improvements as globalization progresses. Others are not so sure. They suggest that "globalization" is merely a happy code-word for American dominance and America's use of its influence, as the only remaining superpower, to now turn the entire world economy to its own profit and advantage. Others worry that the countries of the Third World—now known as "underdeveloped" or "developing" countries—are starting from a position so far behind that of the developed countries that they stand to gain little from the flurry of international trading activity, financial exchange and market development. The relationship between trade and rights, and between rights and development, is a controversial and increasingly important one for the future. As leaders of nations sign more and more trade agreements, more and more objectors seem to take to the streets in protest. Defenders of trade argue that long-term economic growth is the best guarantee of rights satisfaction and poverty alleviation, whereas opponents doubt whether the benefits will really flow back to those who need them most. There can be little doubt that the presence of widespread poverty and deep deprivation must be of concern to any who take seriously the human rights idea that everyone deserves to live a life of at least minimal value in the modern world. The grim conditions in parts of the developing world further give rise to questions whether people there may immigrate to, or become refugees in, developed countries. As a rule, developed countries jealously guard their borders so as not to be swamped. But the global economy, and its associated mobility, are beginning to highlight questions of immigration and refugee status as possible matters for human rights advocates. Can there be a human right to enter the country of one's choice? Are there, conversely, any limits to an established community's right to let in only those it chooses?[18]

The developed world has few grounds for complacency on the human rights front, even if most of its people do indeed enjoy minimally decent lives. For even the richest countries have their own pockets of deep poverty, homelessness and deprivation. The vulnerability of children, the elderly and the mentally ill to these phenomena, and to physical abuse, is of special concern. The wealthiest countries also have their own kinds of crime, and even official corruption, that call out for rights-respecting reform. Debates continue, as noted in Chapter 4, regarding the full specification of the foundational five objects of our human rights: security, subsistence, liberty, equality, and recognition. There are, in particular, substantial issues of equality and non-discrimination yet to be resolved. Such issues involve references to gender, sexual orientation, and visible and cultural minorities. There are related, yet broader, issues of how to ensure that we all manage to get along peacefully as our societies become more free and diverse; how to cherish individual and group differences while at the same time retaining the cohesion and order needed to ensure security and stability; how to use institutions to preserve democracy and majority rule, yet also secure fair treatment for minorities. The developed world's technological prowess—one of the sources of its very prosperity—also poses human rights perplexities, especially in connection with health care, human reproduction and biomedical ethics. How to treat the sick in a dignified way can at times be difficult, and some new technologies, such as cloning, stretch the boundaries of thought regarding the moral status of what is being experimented with. There are also questions of the right to personal privacy in an age dominated by invasive information technology, driven by the latest developments in computers. The legal systems of most developed countries are frequently the site on which these and other issues are debated and resolved. It follows that the legal arena is one of special concern, attention and energy for human rights advocates. In the political arena the extent of state intervention in the economy and society and the connection such intervention has to a level of vitally needed subsistence and decent treatment is rarely far from the surface of debate. Also enduring and difficult is the foreign policy question of how best to use one's influence to promote respect for human rights in other countries. There may actually be issues not merely of policy preference but positive obligation in this regard, as discussed in Chapter 5. The terrorist strikes on America in 2001 highlighted concerns with security. On the one hand, we have a human right to it; on the other, stringent security arrangements can sometimes violate civil liberties. The strikes, and the response, underlined enduring questions about a just war and the complex connection between force and human rights. An important connection between the economy, technology, health care, and even security and foreign policy, can be seen in environmental issues. Most countries face real challenges regarding the use of vitally needed natural resources (such as drinkable water), the exploitation of sources of energy, the trade-off between economic activity and pollution, and the need to ensure a non-toxic environment for ourselves and future generations.[19]

These last two chapters have been but a brief tour of how human rights shape our present and frame our future. The historical details, of course, are deep and diverse, but going further would divert us from our main goal. That goal, all along, has been this: to develop an adequate understanding of the conceptual elements of human rights, as well as the historical, legal and political context within which such rights have been respected, or else violated. The goal was to provide a comprehensive and substantive look at human rights, in both theory and practice. That goal, I think, has now been achieved.[20]

Notes

1 J. Keegan, *The First World War* (New York: Vintage, 2000).

2 M. Boemeke, ed., *The Treaty of Versailles* (Cambridge: Cambridge University Press, 1998); M.E. Howard, *et al.*, eds., *The Oxford History of the 20th Century* (Oxford: Oxford University Press, 2000).

3 Howard, *et al.*, ed., *Oxford History, passim*; E. Birkowitz and K. McQuaid, *Creating the Welfare State*, 2nd ed. (New York: Praeger, 1988); D. Gladstone, *The 20th Century Welfare State* (London: Palgrave, 1999).

4 J. Keegan, *The Second World War* (New York: Vintage, 1990); M. Gilbert, *The Holocaust* (New York: Henry Holt, 1987); J. Glover, *Humanity: A Moral History of the 20th Century* (New Haven: Yale University Press, 2000).

5 Howard, *et al.*, ed., *Oxford History, passim*; H.J. Steiner and P. Alston, eds., *International Human Rights in Context* (New York: Oxford, 2000), 56-135; W. Reisman and C. Antoniou, eds., *The Laws of War* (New York: Vintage, 1994), 318-50; G. Best, *War and Law Since 1945* (Oxford: Clarendon, 1994).

6 Steiner and Alston, eds., *International Rights, passim*; M. Ishay, ed., *The Human Rights Reader* (New York: Routledge, 1997), 403-11, 424-40; M.A. Glendon, *A World Made New: Eleanor Roosevelt and the Universal Declaration of Human Rights* (New York: Random House, 2001).

7 M. Walker, *The Cold War: A History* (New York: Henry Holt, 1995).

8 S. Courtois, *et al.*, *The Black Book of Communism: Crimes, Terror, Repression* (Cambridge, MA: Harvard University Press, 1999).

9 Conference on Security and Cooperation in Europe, Final Act 1975, 1(a). See Ishay, ed., *The Human Rights Reader*, 452-61. A prominent human rights group, Helsinki Watch, was formed to monitor compliance. Today it is better known as Human Rights Watch.

10 Walker, *Cold War*, 28-29.

11 *Twenty-Five Human Rights Documents* (New York: Columbia University Center for the Study of Human Rights, 1995), 210-19.

12 We talked about these requirements in Chapter 5.

13 Walker, *Cold War, passim*; Howard, *et al.*, eds., *Oxford History, passim*; Birkowitz and McQuaid, *Welfare State, passim*; J. Schumpeter, *Capitalism, Socialism and Democracy*, 3rd ed. (New York: HarperCollins, 1984); F. Furet, *The Passing of an Illusion: The Idea of Communism in the 20th Century* (Chicago: University of Chicago Press, 1999).

14 Steiner and Alston, eds., *International Rights*, 592-937.

15 R. Foot, *Rights Beyond Borders: The Global Community and The Struggle over Human Rights in China* (Oxford: Oxford University Press, 2001).

16 R.F. Drinan, *The Mobilization of Shame: A World View of Human Rights* (New Haven: Yale University Press, 2001); W. Korey, *NGOs and the Universal Declaration of Human Rights* (New York: Palgrave, 1998); S. Power and G. Allison, eds., *Realizing Human Rights* (New York: Palgrave, 2000).

17 F. Fukuyama, "The End of History?" *The National Interest* 16 (1989): 3-18; H. Williams, *et al.*, *Francis Fukuyama and The End of History* (Cardiff: University of Wales Press, 1997).

18 See the following pieces of international law: The Convention Relating to the Status of Refugees (1954), pp. 57-70 in *Twenty Five Human Rights Documents*; and The United Nations Declaration on the Right to Development (1986), pp. 469-73 of Ishay, ed., *Reader*.

19 Other relevant sources for the future of human rights include R. Falk, *Human Rights Horizons* (Princeton: Princeton University Press, 2000); M. Ignatieff, *The Rights Revolution* (Toronto: Anansi, 2000); D. Forsythe, *Human Rights in International Relations* (Cambridge: Cambridge University Press, 2000); R. McRae and D. Hubert, eds., *Human Security and The New Diplomacy* (Montreal: McGill-Queens University Press, 2001); T. Risse, ed., *The Power of Human Rights* (Cambridge: Cambridge University Press, 1999); and T. Dunne, ed., *Human Rights in Global Politics* (Cambridge: Cambridge University Press, 1999).

20 Other histories on various aspects of human rights include P.G. Lauren, *The Evolution of International Human Rights* (Philadelphia: University of Pennsylvania Press, 1998); L. Henkin, *The Age of Rights* (New York: Columbia University Press, 1990); R. Drinan, *Cry of the Oppressed* (New York: Palgrave, 1987); S. Davidson, *Human Rights* (London: Open University Press, 1993); L.J. MacFarlane, *The Theory and Practice of Human Rights* (London: Temple Smith, 1985); and I. Shapiro, *The Evolution of Rights in Liberal Theory* (Cambridge: Cambridge University Press, 1986). There are also histories to be found in various encyclopaedic entries on human rights. There is even an *Encyclopedia of Human Rights*, edited by E. Lawson (New York: Taylor & Francis, 1991).

Appendix A

The American Bill of Rights
(1789)

First Amendment: Congress shall make no law respecting an establishment of religion, or prohibiting the free exercise thereof; or abridging the freedom of speech, or of the press; or the right of the people peaceably to assemble, and to petition the government for a redress of grievances.

Second Amendment: A well regulated militia being necessary to the security of a free state, the right of the people to keep and bear arms shall not be infringed.

Third Amendment: No soldier shall, in time of peace, be quartered in any house, without the consent of the owner, nor in time of war, but in a manner to be prescribed by law.

Fourth Amendment: The right of the people to be secure in their persons, houses, papers, and effects, against unreasonable searches and seizures, shall not be violated, and no warrants shall issue, but upon probable cause, supported by oath or affirmation, and particularly describing the place to be searched, and the persons or things to be seized.

Fifth Amendment: No person shall be held to answer for a capital, or otherwise infamous crime, unless on a presentment or indictment of a grand jury, except in cases arising in the land or naval forces, or in the militia, when in actual service in time of war or public danger; nor shall any person be subject for the same offense to be twice put in jeopardy of life or limb; nor shall be compelled in any criminal case to be a witness against himself, nor be deprived of life, liberty, or property, without due process of law; nor shall private property be taken for public use, without just compensation.

Sixth Amendment: In all criminal prosecutions, the accused shall enjoy the right to a speedy and public trial, by an impartial jury of the state and district wherein the crime shall have been committed, which district shall have been previously ascertained by law, and to be informed of the nature and cause of the accusation; to be confronted with the witnesses against him; to have compulsory process for obtaining witnesses in his favor, and to have the assistance of counsel for his defense.

Seventh Amendment: In suits at common law, where the value in controversy shall exceed twenty dollars, the right of trial by jury shall be preserved, and no fact tried by a jury, shall be otherwise reexamined in any court of the United States, than according to the rules of the common law.

Eighth Amendment: Excessive bail shall not be required, nor excessive fines imposed, nor cruel and unusual punishments inflicted.

Ninth Amendment: The enumeration in the Constitution of certain rights shall not be construed to deny or disparage others retained by the people.

Tenth Amendment: The powers not delegated to the United States by the Constitution, nor prohibited by it to the states, are reserved to the states respectively, or to the people.

French Declaration
of The Rights of Man and Citizen
(1789)

The representatives of the French people, organized as a National Assembl[y] believing that the ignorance, neglect, or contempt of the rights of man are the so[le] cause of public calamities and of the corruption of governments, have determine[d] to set forth in a solemn declaration the natural, unalienable, and sacred rights [of] man, in order that this declaration, being constantly before all the members of th[e] Social body, shall remind them continually of their rights and duties; in order th[at] the acts of the legislative power, as well as those of the executive power, may b[e] compared at any moment with the objects and purposes of all political institutio[n] and may thus be more respected, and, lastly, in order that the grievances of the ci[t]izens, based hereafter upon simple and incontestable principles, shall tend to th[e] maintenance of the constitution and redound to the happiness of all. Therefore th[e] National Assembly recognizes and proclaims, in the presence and under the au[s]pices of the Supreme Being, the following rights of man and of the citizen:

1. Men are born and remain free and equal in rights. Social distinctions may be founded only upon the general good.

2. The aim of all political association is the preservation of the natural and imprescriptible rights of man. These rights are liberty, property, security, and resistance to oppression.

3. The principle of all sovereignty resides essentially in the nation. No body nor individual may exercise any authority which does not proceed directly from the nation.

4. Liberty consists in the freedom to do everything which injures no one else; hence the exercise of the natural rights of each man has no limits except those which assure to the other members of the society the enjoyment of the same rights. These limits can only be determined by law.

5. Law can only prohibit such actions as are hurtful to society. Nothing may be prevented which is not forbidden by law, and no one may be forced to do anything not provided for by law.

6. Law is the expression of the general will. Every citizen has a right to participate personally, or through his representative, in its foundation. It must be the same for all, whether it protects or punishes. All citizens, being equal in the eyes of the law, are equally eligible to all dignities and to all public positions and occupations, according to their abilities, and without distinction except that of their virtues and talents.

7. No person shall be accused, arrested, or imprisoned except in the cases and according to the forms prescribed by law. Any one soliciting, transmitting, executing, or causing to be executed, any arbitrary order, shall be punished. But any citizen summoned or arrested in virtue of the law shall submit without delay, as resistance constitutes an offense.

8. The law shall provide for such punishments only as are strictly and obviously necessary, and no one shall suffer punishment except it be legally inflicted in virtue of a law passed and promulgated before the commission of the offense.

9. As all persons are held innocent until they shall have been declared guilty, if arrest shall be deemed indispensable, all harshness not essential to the securing of the prisoner's person shall be severely repressed by law.

10. No one shall be disquieted on account of his opinions, including his religious views, provided their manifestation does not disturb the public order established by law.

(?) [handwritten margin note]

11. The free communication of ideas and opinions is one of the most precious of the rights of man. Every citizen may, accordingly, speak, write, and print with freedom, but shall be responsible for such abuses of this freedom as shall be defined by law.

12. The security of the rights of man and of the citizen requires public military forces. These forces are, therefore, established for the good of all and not for the personal advantage of those to whom they shall be intrusted.

13. A common contribution is essential for the maintenance of the public forces and for the cost of administration. This should be equitably distributed among all the citizens in proportion to their means.

14. All the citizens have a right to decide, either personally or by their representatives, as to the necessity of the public contribution; to grant this freely; to know to what uses it is put; and to fix the proportion, the mode of assessment and of collection and the duration of the taxes.

15. Society has the right to require of every public agent an account of his administration.

16. A society in which the observance of the law is not assured, nor the separation of powers defined, has no constitution at all.

17. Since property is an inviolable and sacred right, no one shall be deprived thereof except where public necessity, legally determined, shall clearly demand it, and then only on condition that the owner shall have been previously and equitably indemnified.

Is this as important [handwritten note]

Universal Declaration of Human Rights
(1948)

Preamble

Whereas recognition of the inherent dignity and of the equal and inalienable rights of all members of the human family is the foundation of freedom, justice and peace in the world,

Whereas disregard and contempt for human rights have resulted in barbarous acts which have outraged the conscience of mankind, and the advent of a world in which human beings shall enjoy freedom of speech and belief and freedom from fear and want has been proclaimed as the highest aspiration of the common people,

Whereas it is essential, if man is not to be compelled to have recourse, as a last resort, to rebellion against tyranny and oppression, that human rights should be protected by the rule of law,

Whereas it is essential to promote the development of friendly relations between nations,

Whereas the peoples of the United Nations have in the Charter reaffirmed their faith in fundamental human rights, in the dignity and worth of the human person and in the equal rights of men and women and have determined to promote social progress and better standards of life in larger freedom,

Whereas Member States have pledged themselves to achieve, in cooperation with the United Nations, the promotion of universal respect for and observance of human rights and fundamental freedoms,

Whereas a common understanding of these rights and freedoms is of the greatest importance for the full realization of this pledge,

Now, therefore The General Assembly proclaims this Universal Declaration of Human Rights as a common standard of achievement for all peoples and all nations, to the end that every individual and every organ of society, keeping this Declaration constantly in mind, shall strive by teaching and education to promote respect for these rights and freedoms and by progressive measures, national and international, to secure their universal and effective recognition and observance, both among the peoples of Member States themselves and among the peoples of territories under their jurisdiction.

Articles

1. All human beings are born free and equal in dignity and rights. They are endowed with reason and conscience and should act towards one another in a spirit of brotherhood.

2. Everyone is entitled to all the rights and freedoms set forth in this Declaration, without distinction of any kind, such as race, colour, sex, language, religion, political or other opinion, national or social origin, property, birth or other status. Furthermore, no distinction shall be made on the basis of the political, jurisdictional or international status of the country or territory to which a person belongs, whether it be independent, trust, non-self-governing or under any other limitation of sovereignty.

3. Everyone has the right to life, liberty and security of person.

4. No one shall be held in slavery or servitude; slavery and the slave trade shall be prohibited in all their forms.

5. No one shall be subjected to torture or to cruel, inhuman or degrading treatment or punishment.

6. Everyone has the right to recognition everywhere as a person before the law.

7. All are equal before the law and are entitled without any discrimination to equal protection of the law. All are entitled to equal protection against any discrimination in violation of this Declaration and against any incitement to such discrimination.

8. Everyone has the right to an effective remedy by the competent national tribunals for acts violating the fundamental rights granted him by the constitution or by law.

9. No one shall be subjected to arbitrary arrest, detention or exile.

10. Everyone is entitled in full equality to a fair and public hearing by an independent and impartial tribunal, in the determination of his rights and obligations and of any criminal charge against him.

11. (1) Everyone charged with a penal offence has the right to be presumed innocent until proved guilty according to law in a public trial at which he has had all the guarantees necessary for his defence.

(2) No one shall be held guilty of any penal offence on account of any act or omission which did not constitute a penal offence, under national or international law, at the time when it was committed. Nor

shall a heavier penalty be imposed than the one that was applicable at the time the penal offence was committed.

12. No one shall be subjected to arbitrary interference with his privacy, family, home or correspondence, nor to attacks upon his honour and reputation. Everyone has the right to the protection of the law against such interference or attacks.

13. (1) Everyone has the right to freedom of movement and residence within the borders of each state.

(2) Everyone has the right to leave any country, including his own, and to return to his country.

14. (1) Everyone has the right to seek and to enjoy in other countries asylum from persecution.

(2) This right may not be invoked in the case of prosecutions genuinely arising from non-political crimes or from acts contrary to the purposes and principles of the United Nations.

15. (1) Everyone has the right to a nationality.

(2) No one shall be arbitrarily deprived of his nationality nor denied the right to change his nationality.

16. (1) Men and women of full age, without any limitation due to race, nationality or religion, have the right to marry and to found a family. They are entitled to equal rights as to marriage, during marriage and at its dissolution.

(2) Marriage shall be entered into only with the free and full consent of the intending spouses.

(3) The family is the natural and fundamental group unit of society and is entitled to protection by society and the State.

17. (1) Everyone has the right to own property alone as well as in association with others.

(2) No one shall be arbitrarily deprived of his property.

18. Everyone has the right to freedom of thought, conscience and religion; this right includes freedom to change his religion or belief, and freedom, either alone or in community with others and in public or private, to manifest his religion or belief in teaching, practice, worship and observance.

19. Everyone has the right to freedom of opinion and expression; this right includes freedom to hold opinions without interference and to seek, receive and impart information and ideas through any media and regardless of frontiers.

20. (1) Everyone has the right to freedom of peaceful assembly and association.

    (2) No one may be compelled to belong to an association.

21. (1) Everyone has the right to take part in the government of his country, directly or through freely chosen representatives.

    (2) Everyone has the right of equal access to public service in his country. *Democracy?*

    (3) The will of the people shall be the basis of the authority of government; this will shall be expressed in periodic and genuine elections which shall be by universal and equal suffrage and shall be held by secret vote or by equivalent free voting procedures.

22. Everyone, as a member of society, has the right to social security and is entitled to realization, through national effort and international co-operation and in accordance with the organization and resources of each State, of the economic, social and cultural rights indispensable for his dignity and the free development of his personality.

23. (1) Everyone has the right to work, to free choice of employment, to just and favourable conditions of work and to protection against unemployment.

    (2) Everyone, without any discrimination, has the right to equal pay for equal work.

    (3) Everyone who works has the right to just and favourable remuneration ensuring for himself and his family an existence worthy of

human dignity, and supplemented, if necessary, by other means of social protection.

(4) Everyone has the right to form and to join trade unions for the protection of his interests.

24. Everyone has the right to rest and leisure, including reasonable limitation of working hours and periodic holidays with pay.

25. (1) Everyone has the right to a standard of living adequate for the health and well-being of himself and of his family, including food, clothing, housing and medical care and necessary social services, and the right to security in the event of unemployment, sickness, disability, widowhood, old age or other lack of livelihood in circumstances beyond his control.

(2) Motherhood and childhood are entitled to special care and assistance. All children, whether born in or out of wedlock, shall enjoy the same social protection.

26. (1) Everyone has the right to education. Education shall be free, at least in the elementary and fundamental stages. Elementary education shall be compulsory. Technical and professional education shall be made generally available and higher education shall be equally accessible to all on the basis of merit.

(2) Education shall be directed to the full development of the human personality and to the strengthening of respect for human rights and fundamental freedoms. It shall promote understanding, tolerance and friendship among all nations, racial or religious groups, and shall further the activities of the United Nations for the maintenance of peace.

(3) Parents have a prior right to choose the kind of education that shall be given to their children.

27. (1) Everyone has the right freely to participate in the cultural life of the community, to enjoy the arts and to share in scientific advancement and its benefits.

(2) Everyone has the right to the protection of the moral and material interests resulting from any scientific, literary or artistic production of which he is the author.

28. *Higher Order Right to Legal Order* Everyone is entitled to a social and international order in which the rights and freedoms set forth in this Declaration can be fully realized.

29. (1) Everyone has duties to the community in which alone the free and full development of his personality is possible.

(2) In the exercise of his rights and freedoms, everyone shall be subject only to such limitations as are determined by law solely for the purpose of securing due recognition and respect for the rights and freedoms of others and of meeting the just requirements of morality, public order and the general welfare in a democratic society.

(3) These rights and freedoms may in no case be exercised contrary to the purposes and principles of the United Nations.

30. Nothing in this Declaration may be interpreted as implying for any State, group or person any right to engage in any activity or to perform any act aimed at the destruction of any of the rights and freedoms set forth herein.

Canadian Charter of Rights and Freedoms
(1982)

Preamble

Whereas Canada is founded upon principles that recognize the supremacy of God and the rule of law:

Articles

1. The *Canadian Charter of Rights and Freedoms* guarantees the rights and freedoms set out in it subject only to such reasonable limits prescribed by law as can be demonstrably justified in a free and democratic society.

2. Everyone has the following fundamental freedoms:

(a) freedom of conscience and religion;

(b) freedom of thought, belief, opinion and expression, including freedom of the press and other media of communication;

(c) freedom of peaceful assembly; and

(d) freedom of association.

3. Every citizen of Canada has the right to vote in an election of members of the House of Commons or of a legislative assembly and to be qualified for membership therein.

4. (1) No House of Commons and no legislative assembly shall continue for longer than five years from the date fixed for the return of the writs at a general election of its members.

(2) In time of real or apprehended war, invasion or insurrection, a House of Commons may be continued by Parliament and a legislative assembly may be continued by the legislature beyond five years if such continuation is not opposed by the votes of more than one-third of the members of the House of Commons or the legislative assembly, as the case may be.

5. There shall be a sitting of Parliament and of each legislature at least once every twelve months.

6. (1) Every citizen of Canada has the right to enter, remain in and leave Canada.

(2) Every citizen of Canada and every person who has the status of a permanent resident of Canada has the right

(a) to move to and take up residence in any province; and

(b) to pursue the gaining of a livelihood in any province.

(3) The rights specified in subsection (2) are subject to

(a) any laws or practices of general application in force in a province other than those that discriminate among persons primarily on the basis of province of present or previous residence; and

(b) any laws providing for reasonable residency requirements as a qualification for the receipt of publicly provided social services.

(4) Subsections (2) and (3) do not preclude any law, program or activity that has as its object the amelioration in a province of conditions of individuals in that province who are socially or economically disadvantaged if the rate of employment in that province is below the rate of employment in Canada.

7. Everyone has the right to life, liberty and security of the person and the right not to be deprived thereof except in accordance with the principles of fundamental justice.

8. Everyone has the right to be secure against unreasonable search or seizure.

9. Everyone has the right not to be arbitrarily detained or imprisoned.

10. Everyone has the right on arrest or detention

    (a) to be informed promptly of the reasons therefor;

    (b) to retain and instruct counsel without delay and to be informed of that right; and

    (c) to have the validity of the detention determined by way of *habeas corpus* and to be released if the detention is not lawful.

11. Any person charged with an offence has the right

    (a) to be informed without unreasonable delay of the specific offence;

    (b) to be tried within a reasonable time;

    (c) not to be compelled to be a witness in proceedings against that person in respect of the offence;

    (d) to be presumed innocent until proven guilty according to law in a fair and public hearing by an independent and impartial tribunal;

    (e) not to be denied reasonable bail without just cause;

(f) except in the case of an offence under military law tried before a military tribunal, to the benefit of trial by jury where the maximum punishment for the offence is imprisonment for five years or a more severe punishment;

(g) not to be found guilty on account of any act or omission unless, at the time of the act or omission, it constituted an offence under Canadian or international law or was criminal according to the general principles of law recognized by the community of nations;

(h) if finally acquitted of the offence, not to be tried for it again and, if finally found guilty and punished for the offence, not to be tried or punished for it again; and

(i) if found guilty of the offence and if the punishment for the offence has been varied between the time of commission and the time of sentencing, to the benefit of the lesser punishment.

12. Everyone has the right not to be subjected to any cruel and unusual treatment or punishment.

13. A witness who testifies in any proceedings has the right not to have any incriminating evidence so given used to incriminate that witness in any other proceedings, except in a prosecution for perjury or for the giving of contradictory evidence.

14. A party or witness in any proceedings who does not understand or speak the language in which the proceedings are conducted or who is deaf has the right to the assistance of an interpreter.

15. (1) Every individual is equal before and under the law and has the right to the equal protection and equal benefit of the law without discrimination and, in particular, without discrimination based on race, national or ethnic origin, colour, religion, sex, age or mental or physical disability.

(2) Subsection (1) does not preclude any law, program or activity that has as its object the amelioration of conditions of disadvantaged individuals or groups including those that are disadvantaged because of

race, national or ethnic origin, colour, religion, sex, age or mental or physical disability.

16. (1) English and French are the official languages of Canada and have equality of status and equal rights and privileges as to their use in all institutions of the Parliament and government of Canada.

(2) English and French are the official languages of New Brunswick and have equality of status and equal rights and privileges as to their use in all institutions of the legislature and government of New Brunswick.

(3) Nothing in the Charter limits the authority of Parliament or a legislature to advance the equality of status or use of English and French.

17. (1) Everyone has the right to use English or French in any debates and other proceedings of Parliament.

(2) Everyone has the right to use English or French in any debates and other proceedings of the legislature of New Brunswick.

18. (1) The statutes, records and journals of Parliament shall be printed and published in English and French and both language versions are equally authoritative.

(2) The statutes, records and journals of the legislature of New Brunswick shall be printed and published in English and French and both language versions are equally authoritative.

19. (1) Either English or French may be used by any person in, or in any pleading in or process issuing from, any court established by Parliament.

(2) Either English or French may be used by any person in, or in any pleading in or process issuing from, any court of New Brunswick.

20. (1) Any member of the public in Canada has the right to communicate with, and to receive available services from, any head or central office of an institution of the Parliament or government of Canada in English or French, and has the same right with respect to any other office of any such institution where

(a) there is a significant demand for communications with and services from that office in such language; or

(b) due to the nature of the office, it is reasonable that communications with and services from that office be available in both English and French.

(2) Any member of the public in New Brunswick has the right to communicate with, and to receive available services from, any office of an institution of the legislature or government of New Brunswick in English or French.

21. Nothing in sections 16 to 20 abrogates or derogates from any right, privilege or obligation with respect to the English and French languages, or either of them, that exists or is continued by virtue of any other provision of the Constitution of Canada.

22. Nothing in section 16 to 20 abrogates or derogates from any legal or customary right or privilege acquired or enjoyed either before or after the coming into force of this Charter with respect to any language that is not English or French.

23. (1) Citizens of Canada

(a) whose first language learned and still understood is that of the English or French linguistic minority population of the province in which they reside, or

(b) who have received their primary school instruction in Canada in English or French and reside in a province where the language in which they received that instruction is the language of the English or French linguistic minority population of the province, have the right to have their children receive primary and secondary school instruction in that language in that province.

(2) Citizens of Canada of whom any child has received or is receiving primary or secondary school instruction in English or French in Canada, have the right to have all their children receive primary and secondary school instruction in the same language.

(3) The right of citizens of Canada under subsections (1) and (2) to have their children receive primary and secondary school instruction in the language of the English or French linguistic minority population of a province

    (a) applies wherever in the province the number of children of citizens who have such a right is sufficient to warrant the provision to them out of public funds of minority language instruction; and

    (b) includes, where the number of those children so warrants, the right to have them receive that instruction in minority language educational facilities provided out of public funds.

24. (1) Anyone whose rights or freedoms, as guaranteed by this Charter, have been infringed or denied may apply to a court of competent jurisdiction to obtain such remedy as the court considers appropriate and just in the circumstances.

(2) Where, in proceedings under subsection (1), a court concludes that evidence was obtained in a manner that infringed or denied any rights or freedoms guaranteed by this Charter, the evidence shall be excluded if it is established that, having regard to all the circumstances, the admission of it in the proceedings would bring the administration of justice into disrepute.

25. The guarantee in this Charter of certain rights and freedoms shall not be construed so as to abrogate or derogate from any aboriginal, treaty or other rights or freedoms that pertain to the aboriginal peoples of Canada including

    (a) any rights or freedoms that have been recognized by the Royal Proclamation of October 7, 1763; and

    (b) any rights or freedoms that may be acquired by the aboriginal peoples of Canada by way of land claims settlement.

26. The guarantee in this Charter of certain rights and freedoms shall not be construed as denying the existence of any other rights or freedoms that exist in Canada.

27. This Charter shall be interpreted in a manner consistent with the preservation and enhancement of the multicultural heritage of Canadians.

28. Notwithstanding anything in this Charter, the rights and freedoms referred to in it are guaranteed equally to male and female persons.

29. Nothing in this Charter abrogates or derogates from any rights or privileges guaranteed by or under the Constitution of Canada in respect of denominational, separate or dissentient schools.

30. A reference in this Charter to a province or to the legislative assembly or legislature of a province shall be deemed to include a reference to the Yukon Territory and the Northwest Territories, or to the appropriate legislative authority thereof, as the case may be.

31. Nothing in this Charter extends the legislative powers of any body or authority.

32. (1) This Charter applies

(a) to the Parliament and government of Canada in respect of all matters within the authority of Parliament including all matters relating to the Yukon Territory and Northwest Territories; and

(b) to the legislature and government of each province in respect of all matters within the authority of the legislature of each province.

(2) Notwithstanding subsection (1), section 15 shall not have effect until three years after this section comes into force.

33. (1) Parliament or the legislature of a province may expressly declare in an Act of Parliament or of the legislature, as the case may be, that the Act or a provision thereof shall operate notwithstanding a provision included in section 2 or sections 7 to 15 of this Charter.

(2) An Act or a provision of an Act in respect of which a declaration made under this section is in effect shall have such operation as it would have but for the provision of this Charter referred to in the declaration.

(3) A declaration made under subsection (1) shall cease to have effect five years after it comes into force or on such earlier date as may be specified in the declaration.

(4) Parliament or a legislature of a province may re-enact a declaration made under subsection (1).

(5) Subsection (3) applies in respect of a re-enactment made under subsection (4).

34. This Part may be cited as the Canadian Charter of Rights and Freedoms

Appendix B

Human Rights Research Tool

There are now thousands of human rights documents, both national and international. This makes for much material to wade through. To aid in this task, I have designed below a research tool. This tool is comprised of an extensive listing, by title, year, and theme, of the most influential human rights documents, both national and international. I also offer some internet web-sites—marked off by the angled brackets "<>"— where interested readers can view these documents, and much else of interest, in their entirety. Some very good research instruments exist on the internet, and readers should feel free to make extensive use of this handy resource. I should add that, at the time of writing, all these web-sites were up and running, of high quality, and were sponsored by organizations of repute.

General Human Rights Research

The sites below are all useful, substantive sites for general human rights-related research. The first is probably the most comprehensive and impressive human rights information web-site in the world.

The Human Rights Library at the University of Minnesota:
<www1.umn.edu/humanrts>. Note in particular the bibliography there, at: <www1.umn.edu/humanrts/bibliog/BIBLIO.htm>
Human Rights Research Program at Harvard Law School:
<www.law.harvard.edu/programs/HRP/guide/rgtoc.html>
Human Rights Research and Education Centre, University of Ottawa:
<www.uottawa.ca/hrrec>
United Nations Human Rights Research Guide:
<www.un.org/Depts/dhl/resguide/spechr.htm>
Human Rights Interactive Network:
<www.webcom.com/hrin/research.html>
American Society of International Law:
<www.asil.org>

DIANA Project, Yale University Law School:
  <http://diana.law.yale.edu>
Human Rights Internet:
  <www.hri.ca>
Derechos:
  <www.derechos.org>

National Human Rights Documents

National human rights documents refer not merely to various national bills, charters or declarations of human and civil rights. They include also, and importantly, court decisions on human rights cases. Of course, every country's national rights document is special and meaningful. The small list offered below is not necessarily of the best documents but, rather, those that have been the most historically influential and well-known. They include The Magna Carta (UK), 1215; The English Bill of Rights, 1689; The American Bill of Rights, 1789; The French Declaration of the Rights of Man and Citizen, 1789; and The Canadian Charter of Rights and Freedoms, 1982. The last three of these documents are contained in Appendix A. All these documents can be found online at The Avalon Project at Yale Law School, at: <www.yale.edu/lawweb/avalon/avalon.htm>

Another important web-site is The Bill of Rights Comparative Law Materials. It features a compilation of national court decisions on human rights topics, and is organized by theme. If one wants to look, e.g., at how the human right to equality has been dealt with nationally by courts in, say, Canada, America, Ireland and India, this information can be readily had at this site. It is located at <www.hrcr.org/safrica>. A web-site that contains a very comprehensive listing of national constitutional and rights-related documents is the International Constitutional Law site at <www.uni-wuerzburg.de/law>.

Various organizations issue annual country-by-country reports regarding how well nations are doing, inside their own borders, with regard to human rights issues. These reports can be interesting and useful, but the source and its own agenda should always be taken into account. These organizations include Human Rights Watch: <www.hrw.org>; Amnesty International: <www.amnesty.org>; The US State Department <www.state.gov/www/global/human_rights/hrp_reports_mainhp.html>; and the reports of the various UN human rights committees: <www.unhcr.ch>. This last option is worth a further comment. There are six important human rights committees at the UN, and they meet to report on how well nations are doing with respect to six international human rights treaties, which are contained in the extensive listing in the next section. These treaties are the ones dealing with civil and political rights; economic, social and cultural rights; torture; racial discrimination; discrimination against women; and the rights of children.

International Human Rights Documents

There are two kinds of international human rights documents. The first, most familiar, kind is a human rights document whose origin rests within the United Nations framework, or within one of the UN's subsidiary bodies. The second, lesser known, kind is a treaty or convention between a particular sub-set of countries outside of the UN framework. Since these sub-sets are usually organized geographically, these documents are often referred to as "regional" human rights documents. The regions in question are Europe, Africa, the Islamic world and the Americas. Asia is the one region that has thus far resisted the development of a regional human rights framework. What follows below is a list of important international human rights documents, organized by theme, title and date. Unless otherwise noted, the documents in the "A" list are all official UN declarations, or UN-sponsored conventions that are full-blown pieces of international law. The regional documents, in the "B" list, are binding only on those nations in that region which signed the treaty in question. The two best on-line sources for locating the full text of these documents are The University of Minnesota Human Rights Library: <www1.umn.edu/humanrts>; and The United Nations Office of the High Commissioner for Human Rights: <www.unhcr.ch>

A. UN Human Rights Documents

The International Bill of Rights
Universal Declaration of Human Rights (1948)
International Covenant on Civil and Political Rights (1966, entered into force 1976)
— First Optional Protocol to the ICCPR, dealing with the formation of an oversight committee (1966, entered into force 1976)
— Second Optional Protocol to the ICCPR, dealing with the abolition of the death penalty (1989, entered into force 1991)
International Covenant on Economic, Social and Cultural Rights (1966, entered into force 1976)

Aboriginal, Indigenous or Native Peoples
Convention Concerning Indigenous and Tribal Peoples in Independent
Countries (1989). This is a convention of the International Labour
Organization (ILO), which is part of the UN framework.

Children
Declaration of the Rights of the Child (1959)
Convention on the Rights of the Child (1989, entered into force 1990)
Convention on the Prohibition and Immediate Action for the Elimina-
tion of the Worst Forms of Child Labour (1999, entered into force
2000)

Development
Declaration on the Granting of Independence to Colonial Countries
and Peoples (1960)
Declaration on Permanent Sovereignty Over Natural Resources (1962)
Declaration on Social Progress and Development (1969)
Declaration on the Right to Development (1986)

Disabled or Challenged Persons
Declaration on the Rights of Mentally Retarded Persons (1971)
Declaration on the Rights of Disabled Persons (1975)
Guidelines on HIV/AIDS and Human Rights (1997). These guidelines
are declarations of the UN Office of the High Commissioner on
Human Rights.

Duties
Declaration on the Right and Responsibility of Individuals, Groups and
Organs of Society to Promote and Protect Universally Recognized
Human Rights and Fundamental Freedoms (1999)

Equality
Convention on the Elimination of All Forms of Racial Discrimination
(1965, entered into force 1969)
Convention on the Elimination of All Forms of Discrimination Against
Women (1979, entered into force 1981)
— Optional Protocol to CEDAW (2000)
Declaration on the Elimination of All Forms of Intolerance and of Dis-
crimination Based on Religion or Belief (1981)

Labour

Convention Concerning Freedom of Association and Protection of the Right to Organize (1948)

Convention Concerning the Application of the Principles of the Right to Organize and Bargain Collectively (1949)

Convention Concerning the Abolition of Forced Labour (1957)

Convention Concerning Minimum Age for Admission to Employment (1976)

Convention on the Protection of the Rights of All Migrant Workers and Their Families (1989)

Minority Groups

Declaration on the Rights of Persons Belonging to National or Ethnic, Religious or Linguistic Minorities (1993)

Prisoners (see also *Security of The Person*)

Standard Minimum Rules for the Treatment of Prisoners (1955). This is a resolution of the UN's Economic and Social council.

Basic Principles for the Treatment of Prisoners (1990)

Refugees

Convention Relating to the Status of Refugees (1951, entered into force 1954)

— Protocol Relating to the Status of Refugees (1966, entered into force 1967)

Declaration on Territorial Asylum (1967)

Convention on the Reduction of Statelessness (1969, entered into force 1975)

Declaration on the Human Rights of Individuals who are Not Nationals of The Country in which They Live (1985)

Security of the Person

Convention on the Prevention and Punishment of the Crime of Genocide (1948, entered into force 1951)

Declaration on the Protection of All Persons from Being Subjected to Torture and Other Cruel, Inhuman or Degrading Treatment or Punishment (1975)

Convention Against Torture and Other Cruel, Inhuman or Degrading Treatment or Punishment (1984, entered into force 1987)

"Beijing Rules" for the Administration of Juvenile Justice (1985)

Declaration of Basic Principles of Justice for Victims of Crime and Abuse of Power (1985)

Declaration on the Protection of All Persons from Enforced Disappearances (1992)

Slavery

Convention to Suppress the Slave Trade and Slavery (1926; additional protocol 1953)

Convention Concerning Forced Labour (ILO Convention, 1930)

Convention for the Suppression of the Traffic in Persons and of the Exploitation and Prostitution of Others (1950)

Convention on the Abolition of Slavery, the Slave Trade and Institutions and Practices Similar to Slavery (1956)

War

The Hague Conventions (1899-1907). These were international conventions agreed to prior to the formation of the League of Nations and the UN, but are still considered a binding part of international law.

"Nuremberg Rules" on the Prosecution of War Criminals (1945)

Geneva Conventions (1949)

— Additional Protocols to the Geneva Conventions (1977)

Convention on the Non-applicability of Statutory Limitations to War Crimes and Crimes Against Humanity (1965, entered into force 1968)

Declaration on the Right of Peoples to Peace (1984)

Rome Statute of the International Criminal Court (1998, not yet entered into force)

Women (see also *Equality*)

Convention on the Political Rights of Women (1953)

Declaration on the Protection of Women and Children in Emergency and Armed Conflict (1974)

CEDAW (1981, with 2000 Protocol)

Declaration on the Elimination of Violence Against Women (1993)

"Beijing Declaration" on Women's Rights as Human Rights (1995)

World Human Rights Conferences

Proclamation of Tehran, Final Act of the International Conference on Human Rights (1968)

Vienna Declaration, World Conference on Human Rights (1993)

B. Regional Human Rights Documents

Africa
African (or "Banjul") Charter on Human and Peoples' Rights (1981, entered into force 1986)

Americas
American Declaration on the Rights and Duties of Man (1948)
Charter of the Organization of American States (1951, amended 1990)
American Convention on Human Rights (1969, entered into force 1978)
— Additional Protocol on Economic, Social and Cultural Rights (1988)
— Additional Protocol on the Death Penalty (1990)
Inter-American Convention to Prevent and Punish Torture (1985, entered into force 1987)

Europe
European Convention for the Protection of Human Rights and Fundamental Freedoms, plus Nine Protocols (1949, entered into force 1953)
European Social Charter (1961, entered into force 1965)
Helsinki Final Act, Conference on Security and Conference in Europe (1975)
European Convention for the Prevention of Torture (1987, entered into force 1989)
Charter of Paris for a New Europe (1990)

Islamic World/Middle East
Cairo Declaration on Human Rights in Islam (1990)

Index

Using 730 lb. of Rolland Enviro100 Print instead
of virgin fibres paper reduces your ecological footprint of:

Trees: 6 ; 0.1 American football field
Solid waste: 394lb
Water: 3,722gal ; a shower of 0.8 day
Air emissions: 866lb ; emissions of 0.1 car per year